ACCA

PRACTICE & REVISION KIT

Paper 2.5

Financial Reporting

BPP Professional Education
January 2003

First edition 2001
Third edition January 2003

ISBN 0 7517 0763 5 (Previous edition 0 7517 0517 9)

British Library Cataloguing-in-Publication Data
A catalogue record for this book
is available from the British Library

Published by

BPP Professional Education
Aldine House, Aldine Place
London W12 8AW

www.bpp.com

Printed in Great Britain by Ashford Colour Press

We are grateful to the Association of Chartered Certified Accountants for permission to reproduce past examination questions. The answers to past examination questions have been prepared by BPP Professional Education.

CONTENTS

The headings in this checklist/index indicate the main topics of questions, but questions often cover several different topics.

Preparation questions, listed in italics, provide you with a firm foundation for attempts at exam-standard questions.

Questions set under the old syllabus Paper 10 *Accounting and Audit Practice* paper are included because their style and content are similar to those which will appear in the Paper 2.5 exam. The questions have generally been amended to reflect the current syllabus exam format.

TOPIC INDEX

Listed below are the key Paper 2.5 syllabus topics and the numbers of the questions in this Kit covering those topics.

If you need to concentrate your practice and revision on certain topics or if you want to attempt all available questions that refer to a particular subject (be they preparation or exam-standard) you will find this index useful.

Key
ME1 = Mock exam 1
ME2 = Mock exam 2

EFFECTIVE REVISION

What you must remember

Effective use of time as you approach the exam is very important. You must remember:

Believe in yourself
Use time sensibly

Believe in yourself

Are you cultivating the right attitude of mind? There is absolutely no reason why you should not pass this exam if you adopt the correct approach.

- **Be confident** – you've passed exams before, you can pass them again
- **Be calm** – plenty of adrenaline but no panicking
- **Be focused** – commit yourself to passing the exam

Use time sensibly

1 **How much study time do you have?** Remember that you must **eat, sleep,** and of course, **relax.**

2 **How will you split that available time between each subject?** A **revision timetable,** covering **what** and **how** you will revise, will help you organise your revision effectively.

3 **What is your learning style?** AM/PM? Little and often/long sessions? Evenings/weekends?

4 **Do you have quality study time?** Unplug the phone. Let everybody know that you're studying and shouldn't be disturbed.

5 **Are you taking regular breaks?** Most people absorb more if they do not attempt to study for long uninterrupted periods of time. A five minute break every hour (to make coffee, watch the news headlines) can make all the difference.

6 Are you **rewarding yourself** for your hard work? Are you leading a **healthy lifestyle**?

What to revise

Key topics

You need to spend most time on, and practise full questions on, **key topics.**

Key topics

- Recur regularly
- Underpin whole paper
- Appear often in compulsory questions
- Discussed currently in press
- Covered in recent articles by examiner
- Shown as high priority in study material
- Tipped by lecturer

Difficult areas

You may also still find certain areas of the syllabus difficult.

Difficult areas

- Areas you find dull or pointless
- Subjects you highlighted as difficult when taking notes
- Topics that gave you problems when you answered questions or reviewed the material

DON'T become depressed about these areas; instead do something about them.

- Build up your knowledge by **quick tests** such as the quick quizzes in your BPP Study Text.
- Work carefully through **numerical examples** and **questions** in the Text, and refer back to the Text if you struggle with computations in the Kit.
- **Note down weaknesses** that your answers to questions contained; you are less likely to make the same mistakes if you highlight where you went wrong.

Breadth of revision

Make sure your revision has sufficient **breadth.** You need to be able to answer all the compulsory questions and enough optional questions on the paper. On certain papers all major topics in the syllabus will be tested, through objective test questions or longer questions. On other papers it will be impossible to predict which topics will be examined in compulsory questions, which topics in optional questions.

Paper 2.5, Financial Reporting, often includes questions with both a discursive and a numerical element, and sometimes there could be an entirely written question. This means that your revision must encompass both numerical techniques and the ability to explain those techniques and the principles involved.

One thing you do know is that question 1 will be a compulsory question on group accounts, so you must get to grips with that, and practise **all** of the group accounts questions.

How to revise

There are four main ways that you can revise a topic area.

Write it!
Read it!
Teach it!
Do it!

Write it!

The Course Notes and the Study Text are too bulky for revision. You need a slimmed down set of notes that summarise the key points. Writing important points down will help you recall them, particularly if your notes are presented in a way that makes it easy for you to remember them.

Read it!

You should read your notes or BPP Passcards actively, testing yourself by doing quick quizzes or writing summaries of what you have just read.

Teach it!

Exams require you to show your understanding. Teaching what you are revising to another person helps you practise explaining topics. Teaching someone who will challenge your understanding, someone for example who will be taking the same exam as you, can help both of you.

Do it!

Remember that you are revising in order to be able to answer questions in the exam. Answering questions will help you practise **technique** and **discipline**, which examiners emphasise over and over again can be crucial in passing or failing exams.

1. First do any **preparation questions** included for the syllabus area. These provide you with a firm foundation from which to attempt exam-standard questions.
2. The more exam-standard questions you do, the more likely you are to pass the exam. At the very least, you should attempt the **key questions** that are highlighted.
3. You should produce **full answers** under **timed conditions,** and don't cheat by looking at the answer! Look back at your notes or at your BPP Study Text instead if you are really struggling. Produce answer plans if you are running short of time.
4. Always read **Tutor's hints** in the answers. They are there to help you, and will show you which points in the answer are the most important.
5. **Don't get despondent** if you didn't do very well. Refer to the **topic index** and try another question that covers the same subject.
6. When you think you can successfully answer questions on the whole syllabus, attempt the **two mock exams** at the end of the Kit. You will get the most benefit by sitting them under strict exam conditions, so that you gain experience of the four vital exam processes.
    - Selecting questions
    - Deciding on the order in which to attempt them
    - Managing your time
    - Producing answers

BPP's *Learning to Learn Accountancy* book gives further invaluable advice on how to approach revision.

BPP has also produced other vital revision aids.

- **Passcards** – Provide you with clear topic summaries and exam tips
- **Success tapes** – Help you revise on the move
- **Videos** – Show you an overview of key topics and how they are related
- **i-Pass CDs** – Offer you tests of knowledge to be completed against the clock

You can purchase these products by completing the order form at the back of this Kit or by visiting www.bpp.com/acca.

REVISION PROGRAMME

Below is a suggested **step-by-step revision programme**. Please note that this is not the only approach – you may prefer to do your revision in a different order, and your college may suggest a different approach. However, **as a minimum you must do the key questions if you want to pass the exam.**

The BPP programme requires you to devote a **minimum of 45 hours** to revision of Paper 2.5. Any time you can spend over and above this should only increase your chances of success. Prepare full answers instead of answer plans to some of the questions if you have any extra revision time.

Suggested approach

1 For the topics covered in each revision period, **review** your notes and the relevant summaries in the **Paper 2.5 Passcards**.

2 Then do the **key questions** for that section. These are **shaded** in the table below, and, as we indicated earlier, are the questions you must attempt, even if you are short of time. Try to complete your answers without referring to our solutions.

3 Because your available study time may be limited, for some questions we have suggested that you prepare **answer plans** rather than full solutions. This means that you should spend about 30% of the full time allowance for that question on brainstorming the question and drawing up a list of points to be included in an answer.

4 Once you have worked through all of the syllabus sections, **attempt at least one of the Mock Exams under strict exam conditions**. Mock Exam 1 is the December 2001 paper for this subject. Mock Exam 2 is BPP's prediction of the topics likely to come up in June 2003. If you don't have time to do both under exam conditions, have a look at the exam you didn't do to get an idea of the style of questions and the likely topics.

Syllabus section	2003 Passcard Chapter	Questions in this Kit	Comments	Done √
Review of basic accounting concepts	1	1	Accounting terminology. A useful question to brush up your knowledge of basic concepts. Prepare an answer plan.	
Regulatory framework	2	2	Accounting standards. Prepare an answer plan. Compare with suggested solution and identify the key learning points.	
Companies Act requirements and formats of accounts	3	4	This question was included in the pilot paper and is therefore an excellent indication of the type of question you may be set. Attempt it in full and then review the answer carefully.	
		6	This question tests your ability to distinguish between accounting policies and estimation techniques. Ensure you can handle a similar question by doing a full answer.	
Fixed assets: tangible assets	4	8	SSAP 19. The question tests your knowledge of both SSAP 19 and FRS 15. Answer the requirements specifically and fully.	
		9	Dawes. An excellent question testing understanding of a number of different standards. The question is fairly time pressured so do rehearse it till you can make good time and good marks on it.	
Fixed assets: intangible assets and investments	5	10	Impairment. A useful question to evaluate your understanding of FRS 11. Prepare a full answer for all parts.	
		12	Investments, goodwill and intangibles. A useful question. Prepare a full answer and if necessary redo parts where you are weak.	

Syllabus section	2003 Passcard Chapter	Questions in this Kit	Comments	Done √
Hire purchase and leasing	6	14	Tracy. An excellent question on finance leases using the actuarial method. Practise till you maximise your marks performance.	
Stocks and WIP	7	16	Shipright. The question requires a firm grasp of long-term contracts. Practise till fully confident.	
		17	Multiplex. This was included in the pilot paper so it is worth doing it in full and revisiting the areas in which you found it difficult to score marks.	
Taxation in company accounts	8	18	Deferred taxation. A key area following introduction of FRS 19. Practise till you have it mastered. Make notes of the key learning points.	
Earnings per share and reporting financial performance	9	21	ABC. Tests your ability to calculate EPS for several scenarios. Note the mark allocation between parts (a), (b) and (c) and ensure you allocate your time judiciously. Prepare a full answer. Identify your weaknesses and remedy through practice.	
		22	Performance reporting. Requires you to explain why FRS 3 was issued and to describe how various elements of FRS 3 have improved reported financial information. Prepare an answer plan.	

Syllabus section	2003 Passcard Chapter	Questions in this Kit	Comments	Done √
		23	Fresno. This tests your ability to prepare FRS 3 statements and requires good understanding of the provisions and required formats of FRS 3. Attempt the question in full and compare carefully with suggested solution.	
Cash flow statements	10	25	Preparation question: cash flows. A good question to bolster your confidence and remedy any weaknesses.	
		26	Ozac. Review the question for an example of the direct method.	
		28	Ladway. A time pressured question, do and redo it till you are really confident you can crack a similar question in good time in an exam. Rich source of marks if you can do them quickly and accurately.	
Liabilities and provision; reporting the substance of transactions	11	29	Preparation question: SSAP 17. Tests your understanding of the standard. Answer plan only.	
		31	Atomic power. Key question. It's quite a complex one, so take the time to prepare a full answer.	
Share capital and reserves; financial instruments	12	32, 33	FRS 4 and FRS 13. Useful questions for an answer plan	
		34	Jedders. Try this one in full. Make sure that you read it carefully and absorb all the information.	

Syllabus section	2003 Passcard Chapter	Questions in this Kit	Comments	Done √
Distributable profits and capital transactions; revenue recognition	13	35	Revenue recognition is quite topical and appeared in the pilot paper. Have a go at planning this question to make sure you understand the principles involved.	
Related parties: segmental information	14	39	Diversity. Ensure that you are fully aware of the pros and cons of segmental reporting in parts (a) and (b). Before answering part (c), you should know the specific disclosures required by SSAP 25. Do a full answer.	
Consolidated balance sheet: basic principles	16	41	Preparation question: Consolidated balance sheet. A high priority question. Attempt the question in full and review the suggested solution.	
Acquisitions of subsidiaries	17	42	Hample. Useful question. Have a bash.	
		43	Hardy and Sibling. This is a fairly straightforward consolidated balance sheet with fair values. Review this question fully.	

Syllabus section	2003 Passcard Chapter	Questions in this Kit	Comments	Done
Profit and loss account; mergers	18	48	Holding. This question includes all the standard adjustments. Practise it till you can do it as easily as falling off the proverbial log.	
		49	Fruit and Vegetables. The question focuses on the difference between acquisition accounting and merger accounting. This is the type of question that you might expect to see on the exam paper Attempt the question in full. Review the suggested solution. If you could not answer part (b) fully, refer back to your Passcards. Remember, practice makes perfect!	
Associates and joint ventures	19	51	Ren. A useful question. Worth a brisk stab at it to reinforce familiarity. Don't neglect the 4 marks available in part (b) for describing the treatment of dividends.	
		52	Jasmin. A useful question to strengthen your skills in this area. Attempt all parts of the question in full in the correct order.	
	19	53	Augment. Attempt all parts. In this question you are required to produce a consolidated balance sheet with a subsidiary and a joint venture. You must also be confident of the accounting procedure as you have to produce journal entries in part (a). Review your solution and then read through the suggested solution If you have dealt with the joint venture incorrectly refer back to the passcards.	

Syllabus section	2003 Passcard Chapter	Questions in this Kit	Comments	Done √
Theoretical aspects of accounting	20	55	Recost. This is an excellent question incorporating current cost accounting and ratios. Note that most of the marks were for discussion elements., but do attempt the calculations in part (c).	
Interpretation of financial statements	22	58	Heywood Bottles. This question is a good basic interpretation and report writing question. Attempt the question in full before reviewing the suggested solutions.	
		60	Omegar. A question that tests if you have a firm grasp of key ratios. Draw up an answer plan then review the question.	

THE EXAM PAPER

The examination is a **three hour paper** divided into **two sections.**

Section A will normally comprise one compulsory question on group financial statements including group cash flows and foreign currency translation. This question will be technically demanding and could have a discursive element in it.

Section B will comprise four questions out of which candidates should select three questions. These questions will involve advising discussing and reporting on issues and topics in corporate financial reporting. The questions will view the subject matter from the perspective of the preparer of financial statements and from the perspective of the accountant as an advisor. Invariably a technical understanding of the subject matter will be required and candidates will have to apply their knowledge to given cases and scenarios.

Advice as to current and future reporting requirements and their impact on reported corporate performance will be an important element of these questions. Additionally current issues and developments in financial reporting will be examined on a discursive basis.

		Number of Marks
Section A:	One compulsory question	25
Section B:	Choice of 3 from 4 questions (25 marks each)	75
		100

Additional information

Candidates need to be aware that questions involving knowledge of new examinable regulations will not be set until at least six months after the last day of the month in which the regulation was issued.

The Study Guide provides more detailed guidance on the syllabus. Examinable documents are listed in the 'Exam Notes' section of *Student Accountant.*

Analysis of past papers

The analysis below shows the topics which have been examined in the first three sittings of the current syllabus and in the Pilot Paper.

December 2002

Section A

1 Consolidated accounts using acquisition accounting; consolidated P+L account and shareholders' funds using merger accounting; FRS 6 criteria for using merger accounting

Section B

2 Financial statements presentation: P+L account, balance sheet, STRGL
3 FRS 5; creative accounting; consignment stock; sale and repurchase arrangements
4 Cash flow statement preparation; comment on financial position of the company
5 Discontinued operations; diluted EPS and explanation. Discussion of tax charge shown in P+L account.

June 2002

Section A

1 Consolidated accounts preparation; criteria for determining associated company status

Section B

2 Redraft of balance sheet after making adjustments; treatment of lease, issue of convertible loan note, deferred tax, bonus issue of shares, using revaluation reserve; dividends; diluted EPS

3 Definition of fixed asset and goodwill impairment loss; indicators of impairment; interpretations of practical scenarios in relation to consolidated financial statements

4 Action analysis and report on a potential acquisition target; identification of points for further investigation

5 Long term contract accounting; fixed asset revaluation, change of estimated life and impairment.

Examiner's comments

The overall performance in this paper was disappointing, and the pass rate was lower than the previous sitting. The main reason for this seemed to be that students did not have sufficient knowledge of the breadth of the syllabus.

The most prevalent of the problem areas was, once again, poor examination technique. Previous issues of not answering the required four questions and poor time allocation between the questions answered were still very much in evidence. Some candidates spent too much time on one question (usually question 2 or 4) and consequently ran short of time on the other questions. It is very difficult to achieve a pass mark if only three questions are attempted or where large parts of questions are not attempted. The computational elements were generally answered better than the written elements.

December 2001

Section A

1 Consolidated balance sheet; non-consolidation of subsidiaries

Section B

2 Preparation of financial statements; closing stock calculation; debt factoring; investment income; deferred tax; EPS

3 FRS 15; cost; subsequent expenditure, revaluation

4 Cash flow statement

5 Various parts: FRS 18; development expenditure; prior period adjustments; intangible assets; investment property; STRGL; stocks, post-balance sheet events; contingent liabilities

Examiner's comments

Candidates showed a good breadth of knowledge and there seemed to be less reliance on learning a few 'banker' topics. However poor technique was still in evidence, especially not answering four questions and poor time allocation between questions.

Computational questions were generally answered better than written questions. A number of markers reported difficulty in reading some scripts – it is necessary to keep handwriting as legible as possible.

Pilot paper

Section A

1 Consolidated P&L account and balance sheet; treatment of an investment

Section B

2 Accounts preparation: P&L account, balance sheet; lease, property, sale and return goods issues
3 Revenue recognition in the operating cycle
4 Adjustment of accounts for comparison; ratio analysis
5 Capital instrument; impairment of asset; closure of loss-making operation

EXAM TECHNIQUE

Passing professional examinations is half about having the knowledge, and half about doing yourself full justice in the examination. You must have the right approach at the following times.

Before the exam
Your time in the exam hall

Before the exam

1 Set at least one **alarm** (or get an alarm call) for a morning exam.

2 Have **something to eat** but beware of eating too much; you may feel sleepy if your system is digesting a large meal.

3 Allow plenty of **time to get to the exam hall**; have your route worked out in advance and listen to news bulletins to check for potential travel problems.

4 **Don't forget** pens, pencils, rulers, erasers, watch. Also make sure you remember **entrance documentation** and **evidence of identity**.

5 Put **new batteries** into your calculator and take a spare set (or a spare calculator).

6 **Avoid discussion** about the exam with other candidates outside the exam hall.

Your time in the exam hall

1 ***Read the instructions (the 'rubric') on the front of the exam paper carefully***

Check that the exam format hasn't changed. Examiners' reports often remark on the number of students who attempt too few - or too many - questions, or who attempt the wrong number of questions from different parts of the paper.

2 ***Select questions carefully***

Read through the paper once, underlining the key words in the question and jotting down the most important points. Select the optional questions that you feel you can answer best. You should base your selection on:

- The **topics** covered
- The **requirements of the whole question**
- How easy it will be to **apply the requirements** to the details you are given
- The availability of **easy marks**

Make sure that you are planning to answer the **right number of questions,** all the compulsory questions plus the correct number of optional questions.

3 ***Plan your attack carefully***

Consider the **order** in which you are going to tackle questions. It is a good idea to start with your best question to boost your morale and get some easy marks 'in the bag'.

4 ***Check the time allocation for each question***

Each mark carries with it a **time allocation** of 1.8 minutes (including time for selecting and reading questions, and checking answers). A 25 mark question therefore should be selected, completed and checked in 45 minutes. When time is up, you **must** go on to the next question or part. Going even one minute over the time allowed brings you a lot closer to failure.

5 ***Read the question carefully and plan your answer***

Read through the question again very carefully when you come to answer it. Plan your answer taking into account how the answer should be **structured**, what the **format** should be and **how long** it should take.

Confirm before you start writing that your plan makes **sense**, covers **all relevant points** and does not include **irrelevant material.** Two minutes of planning plus eight minutes of writing is virtually certain to earn you more marks than ten minutes of writing.

6 ***Answer the question set***

Particularly with written answers, make sure you **answer the question set**, and not the question you would have preferred to have been set.

7 ***Gain the easy marks***

Include the obvious if it answers the question and don't try to produce the perfect answer.

Don't get bogged down in small parts of questions. If you find a part of a question difficult, get on with the rest of the question. If you are having problems with something, the chances are that everyone else is too.

8 ***Produce an answer in the correct format***

The examiner will **state in the requirements** the format in which the question should be answered, for example in a report or memorandum.

9 ***Follow the examiner's instructions***

You will **annoy** the examiner if you ignore him or her.

10 ***Lay out your numerical computations and use workings correctly***

Make sure the layout fits the **type of question** and is in a style the examiner likes. Show all your **workings** clearly and explain what they mean. **Cross reference** them to your solution. This will help the examiner to follow your method (this is of particular importance where there may be several possible answers).

11 ***Present a tidy paper***

You are a professional, and it should show in the **presentation of your work**. Students are penalised for poor presentation and so you should make sure that you write legibly, label diagrams clearly and lay out your work neatly. Markers of scripts each have hundreds of papers to mark; a badly written scrawl is unlikely to receive the same attention as a neat and well laid out paper.

12 ***Stay until the end of the exam***

Use any spare time **checking and rechecking** your script. This includes checking:

- You have **filled out** the **candidate details correctly.**
- Question parts and workings are **labelled clearly.**
- Aids to navigation such as **headers and underlining** are used effectively.
- **Spelling, grammar** and **arithmetic** are correct.

13 ***Don't discuss an exam with other candidates afterwards***

There's nothing more you can do about it so why discuss it?

14 ***Don't worry if you feel you have performed badly in the exam***

It is more than likely that the other candidates will have found the exam difficult too. Don't forget that there is a competitive element in these exams. As soon as you get up to leave the exam hall, ***forget* that exam** and think about the next - or, if it is the last one, celebrate!

> BPP's *Learning to Learn Accountancy* book gives further invaluable advice on how to approach the day of the exam.

CURRENT ISSUES

If you have been studying with the latest edition of the BPP *Financial Reporting* Study Text you will already be up to date for developments up to June 2002. Since then there have been no developments of which you should be aware.

The following notes give guidance on the material which is examinable in this paper, and also suggest some recent articles in areas of topical interest.

Current accounting standards and other documents

The following standards are those which are examinable in paper 2.5 at the date of writing. The SSAPs which were in force at the date the ASB was formed have been adopted by the Board. They are gradually being superseded by the new Financial Reporting Standards (FRSs).

Accounting standards

No	*Title*	*Issue date*
	Foreword to accounting standards	Jun 93
FRS 1	Cash flow statements (revised) (excluding group cash flow statements and cash flow statements involving foreign currency)	Oct 96
FRS 2	Accounting for subsidiary undertakings	Jul 92
FRS 3	Reporting financial performance	Oct 92
FRS 4	Capital instruments	Dec 93
FRS 5	Reporting the substance of transactions (amended Sept 1998)	Apr 94
FRS 6	Acquisitions and mergers	Sep 94
FRS 7	Fair values in acquisition accounting	Sep 94
FRS 8	Related party disclosures	Oct 95
FRS 9	Associates and joint ventures	Nov 97
FRS 10	Goodwill and intangible assets	Dec 97
FRS 11	Impairment of fixed assets and goodwill	July 98
FRS 12	Provisions, contingent liabilities and contingent assets	Sept 98
FRS 13	Derivatives and other financial instruments: disclosures (NE)	Sept 98
FRS 14	Earnings per share	Oct 98
FRS 15	Tangible fixed assets	Feb 99
FRS 16	Current tax	Dec 99
FRS 17	Retirement benefits (NE)	Nov 00
FRS 18	Accounting policies	Dec 00
FRS 19	Deferred tax	Dec oo
SSAP 4	Accounting for government grants	Jul 90
SSAP 5	Accounting for value added tax	Apr 74
SSAP 9	Stocks and long-term contracts	Sep 88
SSAP 13	Accounting for research and development	Jan 89
SSAP 17	Accounting for post balance sheet events	Aug 80
SSAP 19	Accounting for investment properties (amended)	Nov 81
SSAP 20	Foreign currency translation (NE)	Apr 83
SSAP 21	Accounting for leases and hire purchase contracts	Aug 84
SSAP 25	Segmental reporting	Jun 90
FRSSE	Financial Reporting Standard for Smaller Entities (revised)	Dec 99

NE = not examinable

Other Accounting Standards Board documents

Title	*Issue date*
Operating and financial review	July 93
Statement of Principles for Financial Reporting	Dec 99

UITF Abstracts

There are 35, but only these are examinable

Number	*Title*	*Issue date*
4	Presentation of long term debtors in current assets	July 92
5	Transfers from current assets to fixed assets	July 92
15	Disclosure of substantial acquisitions	November 92
30	Date of award to employees of shares or profits to shares	March 01

Recent articles

The content of any relevant articles published before June 2002 is reflected in the BPP Study Text for *Financial Reporting*. Articles published since then which are of direct relevance to the syllabus are listed below.

'Convergence of UK GAAP to IAS Part 1' by Steve Lawrence, *Student Accountant*, August 2002

'Convergence of UK GAAP to IAS Part 2' by Steve Lawrence, *Student Accountant*, September 2002

'Convergence of UK GAAP to IAS Part 3' by Steve Lawrence, *Student Accountant*, October 2002

'Consolidation adjustments' by Ronnie Patton and Simon McCarthy, *Student Accountant*, August 2002

'Deferred tax' by Paul Robins, *Student Accountant*, August 2002

'Convergence of UK GAAP to IAS: group accounting' by Steve Lawrence, *Student Accountant*, January 2003

USEFUL WEBSITES

The websites below provide additional sources of information of relevance to your studies for *Financial Reporting.*

• ACCA	www.accaglobal.com
• BPP	www.bpp.com
• Financial Times	www.ft.com
• Accounting Standards Board	www.asb.org.uk
• International Accounting Standards Board	www.iasb.org.uk

SYLLABUS MINDMAP

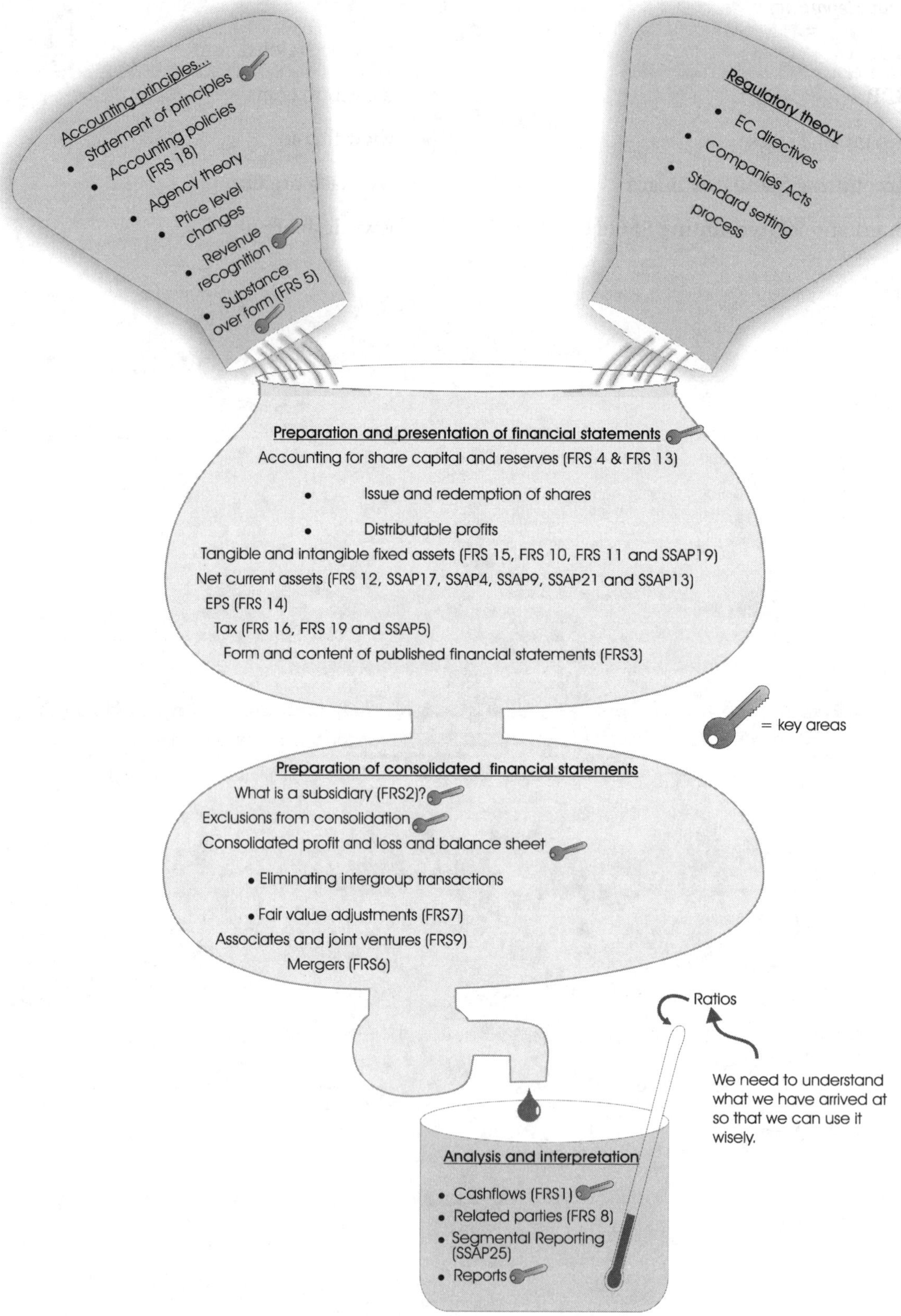

OXFORD BROOKES BSc IN APPLIED ACCOUNTING

The standard required of candidates completing Part 2 is that required in the final year of a UK degree. Students completing Parts 1 and 2 will have satisfied the examination requirement for an honours degree in Applied Accounting, awarded by Oxford Brookes University.

To achieve the degree, you must also submit two pieces of work based on a **Research and Analysis Project.**

- A 5,000 word **Report** on your chosen topic, which demonstrates that you have acquired the necessary research, analytical and IT skills.
- A 1,500 word **Key Skills Statement**, indicating how you have developed your interpersonal and communication skills.

BPP was selected by the ACCA and Oxford Brookes University to produce the official text *Success in your Research and Analysis Project* to support students in this task. The book pays particular attention to key skills not covered in the professional examinations.

AN ORDER FORM FOR ALL ACCA MATERIAL, INCLUDING THE OXFORD BROOKES PROJECT TEXT, CAN BE FOUND AT THE END OF THIS STUDY TEXT.

OXFORD INSTITUTE OF INTERNATIONAL FINANCE MBA

The Oxford Institute of International Finance (OXIIF), a joint venture between the ACCA and Oxford Brookes University, offers an MBA for finance professionals.

For this MBA, credits are awarded for your ACCA studies, and entry to the MBA course is available to those who have completed their ACCA professional stage studies. The MBA was launched in 2002 and has attracted participants from all over the world.

The qualification features an introductory module (*Markets, Management and Strategy*). Other modules include *Global Business Strategy, Managing Self Development,* and *Organisational Change & Transformation.*

Research Methods are also taught, as they underpin the **research dissertation.**

The MBA programme is delivered through the use of targeted paper study materials, developed by BPP, and taught over the Internet by OXIIF personnel using BPP's virtual campus software.

For further information, please see the Oxford Institute's website: www.oxfordinstitute.org

Questions

THE REGULATORY FRAMEWORK

Questions 1 and 2 cover the regulatory framework, the subject of Part A of the BPP Study Text for Paper 2.5.

1 ACCOUNTING TERMINOLOGY *36 mins*

(a) What is the nature of an expense? Explain with particular reference to the accruals concept. Discuss what is meant by a liability. (10 marks)

(b) Costs may be recognised as either expenses or assets. Describe briefly the conceptual tensions which are involved in the treatment of costs. You should illustrate your answer by reference to any two existing accounting standards. (10 marks)

(20 marks)

2 ACCOUNTING STANDARDS (6/94, amended) *36 mins*

The Accounting Standards Committee (ASC) was criticised heavily prior to its replacement by the Accounting Standards Board (ASB). The principal intention of the ASC was to create greater uniformity in the preparation of financial reports in order that there should be more comparability between the results of different companies. Many commentators felt that the ASC failed to achieve their intentions and criticised the role of the ASC because of the following reasons.

(i) A failure to develop an agreed conceptual framework and to specify user needs.

(ii) The composition of the ASC. The ASC had little representation from independent user groups, with the majority of its members coming from the accounting profession.

(iii) The inadequate enforcement of standards. Some writers criticised the ASC for limiting the enforcement of standards to the qualification of the audit report.

(iv) The ASC was too open to pressure from various interested groups who had a direct interest in the work of the committee. This led to political interference in the standard setting process.

(v) A failure to respond quickly to emerging issues.

When the Dearing Committee's recommendations on a whole new structure to replace the ASC were adopted, it was hoped that the new structures would lead to the elimination of the above criticisms. However, there are those who feel that there is no need for a standard setting body and that there is no need for accounting standards. In contrast, others feel that standards should be set by the government and be incorporated in the law.

Required

(a) Explain why there is a need for regulation of financial information in the form of accounting standards. (7 marks)

(b) Discuss the extent to which you feel that the criticisms of the Accounting Standards Committee set out above apply also to the structure for regulating accounting standards that replaced it. (13 marks)

(20 marks)

PREPARATION OF FINANCIAL STATEMENTS OF LIMITED LIABILITY COMPANIES

Questions 3 to 39 cover preparation of financial statements of limited liability companies, the subject of Part B of the BPP Study Text for Paper 2.5.

3 PREPARATION QUESTION: COMPANY REPORTS

In financial reporting it is essential to ensure that information is communicated in a manner which can be understood by the recipients of the report, it is of the utmost importance that company statutory reports do not become over-burdened with unnecessary detail and that the costs of collecting and publishing the information are kept within reasonable bounds.

What is the reasoning behind this statement and what are its implications?

4 WINGER (Pilot paper) *45 mins*

The following trial balance relates to Winger plc at 31 March 20X1:

	£'000	£'000
Turnover (note i)		358,450
Cost of sales	185,050	
Distribution costs	28,700	
Administration expenses	15,000	
Lease rentals (note ii)	20,000	
Debenture interest paid	2,000	
Interim dividends (note vi)	12,000	
Land and buildings - cost (note iii)	200,000	
Plant and equipment - cost	154,800	
Depreciation 1 April 20X0 - plant and equipment		34,800
Development expenditure (note iv)	30,000	
Profit on disposal of fixed assets		45,000
Trade debtors	55,000	
Stocks - 31 March 20X1	28,240	
Cash and bank	10,660	
Trade creditors		29,400
Taxation - over provision in year to 31 March 20X0		2,200
Ordinary shares of 25p each		150,000
8% Debenture (issued in 20W8)		50,000
Profit and loss reserve 1 April 20X0		71,600
	741,450	741,450

The following notes are relevant:

(i) Included in the turnover is £27 million, which relates to sales made to customers under sale or return agreements. The expiry date for the return of these goods is 30 April 20X1. Winger plc has charged a mark-up of 20% on cost for these sales.

(ii) A lease rental of £20 million was paid on 1 April 20X0. It is the first of five annual payments in advance for the rental of an item of equipment that has a cash purchase price of £80 million. The auditors have advised that this is a finance lease and have calculated the implicit interest rate in the lease as 12% per annum. Leased assets should be depreciated on a straight-line basis over the life of the lease.

(iii) On 1 April 20X0 Winger plc acquired new land and building at a cost of £200 million. For the purpose of calculating depreciation only, the asset has been separated into the following elements:

Separate asset	Cost	Life
	£'000	
Land	50,000	Freehold
Heating system	20,000	10 years
Lifts	30,000	15 years
Building	100,000	50 years

The depreciation of the elements of the building should be calculated on a straight-line basis. The new building replaced an existing building that was sold on the same date for £95 million. It had cost £50 million and had a carrying value of £80 million at the date of sale. The profit on this building has been calculated on the original cost. It had not been depreciated on the basis that the depreciation charge would not be material.

Plant and machinery is depreciated at 20% on the reducing balance basis.

(iv) The figure for development expenditure in the trial balance represents the amounts capitalised in previous years in respect of the development of a new product. Unfortunately, during the current year, the Government has introduced legislation which effectively bans this type of product. As a consequence of this the project has been abandoned. The directors of Winger plc are of the opinion that writing off the development expenditure, as opposed to its previous capitalisation, represents a change of accounting policy and therefore wish to treat the write off as a prior period adjustment.

(v) A provision for corporation tax for the year to 31 March 20X1 of £15 million is required.

(vi) The company has paid an interim ordinary dividend and half of the annual debenture interest. The average annual dividend yield (interim plus final) for companies in Winger plc's market sector is 4%. The current market price of Winger plc's equity shares is £1.25. The directors are to propose a final dividend which will give Winger plc's equity shareholders a return equal to the average gross yield for the sector.

Required

(a) Prepare the profit and loss account of Winger plc for the year to 31 March 20X1. (9 marks)

(b) Prepare a balance sheet as at 31 March 20X1 in accordance with the Companies Acts and current accounting standards so far as the information permits. (11 marks)

Notes to the financial statements are not required.

(c) Discuss the current acceptability of the company's previous policy in respect of non-depreciation of buildings. (5 marks)

(25 marks)

5 LARCHER (12/98 amended) *45 mins*

The following trial balance relates to Larcher plc at 30 September 20X8.

	£'000	£'000
Ordinary shares of £1 each		100,000
10% debenture (issued in 20X6)		30,000
Profit and loss reserve 1 October 20X7		23,440
Land and buildings: cost (note (i))	92,000	
Plant and equipment: cost (note (i))	124,740	
Depreciation 1 October 20X7: building		16,000
plant		34,740
Trade debtors (note (ii))	25,500	
Trade creditors		8,540
Lease rentals (note (iii))	800	
Turnover		247,450
Cost of sales	165,050	
Distribution costs	14,200	
Administration expenses (note (ii))	12,300	
Interim dividends (note (v))	3,200	
Debenture interest paid (note (v))	1,500	
Stock at 30 September 20X8	16,240	
Cash and bank	4,640	
	460,170	460,170

The following notes are relevant.

(i) *Fixed assets*

The land had an original cost of £12m and the buildings £80m. The land and buildings were revalued on 1 October 20X7 on the basis of open market values at £120m in total. This was made up of £20m attributed to the land and £100m to the buildings. The building's original estimated life of 50 years (with a nil residual value) has not changed. From the date of the revaluation there were 40 years of life remaining. The directors wish to include the revalued amounts (including the depreciation effects) in the financial statements for the year to 30 September 20X8. Plant and equipment is depreciated at 15% per annum on the reducing balance.

(ii) *Factoring of trade debtors*

The trade debtors figure in the trial balance of £25.5m is a net figure after £10m of trade debtors were sold for £9.5m to Merchant Financing on 30 September 20X8. The £9.5m was paid into the bank on the same date. The difference of £500,000 has been charged to administration as a financing cost. Larcher plc will have to refund Merchant Financing any amounts relating to trade debtors that remain uncollected by Merchant Financing after a period of six months.

(iii) *Lease rentals*

A lease rental of £800,000 was paid on 30 September 20X8. It is the first of five annual payments in arrears for the rental of an item of equipment that has a cash purchase price of £3m. The auditors have advised that this is a finance lease and have calculated that the implicit interest rate in the lease is 10% per annum.

(iv) *Tax*

A provision for corporation tax for the year to 30 September 20X8 of £9m is required.

(v) *Dividends and debenture interest*

The company has paid an interim ordinary dividend and half of the annual debenture interest. The average annual dividend yield (interim plus final) for companies in

Larcher plc's market sector is 6%. The yield is calculated as the dividend paid expressed as a percentage of the market price of the share. The current market price of Larcher plc's equity shares is £2.25. The directors are to propose a final dividend which will give Larcher plc's equity shareholders a dividend yield equal to the average for the sector.

Required

(a) The profit and loss account for Larcher plc for the year to 30 September 20X8 reflecting the adjustments required by notes (i) to (v) above (8 marks)

(b) A statement of total recognised gains and losses for the same period (3 marks)

(c) A balance sheet as at 30 September 20X8 (14 marks)

Note. Ignore deferred tax and the notes to the financial statements. **(25 marks)**

6 ACCOUNTING POLICIES AND ESTIMATION TECHNIQUES *45 mins*

FRS 18 *Accounting policies* distinguishes between accounting policies and estimation techniques and the accounting for changes in each is very different.

Required

(a) Distinguish between accounting policies and estimation techniques, as defined by FRS 18 and state the differences in accounting for a change in accounting policy and a change in an estimation technique. (7 marks)

(b) For items (i) to (vi) below, state in each case whether the proposed changes represent changes in accounting policies or estimation techniques, giving brief reasons.

(i) **Capitalised finance costs**

An entity has previously charged to the profit and loss account interest incurred in connection with the construction of tangible fixed assets. It now proposes to capitalise such interest, as permitted by FRS 15 *Tangible fixed assets*, since it believes this better reflects the cost of constructing those assets. (2 marks)

(ii) **Indirect overheads recorded in the value of stock**

A manufacturing entity has three indirect cost centres (A, B and C). It has previously assessed that the indirect costs attributable to production are 30% of A and 40% of B. Having reassessed the nature of those cost centres' activities, it now assesses that the indirect costs attributable to production are 25% of A, 40% of B and 10% of C. (3 marks)

(iii) **Classification of overheads**

An entity has previously shown certain overheads within cost of sales. It now proposes to show those overheads within administrative expenses. (2 marks)

(iv) **Depreciation of vehicles**

(1) An entity has previously depreciated vehicles using the reducing balance method at 40% per year. It now proposes to depreciate vehicles using the straight-line method over five years, since it believes this better reflects the pattern of consumption of economic benefits. (2 marks)

(2) As in (1), an entity has previously depreciated vehicles using the reducing balance method at 40% per year and now proposes to depreciate vehicles using the straight-line method over five years. In addition, it has previously

recorded the depreciation charge within cost of sales, but now proposes to include it within administration expenses. (2 marks)

(v) **Accounting for fungible stocks**

An entity has fungible stocks and its accounting policy has previously been to consider those stocks in aggregate, measuring them at weighted average historical cost. However, it determines that the normal accounting policy in its industry is to measure such stocks at historical cost on a FIFO basis. It concludes, for reasons of comparability, that it should adopt the normal industry policy. (2 marks)

(vi) **Discounting**

(1) An entity has previously reported deferred tax on an undiscounted basis. However, the norm in its industry is to report deferred tax on a discounted basis. It concludes, for reasons of comparability, that it should adopt the normal industry approach. (2 marks)

(2) An entity has previously measured a particular provision on an undiscounted basis, in accordance with FRS 12 *Provisions, contingent liabilities and contingent assets*, as the effect of discounting was not material. However, this year it has revised upwards its estimates of future cash flows associated with the provision and, as a result, the effect of discounting is now material. FRS 12 therefore requires it to report the provision at the discounted amount. (3 marks)

(25 marks)

7 PREPARATION QUESTION: DEPRECIATION

(a) (i) FRS 15 *Tangible fixed assets* was published in February 1999. How does the standard define tangible fixed assets?

(ii) How should tangible fixed assets be measured initially?

(b) Kabin Ltd, a retail company has previously not depreciated its land and buildings, including shop facias (which have all been treated as one asset) on the grounds that they were regularly maintained. Following FRS 15, the company has revised its policy and split its property into three separate components with different useful economic lives, which are to be depreciated as follows

Land	No depreciation
Buildings	Depreciation over useful economic life of 40 years
Shop facias	Depreciation over useful economic life of 10 years

Required

Comment on these proposals, stating how the change should be reflected in the accounts.

8 SSAP 19 *36 mins*

Kumar Enterprise plc owns three identical properties, North, South and East. North is used as the head office of Kumar Enterprises plc. South is let to, and is occupied by, a subsidiary. East is let to, and is occupied by, an associated company. A fourth property, West, is leased by Kumar Enterprises plc and the unexpired term on the lease is 15 years. West is let to, and is occupied by, a company outside the group.

Required

(a) Which, if any, of these properties is likely to be an investment property of Kumar Enterprises plc and what additional information may be necessary for a final decision? State your reasons. (10 marks)

(b) Identify and justify the appropriate depreciation policy for each of the properties. (10 marks)

(20 marks)

9 DAWES (12/97) *45 mins*

The following problems and issues have arisen during the preparation of the draft financial statements of Dawes plc for the year to 30 September 20X7.

(a) The following schedule of the movement of plant has been drafted.

	Cost	*Depreciation*
	£m	£m
At 1 October 20X6 (including leased assets	81.20	32.50
Additions at cost excluding leased asset (see (i) and (ii) below)	23.00	-
Depreciation charge for year	-	19.84
Disposal (see (iii) below)	(5.00)	-
Balance 30 September 20X7	99.20	52.34

(i) The addition to plant is made up of:

	£m
Basic cost from supplier	20.00
Value added tax	3.50
Installation costs	1.00
Pre-production testing	0.50
Annual insurance and maintenance contract	1.00
Less government grant (see (iv) below)	(3.00)
	23.00

(ii) During the year some assets were acquired under finance leases. The fair value of these assets is represented by the movement on finance lease obligations. These increased from £21.4 million at 1 October 20X6 to £29 million at 30 September 20X7 after capital repayments during the year of £8.4 million. All finance leases for plant are for five years.

(iii) The disposal figure of £5 million is the *proceeds* from the sale of an item of plant during the year. It had cost £15 million on 1 October 20X3 and had been correctly depreciated prior to disposal. Dawes plc charges depreciation of 20% per annum on the cost of plant held at the year end.

(iv) The company policy for government grants is to treat them as deferred credits in the balance sheet.

Required

Prepare a corrected schedule of the movements on the cost and depreciation of plant, including leased assets. (7 marks)

(b) On 1 October 20X6 Dawes plc issued £20 million 5% loan stock at a discount of 10%. The issue costs were £1.5 million made up of apportioned administration costs of £500,000 and professional and underwriting costs of £1 million. The loan stock will be repaid on 30 September 20Y6 (ie ten years after issue) at a premium of 20%.

Required

Calculate the amounts that would appear in the profit and loss account and balance sheet of the current year in respect of the issue of the loan stock.

Note. You may calculate the finance costs on a straight line basis. (5 marks)

(c) On 1 July 20X7 Dawes plc entered into a binding agreement to sell its loss making engineering operation to Manulite plc. Dawes plc accounts for its various operations on a divisional basis, but they are not separate legal entities. The sale will be completed on 10 January 20X8 at an agreed value of £30 million. Associated disposal costs are estimated at £2 million. The book value of the division's net assets at the date of sales are expected to be £46 million. Estimated operating losses for the period from 1 October 20X7 to the date of sale are £4.5 million.

The engineering division is currently being sued for damages relating to a faulty product it manufactured. Independent engineering consultants have prepared a report which confirms that the product was faulty, but this was partly due to the failure of a component that was manufactured by Holroyd Ltd as a sub-assembly. The damages and costs are estimated at £5 million and the level of contributory negligence of Holroyd Ltd is considered to be 40%.

The directors of Dawes plc believe that the disposal should be accounted for in next year's financial statements, and, as the division is to be sold, they do not propose to provide for the damages claim.

The above amounts are material in the context of Dawes plc's financial statements.

Required

Advise the directors on the correct treatment of the disposal of the engineering division and the claim for damages. Your answer should consider the requirements of FRS 3 *Reporting financial performance* and be supported by appropriate calculations. (7 marks)

(d) On 1 October 20X1 Dawes plc purchased a 25 year lease on a new industrial storage building for £4 million. Prior to the current year this property was being amortised over its life. The directors are now questioning the necessity for this as a 20 year lease on an almost identical building was sold on 1 October 20X6 by the builders for £6 million. With effect from the same date (1 October 20X6) the directors wish to value the lease at £6 million and cease depreciating it.

Required

Discuss whether it is acceptable not to depreciate the leasehold property; and show balance sheet, profit and loss account and statement of total recognised gains and losses extracts in respect of the property for the year ended 30 September 20X7 assuming:

(i) There is no revaluation of the property
(ii) The property is revalued to £6 million at 1 October 20X6. (6 marks)

(25 marks)

Note. Your answers for (a) to (d) above should be based on current companies legislation and accounting standards.

10 IMPAIRMENT OF ASSETS *45 mins*

FRS 11 *Impairment of fixed assets and goodwill* was published in July 1998. It deals with an important aspect of accounting for fixed assets for which there had previously been no guidance.

Required

(a) According to FRS 11, when is an asset impaired and how is that impairment calculated? (4 marks)

(b) FRS 11 recognises that it will not always be easy to tell when a fixed asset might be impaired. Briefly list the indicators of impairment noted in the standard. (4 marks)

(c) Entity R has a single substantial asset, the ST, which it uses to manufacture UVs. The carrying value of the ST after 4 years (in 20X9) is £5m (cost £7m, accumulated depreciation on a straight line basis of £2m). There is no expected residual value. Due to a breakthrough in technology in the manufacture of UVs, Entity R now expect the machine to produce 30% less in revenue terms than expected over the rest of its estimated useful life of 10 years. Net future cash flows for the next 5 years, based on management's best estimate after taking the 30% cut into account are (£'000):

Year	*1*	*2*	*3*	*4*	*5*
Future cash flows	600	660	710	755	790

The expected growth rates for the following years are:

Year	*6*	*7*	*8*	*9*	*10*
Rate of growth	2%	(1)%	(7)%	(16)%	(30)%

If the machine was sold now it would realise £3.2m, net of selling costs.

Calculate the recoverable amount of the ST and hence any impairment loss.

(10 marks)

(d) FRS 11 introduced the term 'income generating unit'.

(i) Define 'income generating unit'. (2 marks)

(ii) Identify the income generating unit in the following cases.

(1) A manufacturer can produce a product at a number of different sites. Not all the sites are used to full capacity and the manufacturer can choose how much to make at each site. However, there is not enough surplus capacity to enable any one site to be closed. The cash inflows generated by any one site therefore depend on the allocation of production across all sites.

(2) A restaurant chain has a large number of restaurants across the country. The cash inflow of each restaurant can be individually monitored and sensible allocations of cost to each restaurant can be made. (5 marks)

(25 marks)

Note. PV factors at 10% are on the next page.

Year	*PV factor @10%*
1	0.90909
2	0.82645
3	0.75131
4	0.68301
5	0.62092
6	0.56447
7	0.51316
8	0.46651
9	0.42410
10	0.38554

11 PREPARATION QUESTION: SSAP 13

Discuss the criteria which SSAP 13 *Accounting for research and development* states should be used when considering whether research and development expenditure should be written off in an accounting period or carried forward.

12 INVESTMENTS, GOODWILL AND INTANGIBLES *45 mins*

(a) Sunfil plc holds a variety of fixed asset investments which, because of their importance, are carried at their revalued amounts determined on an item-by-item basis. Due to a lack of clear guidance by the Companies Acts or accounting standards Sunfil plc has adopted the following policy which it believes fairly accounts for the increases or decreases in the value of its investments.

(i) Increases in value of fixed asset investments, other than those relating to investment properties and subsidiary companies, are credited to an investment revaluation reserve.

(ii) If an increase reverses a previous revaluation deficit on the same investment that was recognised as an expense (see below), the increase is credited to the profit and loss account to the extent of the reversal.

(iii) A decrease in the value of an investment is recognised as an expense unless, and to the extent, it offsets an existing previous revaluation surplus for the same investment that has been credited to reserves.

(iv) Permanent decreases in values are written off to the profit and loss account in accordance with the Companies Act.

The opening credit balance on the investment revaluation reserve at 1 October 20X7 was £1,500,000. Details relating to the investments are as follows.

Investment	*Cost*	*Valuation 30 September 20X7*	*Valuation 30 September 20X8*
	£000	£000	£000
Alto	2,100	3,200	5,300
Bedo	8,600	9,000	7,600
Celtic	6,000	4,700	5,100
Dalmo	8,500	7,300	9,100
	25,200	24,200	27,100

Note: none of the falls in value are considered to be permanent.

The investments are made up of the following assets.

(i) Alto and Bedo are investments of a substantial number of shares in public listed companies. They have been valued at the relevant Stock Market price at each year end.

(ii) Celtic is an investment in a private limited company carried at the directors' valuation.

Note. None of the investments qualify as subsidiary companies.

(iii) Dalmo is a valuable oil painting by a Dutch 'old master'. It was listed as such when it was purchased at a reputable auction by the managing director of Sunfil plc who keeps it as his private home for security reasons. The painting has been valued by a specialist recommended by the company that insures the painting; however it is the subject of recent publicity as a private collector has claimed that he owns the original of this painting and that Sunfil plc's must be a fake. The collector has the testimony of two leading independent art experts that support his claim.

Required

Prepare a schedule detailing how the movements in the value of the investments for the year to 30 September 20X8 would be treated (ie reported in the profit and loss account or as reserve movements). Ignore deferred tax. (7 marks)

(b) The problems of identifying, valuing and subsequently accounting for goodwill and other intangible assets has been an area of inconsistent practice that has led to great debate within the accountancy profession. The Accounting Standards Board (ASB) issued FRS 10 *Goodwill and intangible assets* in December 1997 with effect from accounting periods ending on or after 23 December 1998.

Required

Discuss the initial recognition criteria, and subsequent accounting treatment for goodwill and intangible assets contained in FRS 10 *Goodwill and intangible assets*.

(9 marks)

(c) On 1 October 20X9 Sunfil plc was finally successful in acquiring the entire share capital of Fast Trak plc. The terms of the bid by Sunfil plc had been improved several times as rival bidders also made offers for Fast Trak plc. The terms of the initial bid by Sunfil plc were:

(i) 20 million £1 ordinary shares in Sunfil, plc. Each share had a stock market price of £3.50 immediately prior to the bid

(ii) A cash element of £15 million

The final bid that was eventually accepted on 1 October 20X9 by Fast Trak plc's shareholders had improved the cash offer to £25 million and included a redeemable loan note of a further £25 million that will be redeemed on 30 September 20Y3. It carried no interest, but market rates for this type of loan note were 13% per annum. There was no increase in the number of shares offered but at the date of acceptance the price of Sunfil plc's share on the stock market had risen to £4.00 each.

The present value of £1 receivable in a future period where interest rates are 13% can be taken as:

At end of year three	£0.70
At end of year four	£0.60

The fair value of Fast Trak plc's net assets, other than its intangible assets, was assessed by Sunfil plc to be £64 million. This value had not changed significantly throughout the bidding process. The details of Fast Trak plc's intangible assets acquired were:

(1) The brand name of 'Kleenwash' a dish washing liquid. A company called 'Brands-R-Us' was commissioned to value the brand. Their report, based on a 'multiple of product turnover', attached a figure of £12 million to the brand.

(2) A Government licence to extract a radioactive ore from a mine for the next ten years. The licence is difficult to value as there was no fee payable for it. However, as Fast Trak plc is the only company that can mine the ore, the directors of Sunfil plc have estimated the licence to be worth £9 million. The mine itself has been included as part of Fast Trak plc's property.

(3) A fishing quota of 10,000 tonnes per annum in European Union waters. A specialist company called Quotasales plc actively trades in these and other EU quotas. The price per tonne of fishing quotas at the date of acquisition was £1,600. The quota is for an indefinite period of time, but in order to preserve fish stocks the European Union has the right to vary the weight of fish that may be caught under a quota. The weights of quotas are reviewed annually.

(4) The remainder of the intangible assets is attributable to the goodwill of Fast Trak plc.

Required

Prepare an extract of the intangible fixed assets of Fast Trak plc that would be separately recognised in the consolidated financial statements of Sunfil plc on 1 October 20X9. Your answer should include an explanation justifying your treatment of each item. (9 marks)

(25 marks)

13 PREPARATION QUESTION: HIRE PURCHASE

On 1 January 20X7, Cuthbert bought a machine costing £20,000 on hire purchase. He paid a deposit of £6,000 on 1 January 20X7 and he also agreed to pay two annual instalments of £5,828 on 31 December in each year, and a final instalment of £5,831 on 31 December 20X9.

The implied rate of interest in the agreement was 12%. This rate of interest is to be applied to the amount outstanding in the hire purchase loan account at the beginning of the year.

The machine is to be depreciated on a straight line basis over five years on the assumption that it will have no residual value at the end of that time.

Required

(a) Write up the hire purchase loan account for each of the three years to 31 December 20X7, 20X8 and 20X9.

(b) Show the balance sheet extracts for the year as at 31 December 20X7, 20X8 and 20X9 respectively for the following items:

(i) Machine at cost
(ii) Accumulated depreciation on the machine
(iii) Long-term liabilities: obligations under hire purchase contract
(iv) Current liabilities: obligations under hire purchase contract

14 TRACY

45 mins

On 1 October 20X3 Tracy plc entered into a non-cancellable agreement whereby Tracy plc would lease a new rocket booster. The terms of the agreement were that Tracy plc would pay 26 rentals of £3,000 quarterly in advance commencing on 1 October 20X3, and that after this initial period Tracy plc could continue, at its option, to use the rocket booster for a nominal rental which is not material.

The cash price of this asset would have been £61,570 and the asset has a useful life of 10 years.

Tracy plc considers this lease to be a finance lease and charges a full year's depreciation in the year of purchase of an asset. The rate of interest implicit in the lease is 2% per quarter.

On 1 July 20X2 Tracy plc entered into another non-cancellable agreement to lease a Zarkov rocket for a period of 10 years at a rental of £5,000 half-yearly to be paid in advance, commencing on 1 July 20X2. Tracy plc considers this lease to be an operating lease.

Required

Show how these transactions would be reflected in the financial statements for the year ended 31 December 20X3. **(25 marks)**

15 PREPARATION QUESTION: STOCKS AND WIP

(a) 'Many of the problems involved in arriving at the amount at which stocks and work in progress are stated in accounts are of a practical nature rather than resulting from matters of principle.' (SSAP 9)

Required

Comment on the above statement identifying and discussing both the problems 'of a practical nature' and the 'matters of principle' that may arise when computing the amount at which stocks and work in progress are stated in financial accounts.

(b) The production manager of a business complains regularly each year that he has to provide details of partly finished goods that have no intrinsic value and are of no use to anyone and which, in the eventuality of discontinuing the business, would have to be scrapped, and someone would probably have to be paid for carrying them away! He does not understand why a value has to be put on these items every year and wonders what costs are included in what he considers to be a worthless valuation.

This last year he has supported his usual complaint by saying that in his sister's construction company, accountants even put a value on a new bridge that was not yet joined in the middle!

Required

Explain to the production manager how and why unfinished goods and contracts are accounted for in the profit and loss account and balance sheet.

16 SHIPRIGHT (6/99 part)

27 mins

Shipright plc's main activity is shipbuilding and it prepares its financial statements to 31 March each year. On 1 July 20X5 it was successful in securing a long-term contract to construct an oil tanker for Petrochem plc. The work was expected to be completed by 31 December 20X8 and would thus span several accounting periods.

The agreed price of the contract was £800 million. There is an incentive clause which allows a 2% increase in this price if the work is completed eight weeks or more ahead of schedule, and a penalty clause which will cost 1% if the contract is more than four weeks late. Due to the length of the contract there is a labour cost escalation clause which comes into effect in the accounting years to 31 March 20X8 and 20X9.

A prolonged combined industry and government enquiry relating to safety standards and oil spillage problems resulted in preliminary findings that led to the introduction on 1 July 20X7 of new interim legislation concerning the construction of oil tankers. The main effect of the legislation is that new oil tankers have to have a 'double skin' construction. This was not part of the original design of the tanker being constructed by Shipright plc. Hurried negotiations with Petrochem plc resulted in a variation to the contract involving a modified construction method in line with the new legislation. Petrochem plc agreed a price of a further £100 million and a two-month extension to the completion date (ie 28 February 20X9). The incentive clause does not apply to the price of the variation. Shipright plc estimated the cost of the variation would be £80 million. The following details relate to the progress of the contract, all estimates are at the end of the relevant year and can be taken as being reliable:

All figures in £ million

Year to 31 March	*20X6*	*20X7*	*20X8*	*20X9*
Estimated total cost	640	660	660	680
Actual costs to date (see below)	128	264	507	680
Rectification costs			20	
Estimated variation costs			80	84
Actual variation cost to date			48	84
Agreed accumulated labour cost escalation			6	10
Estimated date of completion	On time	On time	10 weeks early	Completed 31 March 20X9
Value of work certified				
- original contract	136	280	570	800
- variation			60	100

Note. The estimated total costs and the actual cost to date **do not** include rectification costs, variation costs or labour escalation costs.

Shipright plc has the following accounting policy in respect of long-term contracts:

(i) Contract costs and revenues are recognised by reference to the stage of completion of the contract at the balance sheet date.

(ii) The stage of completion is determined by the proportion that the cost incurred to date (excluding rectification costs and labour cost escalation) bears to the total estimated contract costs.

(iii) Contract revenues should include the appropriate proportion of cost escalations and incentives/penalties from the time they are reasonably foreseeable.

(iv) Variations are considered to be part of the original contract (from the date they are agreed), and not treated as a separate contract.

(v) No estimated profits are recognised until the contract is 20% complete. Any expected losses are recognised immediately.

Required

(a) Prepare extracts of the profit and loss account of Shipright plc for the years to 31 March 20X6, 20X7, 20X8, and 20X9 in respect of the above contract applying Shipright plc's accounting policies. (10 marks)

Note. Balance sheet extracts are not required.

(b) Calculate the contract's stage of completion at each of the above year ends using the alternative measure of the agreed sales value completed as a proportion of the contract price. Comment on a comparison of this with the stage of completion in (a) above.

(5 marks)

Note: For this method the contract price should include the variation, but not any incentives or recovered cost escalation revenue. You are NOT required to prepare profit and loss accounts extracts for part (b). **(15 marks)**

17 MULTIPLEX (Pilot paper) *45 mins*

The following transactions and events have arisen during the preparation of the draft financial statements of Multiplex plc for the year to 31 March 20X1:

(a) On 1 April 20X0 Multiplex plc issued £80 million 8% loan stock at a discount of 10%. The issue costs were £1.4 million made up of apportioned costs of the finance and acquisitions department of £1 million and professional and underwriting costs of £400,000 relating directly to this issue. The loan stock will be redeemed on 31 March 20X5 at a premium of 12%.

Required

Calculate the profit and loss account finance charge for the year to 31 March 20X1 and the balance sheet extracts at 31 March 20X1 in respect of the issue of the loan stock.

(5 marks)

Note: you may calculate the finance costs on a straight-line basis.

(b) On 1 January 20X1 Multiplex plc acquired Steamdays Ltd, a company that operates a scenic railway along the coast of a popular tourist area. The summarised balance sheet at fair values of Steamdays Ltd on 1 January 20X1, reflecting the terms of the acquisition was:

	£'000
Goodwill	200
Operating licence	1,000
Property - train stations and land	250
Rail track and coaches	250
Two steam engines	1,000
Other net assets	300
Purchase consideration	3,000

The operating licence is for ten years. It was renewed on 1 January 20X1 by the transport authority and is stated at the cost of its renewal. The carrying values of the property and rail track and coaches are based on their value in use. The engines, and other net assets are valued at their net selling prices.

On 1 February 20X1 the boiler of one of the steam engines exploded, completely destroying the whole engine. Fortunately no one was injured, but the engine was beyond repair. Due to its age a replacement could not be obtained. Because of the reduced passenger capacity the estimated value in use of the whole of the business after the accident was assessed at £2 million.

Passenger numbers after the accident were below expectations even after allowing for the reduced capacity. A market research report concluded that tourists were not using the railway because of their fear of a similar accident occurring to the remaining engine. In the light of this the value in use of the business was re-assessed on 31 March 20X1 at £1.8 million. On this date Multiplex plc received an offer of £600,000 in respect of the operating licence (it is transferable). The realisable value of the other net assets has not changed significantly.

Required

Calculate the carrying value of the assets of Steamdays Ltd (in Multiplex plc's consolidated balance sheet) at 1 February 20X1 and 31 March 20X1 after recognising the impairment losses. (6 marks)

(c) On 1 January 20X1 the Board of Multiplex plc approved a resolution to close the whole of its loss-making engineering operation. A binding agreement to dispose of the assets was signed shortly afterwards. The sale will be completed on 10 July 20X1 at an agreed value of £30 million. The costs of the closure are estimated at:

(i) £2 million for redundancy

(ii) £3 million in penalty costs for non-completion of contracted orders

(iii) £1.5 million for associated professional costs

(iv) Losses on the sale of the net assets whose book value at 31 March 20X1 was £46 million

(v) Operating losses for the period from 1 April 20X1 to the date of sale are estimated at £4.5 million.

Multiplex plc accounts for its various operations on a divisional basis.

Required

Advise the directors on the correct accounting treatment of the closure of the engineering division. (5 marks)

(d) Multiplex plc is in the intermediate stage of a long-term, construction contract for the building of a new privately owned road bridge over a river estuary. The original details of the contract are:

Approximate duration of contract:	3 years
Date of commencement:	1 October 20W9
Total contract price:	£40 million
Estimated total cost:	£28 million

An independent surveyor certified the value of the work in progress as follows.

- On 31 March 20X0 — £12 million
- On 31 March 20X1 — £30 million (including the £12 million in 20X0)

Costs incurred at:

- 31 March 20X0 — £9 million
- 31 March 20X1 — £28.5 million (including the £9 million in 20X0)

Payments received on account by 31 March 20X1 were £25 million

On 1 April 20X0 Multiplex plc agreed to a contract variation that would involve an additional fee of £5 million with associated additional estimated costs of £2 million.

The costs incurred during the year to 31 March 20X1 include £2.5 million relating to the replacement of some bolts which had been made from material that had been incorrectly specified by the firm of civil engineers who were contracted by Multiplex plc to design the bridge. These costs were not included in the original estimates, but Multiplex plc is hopeful that they can be recovered from the firm of civil engineers.

Multiplex plc calculates profit on long-term contracts using the percentage of completion method. The percentage of completion of the contract is based on the value of the work certified to date compared to the total contract price.

Required

Prepare the profit and loss account and balance sheet extracts in respect of the contract for the year to 31 March 20X1 only. (9 marks)

(25 marks)

18 DEFERRED TAXATION *36 mins*

(a) Explain, with examples, the nature and purpose of deferred taxation. (10 marks)

(b) Relax plc, a company that operates solely in the UK, depreciates its plant and machinery on a straight-line basis over 10 years. Residual value is estimated to be 1/11th of cost (at which point assume the asset will be sold). The company receives capital allowances at a rate of 25% per annum on a reducing balance basis. It is taxed on its profit at 30%.

The company has three assets that cost £1.1m each, purchased six years, three years and one year ago (in each case at the end of the financial year). The net book value of plant and machinery at 31 March 20X1 is:

	£'000
Original cost	3,300
Cumulative depreciation	(1,000)
Net book value	2,300

The tax written down values of the plant and machinery pool, and the consequential timing difference, at the balance sheet date are:

	£'000
Net book value	2,300
Tax written-down value	(1,114)
Timing difference at 31 March 20X1	1,186

Required

(i) Produce a schedule of the future reversals of the deferred liability and calculate the undiscounted deferred tax liability of Relax plc as at 31 March 20X1 as required by FRS 19 *Deferred tax*. (You should assume that the plant and machinery pool on which writing-down allowances are claimed will continue beyond year 20Y0.) (6 marks)

(ii) Relax plc has decided that it will adopt a policy of discounting its deferred tax liability at a rate of 4% as permitted by FRS 19.

The discount factors for the years 20X2 to 20Y0 are as follows.

20X2	0.962
20X3	0.925
20X4	0.889
20X5	0.855
20X6	0.822
20X7	0.790
20X8	0.760
20X9	0.731
20Y0	0.703

Required

Using the information in (i) above, calculate the discounted deferred tax liability of Relax plc as at 31 March 20X1, as required by FRS 19. (4 marks)

(20 marks)

19 ABROAD LTD *45 mins*

Abroad Ltd is a 100% owned subsidiary of Home plc, a UK based company. Abroad Ltd is located in a foreign country and was purchased on 1 November 20X5. The financial statements of Abroad Ltd are drawn up in accordance with the local accounting regulations. The following translated profit and loss account related to Abroad Ltd for the year ended 31 October 20X6.

ABROAD LIMITED
PROFIT AND LOSS ACCOUNT FOR THE YEAR ENDED 31 OCTOBER 20X6

		£'000	£'000
Turnover			8,900
Cost of sales			(7,094)
Gross profit			1,806
Sales and distribution costs		(633)	
Motor lorry depreciation		(32)	
Administration and finance costs		(541)	
Interest received		161	
Interest paid		(172)	
			(1,217)
Profit before taxation			589
Taxation:	corporation tax	(20)	
	Deferred taxation	(68)	
			(88)
Profit after taxation			501
Extraordinary profit		103	
Less taxation		(33)	
			70
Profit after tax and extraordinary items			571
Dividends paid and proposed			(52)
Retained profit for the year			519

The following notes are relevant to the above profit and loss account.

(a) The extraordinary profit comprises the following elements. The company had withdrawn from a contract to develop property. As a result, it was felt that there were costs to be incurred of £50,000 before taxation relief (32%). Additionally the company had made profits on the sale of a factory. This factory had not been used for production purposes for several years. The profit on the sale of the factory was calculated using depreciated historical cost of £85,000. The carrying value in the accounting records after a recent revaluation was £180,000. The tax charge provided for on this transaction was £49,000 under the law of the overseas country.

(b) Abroad Ltd has revalued its properties held as tangible fixed assets in line with the UK group policy. It has recorded a gain on revaluation of £37,500 during the year and has provided deferred tax on this gain at 32%, on the basis of full provision. Abroad Ltd has no intention of selling the asset in the foreseeable future.

(c) The closing stock of Abroad Ltd includes stock of £2 million held on consignment from suppliers. The main terms of the consignment agreement, which can be terminated by either side, are such that Abroad Ltd can return any or all of the stock to the supplier without any penalty and the price paid to the supplier when goods are sold will depend upon the current price list of the supplier. The opening stock held on consignment from the same supplier was £1.25 million. No other accounting entries had been made regarding this stock.

(d) Abroad Ltd had issued £2 million of 8% debenture stock on 1 November 20X5. This stock is repayable on 31 October 20X9 and costs of £12,000 were incurred. The issue costs and interest paid for the year were both included in the interest paid figure of £172,000 in Abroad Ltd's profit and loss account.

The auditors of Home plc have been asked to make the necessary adjustments to the financial statements in order to ensure that they comply with the UK Accounting Standards and the Companies Acts.

Required

(a) Prepare a revised profit and loss account for the year ended 31 October 20X6 for Abroad Ltd in accordance with UK Accounting Standards and the Companies Acts. (9 marks)

(b) State the main requirements of FRS 19 Deferred tax. (10 marks)

(c) Why did the ASB consider it necessary to introduce a standard that requires full provision for deferred tax, compared to the old standard. (6 marks)

(25 marks)

20 PREPARATION QUESTION: EARNINGS PER SHARE

In connection with FRS 14 *Earnings per share* (EPS):

(a) How should basic EPS be calculated according to FRS 14?

(b) (i) What are contingently issuable shares? How and when should they be reflected in the calculation of basic EPS?

(ii) A company acquires a retail operation. Deferred consideration on acquisition is payable, as shares, to the extent that the acquirer opens new retail outlets. If 20,000 shares were issued in January 1999 for each new outlet opened during the year ended 31 December 1998, and one was opened on 1 April 1998, how many shares would be included in the basic EPS calculation for 1998?

(c) Explain the relationship between EPS and the price/earnings ratio (P/E). Why may the P/E ratio be considered important as a stock market indicator?

(d) Why is diluted earnings per share also considered important?

21 ABC (6/95) *45 mins*

ABC (Group) plc has traded for many years. The issued share capital on 1 January 20X2 was 300,000 £1 ordinary shares. Of this amount, there were 50,000 £1 ordinary shares which were only paid up to the amount of 75p. The shares were issued at par value. The following information relates to the period 1 January 20X2 to 31 December 20X4.

(a) On 1 April 20X2, the outstanding moneys on the partly paid shares were received.

(b) During 20X3 ABC (Group) plc decided to raise further capital by making a rights issue. The rights issue took place on 31 August 20X3 on a 1 for 2 basis at £1.20 per share. The actual cum rights price on the last day of quotation cum rights was £1.80.

(c) ABC (Group) plc suffered from adverse publicity in 20X4 and in order to prevent a significant loss of profits, a new company XYZ (Group) plc was formed on 1 July 20X4 to take over the business of ABC (Group) plc. In order to gain acceptance from existing shareholders, XYZ (Group) plc issued 2 shares for every 1 held in ABC (Group) plc. Merger accounting principles have been adopted in XYZ (Group) plc's accounts in order to maintain the comparability of reported earnings.

The following are the profit and loss accounts of ABC (Group) plc and XYZ (Group) plc for years ending on 31 December.

	ABC Group plc		*XYZ Group plc*
	20X2	*20X3*	*20X4*
	£'000	£'000	£'000
Sales	800	1,100	1,800
Cost of goods sold	(300)	(500)	(800)
Gross profit	500	600	1,000
Administrative expenses	(120)	(130)	(200)
Distribution costs	(40)	(50)	(100)
Profit on ordinary activities before tax	340	420	700
Tax on profit on ordinary activities	(140)	(170)	(250)
Profit on ordinary activities after tax	200	250	450
Dividends	(50)	(70)	(200)
Profit for the financial year	150	180	250

Required

(a) Calculate the earnings per share figures which would appear in the group financial statements for each of the years ending 31 December 20X2, 20X3 and 20X4, showing the comparative figures for 20X3 and 20X4. (13 marks)

(b) Explain the reasons underlying the earnings per share calculation in a financial year when there has been a rights issue at a discount to the market price. (7 marks)

(c) Explain the reasons why quoted companies place so much importance on the level of reported earnings per share and whether you feel that these reasons are justified. (5 marks)

(25 marks)

22 PERFORMANCE REPORTING (6/97) *45 mins*

FRS 3 *Reporting financial performance* became effective for accounting periods ending on or after 22 June 1993.

The objective of financial statements is to provide information about the financial position and performance of an enterprise that is useful to a wide range of users.

The ASB's *Statement of Principles for Financial Reporting* states: 'Financial reporting gives an account of the results of stewardship of management to enable users to assess the past performance of management and to form a basis for developing future expectations about financial performance'.

In relation to the income statement there are basically two potentially conflicting views of what is the most useful form of presentation of information.

(a) The concept of 'comprehensive income' or 'all-inclusive income' in which the underlying principle is that all gains and losses, irrespective of their nature, are relevant and should be reported in the period in which they occur.

Effectively this is a statement of the change in the owners' equity, other than by injections and withdrawals of capital.

(b) The 'current operating performance concept' or 'maintainable earnings concept' in which the emphasis is on ordinary, normal, recurring earnings. Only those gains and, more particularly losses, which have occurred, and are likely to occur, or 'be maintained' in the future should be reported as income for the period.

Required

(a) Discuss the contribution of FRS 3 to the debate over whether the 'comprehensive income' or 'current operating performance' concepts is preferable. (6 marks)

(b) Describe how the following requirements of FRS 3 improve the informational content of financial statements:

(i) The analysis of results between continuing and discontinued activities
(ii) The treatment of extraordinary and exceptional items
(iii) The calculation of the profit or loss on disposal of a fixed asset
(iv) The inclusion of a 'statement of total recognised gains and losses'
(v) The 'note of historical cost profits and losses' (12 marks)

(c) Describe the criticisms that have been made of FRS 3 in relation to the areas in (b) above. (7 marks)

(25 marks)

23 FRESNO (6/94, amended) *45 mins*

Fresno Group plc have prepared their financial statements for the year ended 31 January 20X4. However, the financial accountant of Fresno Group plc had difficulty in preparing the statements required by FRS 3 *Reporting financial performance* and approached you for help in preparing those statements. The financial accountant furnished you with the following information.

(a) FRESNO GROUP PLC
PROFIT AND LOSS ACCOUNT EXTRACT
FOR THE YEAR ENDED 31 JANUARY 20X4

	£m
Operating profit - continuing operations	290
Profit on sale of property in continuing operations	10
Profit on ordinary activities before taxation	300
Tax on ordinary activities	(90)
Profit after taxation	210
Dividends	(15)
Retained profit for year	195

The financial accountant did not provide for the loss on any discontinued operations in the profit and loss account. (However, you may assume that the taxation provision incorporated the effects of any provision for discontinued operations.)

(b) The shareholders' funds at the beginning of the financial year were as follows.

	£m
Share capital - £1 ordinary shares	350
Merger reserve	55
Revaluation reserve	215
Profit and loss reserve	775
	1,395

(c) Fresno Group plc regularly revalues its fixed assets and at 31 January 20X4, a revaluation surplus of £375 million had been credited to revaluation reserve. During the financial year, a property had been sold on which a revaluation surplus of £54 million had been credited to reserves. Further, if the company had charged depreciation on a historical cost basis rather than the revalued amounts, the depreciation charge in the profit and loss account for fixed assets would have been £7 million. The current year's charge for depreciation was £16 million.

(d) The group has a policy of writing off goodwill on the acquisition of subsidiaries over 10 years. The goodwill arising in the period amounted to £250 million. Amortisation has yet to be charged to profit. In order to facilitate the purchase of subsidiaries, the company had issued £1 ordinary shares of nominal value £150 million and share premium of £450 million. The premium had been taken to the merger reserve. All subsidiaries are currently 100% owned by the group.

(e) During the financial year to 31 January 20X4, the company had made a decision to close a 100% owned subsidiary, Reno plc. However, the closure did not take place until May 20X4. Fresno Group plc estimated that as at 31 January 20X4 the operating loss for the period 1 February 20X4 to 31 May 20X4 would be £30 million and that, in addition, redundancy costs and stock and plant write downs would amount to £15 million. In the event, the operating loss for the period 1 February 20X4 to 31 May 20X4 was £65 million, but the redundancy costs, stock and plant write downs only amounted to £12 million.

(f) The following information relates to Reno plc for the period 1 February 20X4 to 31 May 20X4.

	£m
Turnover	175
Cost of sales	(195)
Gross loss	(20)
Administrative expenses	(15)
Selling expenses	(30)
Operating loss before taxation	(65)

Required

(a) Prepare the following statements in accordance with current statutory requirements and FRS 3 *Reporting financial performance* for Fresno Group plc for the year ending 31 January 20X4.

(i) Statement of total recognised gains and losses (3 marks)
(ii) Reconciliation of movements in shareholders' funds (4 marks)
(iii) Analysis of movements on reserves (6 marks)
(iv) Note of historical cost profits and losses (3 marks)

(b) Explain to the financial accountant:

(i) How the decision to close the subsidiary, Reno plc, affects the financial statements of Fresno Group plc for the year ended 31 January 20X4. (5 marks)

(ii) How the subsidiary, Reno plc, should be dealt with in the financial statements of Fresno Group plc for the year ended 31 January 20X5. (4 marks)

(25 marks)

24 VENTNOR (6/99) *45 mins*

FRS 3 *Reporting financial performance* contains detailed requirements relating to discontinued operations. Many commentators feel that these requirements were prompted by a previous lack of a definition of such operations and inconsistencies in their accounting treatment including the timing of their recognition. The standard also requires a 'primary' statement of total recognised gains and losses and a reconciliation of the movement on shareholders' funds.

Required

(a) (i) List and comment on FRS 3's criteria for classification of discontinued operations (7 marks)

(ii) Discuss the relevance of the comparative information that has to be disclosed in relation to discontinued operations (3 marks)

(iii) Describe how users of accounts can expect to benefit from information relating to discontinuing operations, a statement of total recognised gains and losses and a reconciliation of the movement on shareholders' funds (5 marks)

(b) For many years Ventnor plc operated with four diversified divisions; engineering, hotels, car retailing and organic fertilisers. As the company's results in recent years have disappointed stock market analysts, a firm of consultants has been employed to reorganise its business activities. On 30 September 1997 Ventnor plc sold its engineering division (reported under discontinuing operations) and acquired a computer software company (reported under acquisitions). The details for the company's turnover and operating profit as reported in its published financial statements to 31 March 20X8 are:

YEAR ENDED 31 MARCH 20X8

	Continuing	*Acquisitions (software)*	*Discontinued (engineering)*	*Total*
	£m	£m	£m	£m
Turnover	500	120	100	720
Cost of sales	(270)	(70)	(108)	(448)
Gross profit	230	50	(8)	272
Other operating expenses	(50)	(10)	(12)	(72)
Profit before tax	180	40	(20)	200

During the year to 31 March 20X9 the Board acted on the advice of the consultants and implemented a strategic decision to change the market sector of its hotel division. The company had previously targeted the upper (expensive) end of the hotel sector aimed mainly at business clients. The new strategy was to aim at the lower end, the tourism and holiday market. The change meant that most of the existing hotels were sold and new ones bought, although some hotels were retained and refurbished to suit the new market. The Board wishes to treat the results from the upper end of the hotel market as a discontinued operation and the results from the new lower end hotel market as a newly acquired business. Details from the draft financial statements for the year to 31 March 20X9 are:

	£m
Turnover	750
Cost of sales	(420)
Gross profit	330
Operating expenses	(80)
Operating profit before tax	250

The results of the hotel division are included in the above figures. Its turnover of £140 million was contributed equally by the old and new market sectors, however the gross profit margin on the new sector was 30% whilst the old sector suffered a gross loss of 20%. Operating expenses were £24 million and allocated on the basis of turnover. In the year to 31 March 20X8 the hotel division had a turnover of £160 million, a gross profit margin of 15% and operating expenses of £18 million.

Required

(i) Adopting the Board's wish with regard to the accounting treatment of the hotel division; prepare an analysis of Ventnor plc's results into continuing and discontinued operations, including the comparative figures, for the year to 31 March 20X9 as required by FRS 3 *Reporting financial performance*. (6 marks)

(ii) Briefly comment on the acceptability of the accounting treatment of the hotel division. (4 marks)

(25 marks)

25 PREPARATION QUESTION: CASH FLOWS

Set out below are the financial statements of Jenny Ltd. You have been asked to prepare the cash flow statement of the company, implementing FRS 1 *Cash flow statements*.

JENNY LIMITED
PROFIT AND LOSS ACCOUNT FOR THE YEAR ENDED 31 DECEMBER 20X2

	£'000
Turnover	2,553
Cost of sales	1,814
Gross profit	739
Distribution costs	125
Administrative expenses	264
Operating profit	350
Interest received	25
Interest paid	75
Profit on ordinary activities before taxation	300
Taxation	140
Profit after tax	160
Dividends	100
Retained profit for the year	60

JENNY LIMITED
BALANCE SHEETS AS AT 31 DECEMBER

	20X2	20X1
	£'000	£'000
Fixed assets		
Tangible assets	380	305
Intangible assets	250	200
Investments	-	25
	630	530
Current assets		
Stocks	150	102
Debtors	390	315
Short-term investments	50	-
Cash in hand	2	1
	592	418
Creditors: amounts falling due in less than one year		
Trade creditors	127	119
Bank overdraft	85	98
Taxation	120	110
Dividends proposed	100	80
	432	407
Net current assets	160	11
Total assets less current liabilities	790	541
Creditors amounts falling due after more than one year		
Long-term loan	100	-
Provisions for liabilities and charges		
Deferred taxation	70	50
	620	491
Capital and reserves		
Share capital (£1 ordinary shares)	200	150
Share premium account	160	150
Revaluation reserve	100	91
Profit and loss account	160	100
	620	491

The following information is available.

(a) The proceeds of the sale of fixed asset investments amounted to £30,000.

(b) Fixtures and fittings, with an original cost of £85,000 and a net book value of £45,000, were sold for £32,000 during the year.

(c) The current asset investments fall within the definition of liquid resources under FRS 1 (revised).

(d) The following information relates to tangible fixed assets.

	31.12.20X2	31.12.20X1
	£'000	£'000
Cost	720	595
Accumulated depreciation	340	290
Net book value	380	305

(e) 50,000 £1 ordinary shares were issued during the year at a premium of 20p per share.

Required

Prepare a cash flow statement for the year to 31 December 20X2 using the format laid out in FRS 1 (revised), together with the relevant notes to the statement.

26 OZAC (12/99 part) *27 mins*

The following information relates to the draft financial statements of Ozac plc.

PROFIT AND LOSS ACCOUNT YEAR TO 30 SEPTEMBER 20X9

	£'000	£'000
Turnover		3,536
Materials consumed	1,079	
Labour costs	758	
Production overheads	453	
Cost of sales		(2,290)
Gross profit		1,246
Selling and distribution costs	(221)	
Administration	(252)	
		(473)
Interest payable	(85)	
Dividends receivable	24	
		(61)
		712
Taxation		(210)
		502
Dividends		(350)
Retained profit for period		152

OZAC PLC BALANCE SHEET AS AT:

	30 September 20X9			30 September 20X8		
	Cost	*Dep'n*	*NBV*	*Cost*	*Dep'n*	*NBV*
	£'000	£'000	£'000	£'000	£'000	£'000
Fixed assets						
Tangible						
Land and buildings	2,000	750	1,250	1,700	745	955
Plant	1,368	525	843	940	310	630
	3,368	1,275	2,093	2,640	1,055	1,585
Investments						
Shares in						
Unquoted company			800			nil
			2,893			1,585
Current assets						
Stocks		758			628	
Debtors: all trade		260			194	
Dividend receivable		15			-	
Bank		22			-	
		1,055			822	
Creditors: amounts falling due within one year						
Creditors – all trade		234			253	
Proposed dividends		200			180	
Taxation		251			204	
Government grants		125			75	
Overdraft		-			28	
		810			740	
Net current assets			245			82
Creditors: amount falling due after more than one year						
Deferred tax		252			141	
Government grants		220			160	
7% debenture		968			Nil	
			(1,440)			(301)
			1,698			1,366
Share capital and reserves:						
Ordinary shares of £1 each			1,100			1,000
Reserves						
Share premium		180			100	
Profit and loss account		418			266	
			598			366
			1,698			1,366

Notes

1 Included in turnover are sales of £500,000 to Petrov, a company located in Bulgarussia. This figure consists of two separate sales transactions, both of which have been translated into sterling. The first transaction, translated at £200,000 was paid in Bulgas, the local currency. Ozac plc had difficulties in converting the Bulgas into sterling. Petrov's main activity relates to the extraction of crude oil, and as a result of previous exchange difficulties, it was agreed that Petrov would pay for the second transaction in barrels of oil. The spot rate for the crude oil at the date it was shipped to Ozac was £10 per barrel. Ozac plc later used the crude oil in one of its manufacturing processes.

2 All depreciation charges and a credit of £80,000 relating to the amortisation of government grants have been included in production overheads. There were no disposals of fixed assets during the year.

3 During the year 10,000 ordinary shares were issued to employees under the company's employee share purchase scheme. The market value of these shares was £50,000. This amount has been correctly recorded in share capital and share premium. The terms of the share scheme meant that the employees were required to contribute only the nominal value of the shares. The net cost to the company of this transaction has been included in labour costs.

4 On 1 October 20X8 Ozac plc issued a £1,000,000 7% debenture at a discount of 5%. The debenture is redeemable on 30 September 20Y3 at a premium of 4%. Ozac plc has amortised the discount and premium on this financial instrument equally (straight-line) over its five-year life and included the amortisation charge in the interest payable figure.

5 On 1 October 20X8 Ozac plc acquired 15% of the share capital of Tilzac Ltd, one of its major materials suppliers. It has treated this as a fixed asset investment. Ozac plc has recently received the financial statements of Tilzac Ltd for the year to 30 September 20X9. These show an interim dividend paid of £60,000 and proposed final dividend of £100,000. Ozac plc received an interim dividend from Tilzac Ltd in March 20X9, and has accrued for its share of the proposed dividend.

Required

Prepare the cash flow statement for Ozac plc for the year to 30 September 20X9. **(15 marks)**

Note. The cash flow from operations must be prepared using the direct method; you are not required to prepare the reconciliation to operating profit nor the notes relating to net debt.

27 BLUE TING (6/95, amended) *45 mins*

The following financial statements relate to Blue Ting plc for the year ended 31 May 20X5.

BLUE TING PLC
PROFIT AND LOSS ACCOUNT FOR THE YEAR ENDED 31 MAY 20X5

	£m	£m
Turnover		335
Cost of sales		(177)
Gross profit		158
Distribution costs	31	
Administrative expenses	27	
		(58)
Operating profit		100
Interest payable	(7)	
Interest receivable	3	
		(4)
Profit before tax		96
Taxation		(22)
Profit for the financial year		74
Dividends		(12)
Retained profit for financial year		62

BLUE TING PLC
BALANCE SHEETS AT 31 MAY

	20X5		20X4	
	£m	£m	£m	£m
Tangible fixed assets		272		196
Intangible fixed assets (development expenditure)		3		4
		275		200
Current assets				
Stock	140		155	
Debtors	130		110	
Short-term investments	80		-	
Cash	22		23	
	372		288	
Creditors: amounts falling due within one year	(249)		(172)	
Net current assets		123		116
Total assets less current liabilities		398		316
Creditors: amounts falling due after more than one year		(80)		(90)
		318		226
Capital and reserves				
Ordinary share capital		120		100
Share premium account		45		35
Capital redemption reserve		12		-
Profit and loss account		141		91
		318		226

The following information relates to the financial statements of Blue Ting plc.

1 *Ordinary share capital*

	£m
£1 shares fully paid at 1.6.X4	100
Issued during year	10
Purchase of own shares	(12)
Shares converted	22
	120

2 *Reserves*

	Share Premium account	*Capital Redemption reserve*	*Profit and loss account*
	£m	£m	£m
At 1.6.X4	35		91
Premium on issue (net of issue costs of £1m)	3		
Premium on conversion of debentures	7		
Transfer to CRR		12	(12)
Profit for period			62
	45	12	141

3 *Creditors: amounts falling due after more than one year*

	20X5	*20X4*
	£m	£m
Obligations under finance leases	49	30
6% debentures 20X5-20Y1	31	60
	80	90

£29m of 6% debentures 20X5-20Y1 were converted into £22m of ordinary shares during the year and interest paid in the year amounted to £2m.

4 *Creditors: amounts falling due within one year*

	20X5	*20X4*
	£m	£m
Bank overdraft	8	20
Obligations under finance leases	5	3
Trade creditors	220	131
Taxation	16	10
Dividends	-	8
	249	172

5 *Tangible fixed assets*

	£m
Carrying value at 1.6.X4	196
Additions: finance leases	28
purchases at cost	104
Disposals at carrying value	(19)
Depreciation for the year	(37)
Carrying value at 31.5.X5	272

The fixed assets disposed of realised £21m.

6 *Short-term investments*

	20X5	*20X4*
Treasury stock 12.5% 20X5 (June)	80	-
	80	-

These investments fall within the definition of liquid resources under FRS 1 (revised). All of the interest due on the Treasury Stock for the year ended 31.5.X5 had been received and there was no interest due on 31.5.X4

7 *Cash*

	20X5	*20X4*
	£m	£m
Loan notes repayable on demand	15	20
Cash at bank and in hand	7	3
	22	23

8 *Interest payable*

	20X5
	£m
Bank overdraft	2
Finance charges payable under finance leases	3
Debentures not wholly repayable within five years	2
	7

9 *Obligations under finance leases*

	20X5	*20X4*
	£m	£m
Amounts payable within one year	6	4
Within two to five years	55	33
	61	37
Less finance charges allocated to future periods	(7)	(4)
	54	33

Interest paid on finance leases in the year to 31 May 20X5 amounted to £3m.

Required

(a) Prepare a cash flow statement for Blue Ting plc for the year ended 31 May 20X5 in compliance with FRS 1 *Cash flow statements.* Students should show the relevant notes to the cash flow statement.

Hint. Leave the reconciliation of cash flow to movements in net debt and the analysis of net debt until the end. Treat 'obligations under finance leases' as a separate item from both 'debt within one year', and 'debt due after one year' as in the second example of the appendix to the revised standard. Work out the capital element of the finance lease repayment first. (20 marks)

(b) Discuss the principal advantages and disadvantages of publishing *forecast* cash flow statements for the next accounting period. (5 marks)

(25 marks)

28 LADWAY PLC *45 mins*

The draft balance sheets for the years to 31 March 20X8 and 20X7 of Ladway plc are shown below.

	20X8		*20X7*	
	£m	£m	£m	£m
Fixed assets				
Intangible assets – goodwill		450		410
Tangible assets		2,480		1,830
		2,930		2,240
Current assets				
Stock	920		763	
Debtors	642		472	
Cash	-		34	
	1,562		1,269	
Creditors: amounts falling due within one year				
Creditors	680		518	
Accrued interest	4		-	
Bank overdraft	63		-	
Proposed dividends	210		180	
Taxation	176		185	
Deferred credit – government grants	50		40	
	1,183		923	
Net current assets		379		346
Creditors: amounts falling due after more than one year				
8% debenture 2003		(200)		-
Provisions for liabilities and charges				
Government grants	210		160	
Deferred tax	52		30	
Environmental provision	76		24	
		(338)		(214)
Net assets		2,771		2,372
Share capital and reserves				
Ordinary shares of £1 each		500		400
10% preference capital		350		350
		850		750
Reserves				
Share premium account	90		70	
Revaluation reserve	170		-	
Profit and loss account	1,661		1,552	
		1,921		1,622
		2,771		2,372

The draft profit and loss account for Ladway plc for the year to 31 March 20X8 is as follows.

		£m	£m
Turnover			3,655
Cost of sales:			
Depreciation of:	tangibles	366	
	goodwill	36	
Other costs		2,522	
			(2,924)
Gross profit for period			731
Other operating income – government grant			50
			781
Distribution costs		75	
Administration		56	
Environmental provision		67	
			(198)
			583
Interest – debenture			(12)
Profit before tax			571
Taxation			(177)
Profit for the period after tax			394
Dividends: ordinary	- interim	40	
	- final	210	
preference		35	
			(285)
Retained profit for period			109

The following information is relevant.

Tangible fixed assets

(i) These include land which was revalued giving a surplus of £170 million during the period.

(ii) The company's motor vehicle haulage fleet was replaced during the year. The fleet originally cost £42 million and had been written down to £11 million at the date of its replacement. The gross cost of the fleet replacement was £180 million and a trade-in allowance of £14 million was given for the old vehicles.

(iii) The company acquired some new plant on 1 July 19X7 at a cost of £120 million from Bromway plc. An arrangement was made on the same day for the liability for the plant to be settled by Ladway plc issuing at par an 8% debenture dated 20Y3 to Bromway plc. The value by which the debenture exceeded the liability for the plant was received from Bromway plc in cash.

Environmental provision

The provision represents an estimate of the cost of environmental improvements relating to the company's mining activities.

Ordinary share issue

During the year Ladway plc made a bonus issue from the share premium account of one for every ten shares held. Later Ladway plc made a further issue for cash.

Required

(a) A cash flow statement for Ladway plc for the year to 31 March 20X8 prepared in accordance with FRS 1 Cash flow statements (revised 1996). (20 marks)

The revision of FRS 1 *Cash flow statements* by the Accounting Standards Board includes a requirement for companies to disclose a note that reconciles the movement of cash in the period with the movement in *net debt*. The statement is not part of the cash flow statement but usually adjoins it.

Required

(b) Describe the composition of the reconciliation to net debt, and discuss the relevance and usefulness of this information to users of financial statements. (5 marks)

(25 marks)

29 PREPARATION QUESTION: SSAP 17

Statement of Standard Accounting Practice No 17 contains the following terms.

Post balance sheet events
Adjusting events
Non-adjusting events

Required

(a) Explain the meaning of each term and give examples of adjusting and non-adjusting events.

(b) State why a Statement of Standard Accounting Practice is needed to regulate the disclosure of post balance sheet events.

(c) What are the disclosure requirements?

30 SUBSTANCE OVER FORM (12/94) *45 mins*

Financial Reporting Standard 5 *Reporting the substance of transactions* requires an entity's financial statements to report the substance of transactions into which it has entered. The FRS sets out how to determine the substance of a transaction and whether any resulting assets and liabilities should be included in the balance sheet. The FRS came about partly as a result of concern over arrangements made by companies whereby assets and liabilities were omitted from the balance sheet.

Required

(a) Explain the reasons why companies may wish to omit assets and liabilities from their balance sheets. (5 marks)

(b) Explain the reasons why the Accounting Standards Board felt it necessary to introduce FRS 5 *Reporting the substance of transactions*. (5 marks)

(c) Discuss the proposed treatment of the following items in the financial statements.

(i) Beak plc sells land to a property investment company, Wings plc. The sale price is £20 million and the current market value is £30 million. Beak plc can buy the land back at any time in the next five years for the original selling price plus an annual commission of 1% above the current bank base rate. Wings plc cannot require Beak plc to buy the land back at any time.

The accountant of Beak plc proposes to treat this transaction as a sale in the financial statements. (7 marks)

(ii) A car manufacturer, Gocar plc, supplies cars to a car dealer, Sparks Ltd, on the following terms.

Sparks Ltd has to pay a monthly fee of £100 per car for the privilege of displaying it in its showroom and is also responsible for insuring the cars. When a car is sold to a customer, Sparks Ltd has to pay Gocar plc the factory price of the car when it was first supplied. Sparks Ltd can only return cars to Gocar plc on the payment of a fixed penalty charge of 10% of the cost of the car. Sparks Ltd has to pay the factory price for the cars if they remain unsold within a four month period. Gocar plc cannot demand the return of the cars from Sparks Ltd.

The accountant of Sparks Ltd proposes to treat the cars unsold for less than four months as the property of Gocar plc and not show them as stock in the financial statements. (8 marks)

(25 marks)

31 ATOMIC POWER (12/00 amended) *45 mins*

You are preparing a technical note to all your clients regarding the effects of FRS 12 *Provisions, contingent liabilities and contingent assets*, which became effective for accounting periods ending on or after 23 March 1999. Amongst other things, FRS 12 replaces SSAP 18 *Accounting for contingencies.*

One of your clients, Atomic Power plc, has asked for further help in applying FRS 12 because the company is concerned it may not be applying the standard correctly.

Atomic Power operates nuclear power stations that supply power to international, national and regional electricity companies. Environmental clear up costs can be a substantial item of expenditure for nuclear power plant operators; in some countries Atomic Power's licences have, by law, environmental clean-up commitments written in as part of the agreement, whereas in other countries there is no legal requirement to provide for them.

Atomic Power has brought into commission, on 1 July 20X1, a new nuclear power station, built at a cost of £600m. The plant has a licence to supply electricity for 12 years, which is the estimated life of the power station. At the end of 12 years, the station must be demolished and all the waste product (ie spent fuel) buried over 100m underground in an area sealed for contamination purposes. During the station's life the company will have to pay for the clean up of any contamination leaks from the plant's water cooling system.

The company has estimated the cost of demolition and waste disposal in 12 years' time at £540m, the discounted value of which, at an appropriate rate, is £360m. Past experience suggests that there is a 30% chance of a contamination leak occurring in any 12 month period, and the cost of cleaning it up will be between £60m and £120m a time, depending on its extent.

The company has sent you extracts from its draft financial statements in relation to the power plant, showing the following:

PROFIT AND LOSS ACCOUNT (EXTRACTS)

	£m
Fixed asset depreciation: power station (1/12 × £600m)	50
Provision for demolition and waste disposal (1/12 × £540m)	45
Provision for contamination leak clean-up (30% × £90m (average))	27
	122

BALANCE SHEET (EXTRACTS)

Tangible fixed assets	£m
Power station at cost	600
Depreciation	(50)
	550
Provisions for liabilities and charges	
Environmental costs (45 + 27)	72

No contamination leaks occurred in the year ended 30 June 20X2.

Required

(a) Draft a technical note for your clients that:

(i) Explains why there is a need for an accounting standard in respect of provisions.

(ii) Describes the main principles of FRS 12 in accounting for provisions, with particular reference to definitions and recognition and measurement criteria.

(12 marks)

(b) Advise Atomic Power plc on the acceptability of its current accounting policy and redraft the extracts of the financial statements for the company in line with FRS 12.

(8 marks)

(c) Explain the effect it would have on your answer to (b) if Atomic Power was operating this nuclear power station in a country that does not legislate in respect of the above types of environmental costs. (5 marks)

(25 marks)

32 PREPARATION QUESTION: FRS 4

Summarise the basic disclosure requirements of FRS 4 *Capital instruments* for:

(a) Debt

(b) Shareholders' funds

Guidance notes

1 This PREPARATION question only asks for the *basic* disclosure requirements. There is no need to list exceptions or alternatives to the requirements.

2 FRS 4 is a complicated standard. The examiner may ask a question on FRS 4 in the context of a brief discussion, or it may affect one aspect of a larger question.

33 PREPARATION QUESTION: FRS 13

FRS 13 *Derivatives and other financial instruments: disclosures* introduces requirements for entities to disclose certain information on the financial instruments they hold. The objective of these requirements is to provide information about:

(a) The impact of financial instruments on an entity's risk profile

(b) How the risks arising from financial instruments might affect the entity's performance and financial condition

(c) How these risks are being managed

Required

(a) Summarise the approach adopted by FRS 13.

(b) Discuss briefly why it was considered necessary to introduce disclosure requirements relating to derivatives and financial instruments.

(c) Discuss the types of risk arising from financial instruments and why information about these risks might be of value to a user of the financial statements.

34 JEDDERS (12/00 amended) *27 mins*

Your assistant at Jedders plc has been preparing the financial statements for the year ended 31 December 20X0 and has raised the following queries.

(a) The company has three freehold properties in different parts of the South of England. As at 1 January 20X0, their original cost, accumulated depreciation to date and carrying (book) values were as follows.

	Cost	*Depreciation*	*Carrying value 1.1.20X0*
	£'000	£'000	£'000
Property in Exeter	3,000	1,800	1,200
Property in Croydon	6,000	1,200	4,800
Property in Dover	3,750	1,500	2,250

All properties had an expected life of 50 years from their date of acquisition and this has not changed.

On 1 January an independent surveyor provided valuation information to suggest that the value of the Dover property was the same as book value, the Exeter property had fallen against carrying value by 20% and the Croydon property had risen by 40% in value against the carrying value.

The directors of the company wish to include the revaluation of the Croydon property in the accounts to 31 December 20X0, whilst leaving the other properties at their depreciated historical cost.

The directors believe that this treatment of the Exeter property is prudent and can be justified because property prices are expected to recover within the next few years, so that this fall in value will be entirely reversed.

Required

(i) Advise the directors whether their proposal is acceptable, assuming they are committed to the use of current value for the Croydon property. (2 marks)

(ii) Calculate the profit and loss account charges and the fixed asset balance sheet extracts for all the properties for the year ended 31 December 20X0. You should follow the requirements of FRS 15 *Tangible fixed assets* (3 marks)

(b) On 1 October 20X0, Jedders plc signed a debt factoring agreement with Fab Factors Ltd. Jedders' debtors are to be split into three groups, as follows.

- **Group A** debtors will not be factored or administered by Fab Factors under the agreement, but instead will be collected as usual by Jedders.
- **Group B** debtors are to be factored and collected by Fab Factors on a 'with recourse' basis. Fab Factors will charge a 1% per month finance charge on the balance outstanding at the beginning of the month. Jedders will reimburse in full any individual balance outstanding after three months.
- **Group C** debtors will be factored and collected by Fab Factors 'without recourse'; Fab Factors will pay Jedders 95% of the book value of the debtors.

Jedders plc has a policy of making a provision for doubtful debts of 20% of a debtor balance when it becomes three months old.

The debtor groups have been analysed as follows.

	Balance @	*% of 1 October 20X0 balance collected in:*		
	1 October 20X0	*October*	*November*	*December*
	£'000			
Group A	1,250	30%	30%	20%
Group B	1,500	40%	30%	20%
Group C	2,000	50%	25%	22%

Required

For the accounts of Jedders plc, calculate the finance costs and charge for doubtful debts for each group of debtors for the period 1 October – 31 December 20X0 and show the balance sheet values for those debtors as at 31 December 20X0. (5 marks)

(c) On 1 January 20X0, Jedders plc issued £15m of 10% debentures at a 5% discount. Direct costs relating to the issue were £300,000. The debentures will be redeemed on 31 December 20X3 at a 10% premium.

Fab Factors have suggested that, if they had been consulted beforehand, they would have suggested an issue of convertible loan stock rather than debentures. The company could have specified a lower interest or coupon rate on the loan stock than on the debentures, by offering advantageous conversion terms to equity. Jedders' gearing would have been improved because the substance of such convertible loan stock is that it will eventually become equity and so should be treated as such. The company's profits would also have been improved by the lower finance costs.

Required

(i) Calculate the finance charge in the profit and loss account and show the balance sheet extracts for the 10% debentures in Jedders' financial statements to 31 December 20X0. (3 marks)

(ii) Comment on the suggestion from Fab Factors regarding the use and treatment of convertible loan stock. (2 marks)

(15 marks)

35 PREPARATION QUESTION: REVENUE RECOGNITION

Telecast Industries plc is preparing its accounts for the year ended 30 September 20X1. In May 20X1 it bought the rights to a film called 'Wind of Change'. It paid a fixed fee and will not incur any further significant costs of commissions. It has entered into the following contracts with:

(a) *Warmer Cinemas plc*

This is a large company with a chain of cinemas throughout the UK. Warmer Cinemas plc has negotiated the right to screen the film during the period from 1 July 20X1 to 31 December 20X1 in as many of its cinemas and as frequently as it chooses. Telecast Industries plc will be paid 15% of gross box office receipts.

(b) *Big Screen Ltd*

This is a small company operating a single cinema. Under the terms of the contract it may screen the film twice a day for the same period as the above contract. It has paid a fixed fee of £10,000.

(c) *Global Satellite plc*

This is a satellite TV company that broadcasts to Europe. It paid £4 million in August 20X1 for the right to screen the film ten times at intervals of not less than one month apart during the period from 1 January 20X2 to 31 December 20X2.

Required

Applying the recommendations in the Statement of Principles describe how Telecast Industries plc should treat the revenue from each of the above contracts in the accounting year to 30 September 20X1.

Note. You are not required to discuss how the cost of the film should be expensed.

36 PREPARATION QUESTION: PURCHASE OF OWN SHARES

In recent years several large listed companies have purchased their own ordinary shares.

You are required to summarise:

(a) The accounting requirements for a public listed company when it purchases its own shares

(b) Six advantages of a company purchasing its own shares.

37 LED (12/94 part) *27 mins*

LED Ltd is a private company, which maintains its accounting records on a computerised system. The financial director has decided that the company will redeem all of the preference shares of the company at a premium of 10% in accordance with the original terms of redemption. In order to assist with the redemption, a new issue of 5,000 £1 ordinary shares at £1.25 will be made and a bank overdraft limit of £10,000 has been negotiated. The redeemable preference shares were originally issued at par value and the preference dividend has been paid up to date.

The financial director has asked your advice on how to treat this matter in the financial statements. He realises that the current redemption plan would reduce the capital of the company and he wondered whether this was possible under the Companies Acts.

The current draft balance sheet of LED Ltd is as follows.

LED LIMITED
DRAFT BALANCE SHEET AS AT 30 NOVEMBER 20X4

	£	£
Ordinary shares of £1 each		25,000
7% redeemable preference shares of £1 each		12,500
Share premium account		7,500
Profit and loss account		5,000
		50,000
Sundry fixed assets		20,000
Sundry net current assets	25,000	
Cash	5,000	
		30,000
		50,000

Required

(a) Explain to the financial director the conditions and safeguards which must be fulfilled when a private company redeems shares out of capital. (5 marks)

(b) Explain the reasons why these conditions and safeguards relating to private companies have been introduced. (4 marks)

(c) Prepare the revised balance sheet of LED Ltd assuming the planned redemption of preference shares takes place. (6 marks)

(15 marks)

38 GLOBELINK (12/96) *45 mins*

The following financial statements relate to Globelink International plc for the year ended 30 November 20X6.

GROUP PROFIT AND LOSS ACCOUNT FOR THE YEAR ENDED 30 NOVEMBER 20X6

	£'000	£'000
Turnover		
Continuing operations		
Ongoing	214,277	
Acquisitions	7,573	
	221,850	
Discontinued operations	54,853	
		276,703
Cost of sales		(220,398)
Gross profit		56,305
Distribution costs	21,886	
Administrative expenses	21,421	
		(43,307)
		12,998
Other operating income		894
Income from interests in associated undertakings		3,575
Operating profit		
Continuing operations		
Ongoing	16,590	
Acquisitions	1,585	
	18,175	
Discontinued operations	(708)	
		17,467
Profit on disposal of fixed assets	1,170	
Discontinued operations		
Loss on sale of operations	(3,168)	
		(1,998)
		15,469
Income from investments	1,648	
Interest payable	(1,432)	
		216
Profit on ordinary activities before taxation		15,685
Tax on profit on ordinary activities		(4,747)
Profit on ordinary activities after taxation		10,938
Minority interests		(404)
Profit attributable to members of the parent company		10,534
Dividends		(2,815)
Retained profit for the year		7,719

GROUP BALANCE SHEET AT 30 NOVEMBER 20X6

	£'000	£'000
Fixed assets		
Intangible assets		2,680
Tangible assets		43,940
Investments in associated undertakings		26,670
		73,290
Current assets		
Stock	33,962	
Debtors	26,470	
Cash at bank and in hand	11,468	
	71,900	
Creditors: amounts falling due within one year	(32,530)	
Net current assets		39,370
Total assets less current liabilities		112,660
Creditors: amounts falling due after more than one year		(16,338)
Accruals and deferred income		
Deferred government grants		(3,530)
Minority interests		(812)
		91,980
Capital and reserves		
Called up share capital		39,600
Share premium account		645
Revaluation reserve		12,725
Profit and loss account		39,010
		91,980

The following information is relevant to the financial statements of Globelink International plc.

(a) The group manufactures and sells printing machinery within the United Kingdom and Asia.

(i) Sales to Asian customers account for 32% of total group turnover.

(ii) Sales originating from Asian subsidiaries account for 34% of the total group turnover including intercompany sales.

(iii) Discontinued activities totally relate to United Kingdom business and operations.

(iv) Items (i) and (ii) above relate solely to continuing activities.

(b) Total intercompany sales from continuing activities were £16.5 million during the year. Asian subsidiary companies originated 20% of these sales.

(c) Asian subsidiaries contributed 24% of the continuing operating profit before taking into account common costs and the profit before tax of associated undertakings. Any apportionment of the common costs of £2.4 million was deemed to be misleading by the directors and therefore no apportionment was to take place. The associated undertakings are all operating from the United Kingdom.

(d) The group has 25% of its tangible and intangible fixed assets located in Asia and 30% of its current assets. No government grants have been received in Asia. The creditors falling due after more than one year relate to a loan obtained by the UK parent company. Additionally, the directors felt that it was not possible to allocate 'creditors falling due within one year' of £7.8 million between the segments. After adjusting for this amount, 30% of the balance related to activities in Asia.

(e) The directors have decided that for the purpose of the disclosure requirements of FRS 3 *Reporting financial performance,* the acquisitions in the year do not have a material impact on a business segment as they relate to UK operations. However, they consider that the discontinued operations have a material impact on the UK operations.

Required

(a) Prepare a segmental report by geographical area for Globelink International plc in accordance with SSAP 25 *Segmental reporting,* FRS 3 *Reporting financial performance* and the Companies Act 1985 as amended by the Companies Act 1989. (All calculations should be to the nearest £'000.) (21 marks)

(b) Briefly describe *four* limitations of SSAP 25 *Segmental reporting.* (4 marks)

(25 marks)

39 DIVERSITY (6/00) *45 mins*

Consolidated financial statements in effect show the performance of a group as if it were a single entity. It is widely recognised that this information is of great value to many user groups, but consolidated financial statements have also been criticised. Many commentators have argued that to aggregate financial information relating to several subsidiaries that may operate in different industries and markets produces information that may conceal important data and has the potential to confuse those who wish to analyse it. A defence of this is that the financial statements of the individual companies within a group are usually publicly available to those who take the trouble to obtain them.

Required

(a) Identify the main items of information that require disclosure under SSAP 25 *Segmental reporting.* (3 marks)

(b) (i) Bearing in mind the above comments, discuss the necessity for, and the benefits of, segmental information. (5 marks)

(ii) Identify the main problem areas relating to the provision of segmental information. (6 marks)

(c) The following information has been extracted from the consolidated financial statements of Diversity plc for the year ended 31 March 20X4.

Note. The consolidated figures exclude inter-segment trading.

	£'000
Turnover	900
Cost of sales	634
Distribution costs	87
Central administration	37
Amortisation of goodwill	20
Finance costs (lease 10, debenture 12)	22
Dividends	50
Consolidated goodwill	60
Tangible fixed assets: owned	370
leased	150
Current assets	160
Current liabilities	90
Finance lease obligations	200
10% debenture (issued in 20X2)	120

The activities of Diversity plc relate to three operational segments: engineering, chemicals and a supermarket chain. Information relating to the segments is as follows.

	Engineering	*Chemicals*	*Supermarkets*
Turnover	420	340	200
Gross profit margin on third party sales	20%	40%	25%
Distribution and administration	24	38	25
Goodwill (see below)			
Owned fixed asset	150	120	100
Leased assets	60%	40%	Nil
Current assets	70	60	30
Current liabilities	40	20	30
Lease obligations	50%	50%	Nil

Notes

(i) The segmental figures include the results of inter-segment trading; all figures (other than the percentages) are in £ million.

(ii) During the year the engineering division manufactured the steelwork for the superstructure of several new supermarkets. This work was invoiced at cost (£20 million) to the supermarket division. The other inter-segment sales (£40 million) were from the chemical division to the engineering division at normal profit margins. There are no unrealised intra-group profits.

(iii) The finance costs comprise interest on finance leases and debenture interest. The management of Diversity plc considers the debenture interest to be a common cost, but not the interest on finance leases. This can be assumed to accrue in proportion to the value of the outstanding lease obligations.

(iv) The consolidated goodwill and its amortisation relate to a subsidiary that has both engineering and chemical operations. Management calculated that, based on the relative profitability at the time of acquisition, the goodwill should be allocated 30% to the engineering operations and 70% to the chemical operation.

Required

Prepare, as far as the information permits, a segment report for Diversity plc commenting on the merit of management's policy of apportioning the finance lease interest and the consolidated goodwill. (11 marks)

(25 marks)

PREPARATION OF CONSOLIDATED FINANCIAL STATEMENTS

Questions 40 to 53 cover the preparation of consolidated financial statements, the subject of Part C of the BPP Study Text for Paper 2.5.

40 PREPARATION QUESTION: CONSOLIDATED FINANCIAL STATEMENTS

'The consolidation of financial statements hides rather than provides information.'

You are required to discuss this statement.

41 PREPARATION QUESTION: CONSOLIDATED BALANCE SHEET

Pappa plc purchased 1,450,000 ordinary shares in Lima plc in 20X0, when the general reserve of Lima plc stood at £400,000 and there was no balance of unappropriated profit.

The balance sheets of the two companies as at 31 December 20X4 are set out below.

	Pappa plc		*Lima plc*	
	£'000	£'000	£'000	£'000
Fixed assets				
Tangible assets				
Buildings	5,000		1,000	
Plant	3,396		543	
Vehicles	472		244	
		8,868		1,787
Investment				
Shares in Lima plc at cost		1,450		-
		10,318		1,787
Current assets				
Stock	1,983		1,425	
Debtors	1,462		1,307	
Cash	25		16	
	3,470		2,748	
Creditors: amounts due within one year				
Overdraft	1,176		840	
Trade creditors	887		1,077	
Tax	540		218	
Dividend	280		-	
	2,883		2,135	
Net current assets		587		613
Total assets less current liabilities		10,905		2,400
Creditors: amounts due after one year				
10% debentures		4,000		-
15% debentures		-		500
		6,905		1,900

	Pappa plc	*Lima plc*
	£'000	£'000
Shareholders' funds		
Ordinary shares of 50p each	5,000	1,000
Share premium account	500	-
General reserve	1,200	800
Unappropriated profit	205	100
	6,905	1,900

At the balance sheet date the current account of Pappa plc with Lima plc was agreed at £23,000 owed by Lima plc. This account is included in the appropriate debtors and trade creditors balances shown above.

Required

(a) Prepare a consolidated balance sheet for the Pappa Lima Group.

(b) Show the alterations necessary to the group balance sheet if the inter-company balance owed by Lima plc to Pappa plc represented an invoice for goods sold by Pappa to Lima at a mark-up of 15% on cost, and still unsold by Lima plc at 31 December 20X4.

Note. You may assume that goodwill does not require amortisation.

42 HAMPLE (6/99 amended) *45 mins*

On 1 April 20X8 Hample plc acquired 90% of the equity shares in Sopel Ltd. On the same day Hample plc accepted a 10% loan note from Sopel Ltd for £200,000 which was repayable at £40,000 per annum (on 31 March each year) over the next five years. Sopel Ltd's retained profits at the date of acquisition were £2,200,000.

BALANCE SHEETS AS AT 31 MARCH 20X9

		Hample Ltd		*Sopel Ltd*
	£'000	£'000	£'000	£'000
Fixed assets				
Intangible – Software		-		1,800
Tangible:				
Property		600		900
Plant and equipment		1,520		1,090
Investments - equity in Sopel Ltd		4,110		-
- 10% loan note Sopel Ltd		200		-
- others		65		210
		6,495		4,000
Current assets				
Stock	719		560	
Debtors	524		328	
Sopel Ltd current account	75		-	
Cash	20		-	
	1,338		888	
Creditors: amounts falling due within one year				
Trade creditors	475		472	
Hample plc current account	-		60	
Taxation	228		174	
Operating overdraft	-		27	
Dividend payable	100		-	
	(803)		(733)	
Net current assets		535		155
Creditors: amounts falling due after more that one year				
10% Loan note		-		(160)
Government grants		(230)		(40)
Net assets		6,800		3,955
Share capital and reserves				
Ordinary shares of £1 each		2,000		1,500
Share premium	2,000		500	
Retaining earnings	2,800		1,955	
		4,800		2,455
		6,800		3,955

The following information is relevant:

(i) Included in Sopel Ltd's property at the date of acquisition was a leasehold property recorded at its depreciated historic cost of £400,000. The leasehold had been sublet for its remaining life of only four years at an annual rental of £80,000 payable in advance on 1 April each year. The directors of Hample plc are of the opinion that the fair value of this leasehold is best reflected by the present value of its future cash flows. An appropriate cost of capital for the group is 10% per annum.

The present value of a £1 annuity received at the end of each year where interest rates are 10% can be taken as:

3 year annuity	£2.50
4 year annuity	£3.20

(ii) The software of Sopel Ltd represents the depreciated cost of the development of an integrated business accounting package. It was completed at a capitalised cost of £2,400,000 and went on sale on 1 April 20X7. Sopel Ltd's directors are depreciating the software on a straight-line basis over an eight-year life (ie £300,000 per annum). However, the directors of Hample plc are of the opinion that a five-year life would be more appropriate as sales of business software rarely exceed this period.

(iii) The stock of Hample plc on 31 March 20X9 contains goods at a transfer price of £25,000 that were supplied by Sopel Ltd who had marked them up with a profit of 25% on cost.

(iv) On 31 March 20X9 Sopel Ltd remitted to Hample plc a cash payment of £55,000. This was not received by Hample plc until early April. It was made up of an annual repayment of the 10% loan note of £40,000 (the interest had already been paid) and £15,000 off the current account balance.

(v) Consolidated goodwill is amortised over a five-year life.

Required

Prepare the consolidated balance sheet of Hample plc at 31 March 20X9.

(25 marks)

43 HARDY AND SIBLING (6/98) *45 mins*

On 1 April 20X5 Hardy plc acquired 4 million of Sibling plc's ordinary shares, paying £4.50 each. At the same time it also purchased, at par, £500,000 of its 10% redeemable preference shares. At the date of acquisition the retained profits of Sibling plc were £8,400,000.

Reproduced below are the draft balance sheets of the two companies at 31 March 20X8.

	Hardy		Sibling	
	£'000	£'000	£'000	£'000
Fixed assets				
Land and buildings		22,000		12,000
Plant and equipment		20,450		10,220
Investment in Sibling plc: equity		18,000		-
preference		500		-
		60,950		22,220
Current assets				
Stock	9,850		6,590	
Debtors	11,420		3,830	
Cash and bank	490		-	
	21,760		10,420	
Creditors: amounts falling due within one year				
Creditors	5,600		3,810	
Bank overdraft	-		570	
Provision for taxation	2,470		1,980	
Provision for dividends - ordinary	800		500	
- preference	-		200	
	8,870		7,060	
Net current assets		12,890		3,360
Creditors: amounts falling due after more than one year				
10% debentures 20Y1		(12,000)		(4,000)
Net assets		61,840		21,580
Share capital and reserves				
Ordinary shares of £1 each		10,000		5,000
10% redeemable preference shares		-		2,000
Profit and loss reserve		51,840		14,580
		61,840		21,580

Extracts from the profit and loss account of Sibling plc, before intra-group adjustments for the year to 31 March 20X8 are as follows.

	£'000
Profit before tax	5,400
Taxation	(1,600)
	3,800

The following information is relevant.

(i) Included in the land and buildings of Sibling plc is a large area of development land at its cost of £5m. Its fair value at the date Sibling plc was acquired was £7m and by 31 March 20X8 this had risen to £8.5m. The group valuation policy for development land is that it should be carried at fair value and not depreciated.

(ii) Also at the date of Sibling plc's acquisition the plant and equipment included plant that had a fair value of £4m in excess of its carrying value. This plant had a remaining life of five years. The group calculates depreciation on a straight-line basis. The fair value of Sibling plc's other net assets approximated to their carrying values.

(iii) During the year Sibling plc sold goods to Hardy plc for £1.8m. Sibling plc adds a 20% mark-up on cost to all its sales. Goods with a transfer price of £450,000 were included in Hardy plc's stock at 31 March 20X8.

The balance on the current accounts of the parent and subsidiary was £240,000 on 31 March 20X8.

(iv) Hardy plc has not accounted for any dividends receivable from Sibling plc.

(v) Consolidated goodwill is written off on a straight-line basis over a five year life.

Required

(a) Prepare the consolidated balance sheet of Hardy plc at 31 March 20X8. (17 marks)

(b) Calculate the minority interest in the adjusted profit of Sibling plc for the year to 31 March 20X8. (4 marks)

(c) Explain why FRS 7 *Fair values in acquisition accounting* considers it important to consolidate the fair values of assets and liabilities of an acquired subsidiary at the date of acquisition. (4 marks)

(25 marks)

44 CLAYMORE PLC *45 mins*

Claymore plc acquired 60% of the ordinary share capital of College Ltd on 1 October 20X6. The purchase cost of the shares was satisfied by issuing 200,000 ordinary £1 shares of Claymore plc at £1.75 per share. Issue costs of £20,000 were incurred. The companies' financial statements for the year ended 30 November 20X6 were as follows.

BALANCE SHEETS AT 30 NOVEMBER 20X6

	Claymore plc	*College Ltd*
	£'000	£'000
Tangible fixed assets	700	140
Investment in College Ltd	350	-
	1,050	140
Current assets		
Stock	60	180
Debtors	95	85
Cash	75	45
	230	310
Creditors: amounts falling due within one year	(160)	(100)
Net current assets	70	210
Total assets less current liabilities	1,120	350
Creditors: amounts falling due after one year	(420)	(70)
	700	280
Capital and reserves		
Ordinary £1 shares	300	40
Share premium account	150	60
Profit and loss reserve	250	180
	700	280

PROFIT AND LOSS ACCOUNTS FOR THE YEAR ENDED 30 NOVEMBER 20X6

	Claymore plc	*College Ltd*
	£'000	£'000
Turnover	1,260	708
Cost of sales	(644)	(426)
Gross profit	616	282
Distribution costs	(248)	(42)
Administrative expenses	(130)	(84)
Operating profit	238	156
Interest payable	(28)	(12)
Income from College Ltd	18	-
Profit before taxation	228	144
Tax on profit	(113)	(54)
Profit after taxation	115	90
Dividends paid	(15)	(30)
Retained profit for year	100	60

The following information is relevant to the preparation of the group financial statements.

(a) At the date of acquisition the value of the tangible fixed assets of College Ltd at open market price was £200,000. The estimated net realisable value of these assets was £160,000. Because of the proximity of the acquisition to the financial year end, no depreciation adjustment is to be made in the group accounts, and the carrying value of the tangible fixed assets in College Ltd's accounts at the date of acquisition is deemed to be the year end value. All other assets and liabilities of College Ltd were stated at their fair values at the time of acquisition.

(b) The issue costs of £20,000 incurred on the issue of ordinary share capital had been charged to the profit and loss account of Claymore plc under the heading of 'administrative expenses'.

(c) College Ltd paid an ordinary dividend of 75p per share on 1 November 20X6. No further dividends were declared for the year ending 30 November 20X6.

(d) Goodwill arising on acquisition is to be amortised against the profit and loss account over a six year period on the straight-line basis. A full year's charge is to be included in administrative expenses for the year ending 30 November 20X6.

(e) There were no intercompany transactions during the financial year and it is assumed that the profit of College Ltd accrues evenly over the year. College Ltd had not issued any shares since the acquisition by Claymore plc.

(f) The company's policy is to account for preacquisition dividends by treating them as a return of the cost of the investment in the subsidiary.

Required

(a) Prepare a consolidated balance sheet and profit and loss account for the Claymore Group plc for the year ending 30 November 20X6. (Notes to the accounts are not required: workings should be to the nearest £'000.) (21 marks)

(b) Explain how the fair value might be estimated where the purchase consideration is in the form of share capital and no suitable market price exists (for example where the shares issued are those of an unquoted company). (4 marks)

(25 marks)

45 PREPARATION QUESTION: BASIC CONSOLIDATION

Beaver plc has owned 80% of Gorilla Ltd's equity since its incorporation. On 31 December 20X8 it despatched goods which cost £80,000 to Gorilla, at an invoiced cost of £100,000. Gorilla received the goods on 2 January 20X9 and recorded the transaction then. The two companies' draft accounts as at 31 December 20X8 are shown below.

PROFIT AND LOSS ACCOUNTS FOR THE YEAR ENDED 31 DECEMBER 20X8

	Beaver	*Gorilla*
	£'000	£'000
Sales	5,000	1,000
Cost of sales	2,900	600
Gross profit	2,100	400
Other expenses	1,700	320
Net profit	400	80
Tax	130	25
Profit after tax	270	55
Dividends proposed	130	40
Retained profit for the year	140	15
Retained profit brought forward	260	185
Retained profit carried forward	400	200

BALANCE SHEETS AT 31 DECEMBER 20X8

	£'000	£'000
Fixed assets	2,000	200
Current assets		
Stock	500	120
Trade debtors	650	40
Bank and cash	390	35
	1,540	195
Current liabilities		
Trade creditors	910	30
Dividend payable	100	40
Tax	130	25
	1,140	95
Net current assets	400	100
Total assets less current liabilities	2,400	300
Capital and reserves		
Share capital	2,000	100
Profit and loss account	400	200
	2,400	300

Required

Prepare draft consolidated financial statements.

Guidance notes

1 This is a very easy example to ease you into the technique of preparing consolidated accounts. There are a number of points to note.

2 Stock in transit should be included in the balance sheet and deducted from cost of sales at cost to the group.

3 Similarly, the intra-group debtor and sale should be eliminated as a consolidation adjustment.

4 Beaver plc must have included its intercompany account in trade debtors as it is not specifically mentioned elsewhere in the accounts. However, it has apparently not yet recorded the dividend receivable from Gorilla as this is not shown in the P&L account. It must therefore be added to group reserves and the creditor can be cancelled from Gorilla's balance sheet.

5 Remember that only the holding company's shares and proposed dividends are shown in the group accounts.

6 The minority interest in the P&L account is easily calculated as 20% of post-tax profit for the year as shown in Gorilla's accounts. However, in the balance sheet, the minority interest represents the minority interest in retained profits and share capital only. The proposed dividend payable to the minority is a current liability.

7 Don't forget that Beaver's accounts must somewhere contain a balance for its investment in Gorilla Ltd (its holding of shares in Gorilla, at cost since no share premium is shown in Gorilla's books). Fixed assets must therefore be reduced by this amount to correspond to the cancellation of Gorilla's share capital. A valid (although less likely) alternative would be to assume that Beta had provided against the cost of the investment in full, thus reducing the value of the investment in its books to nil. This provision would be reversed as a consolidation adjustment, thus increasing group reserves by the amount of the provision.

46 PREPARATION QUESTION: MERGER

The summarised balance sheets of Kool Ltd and Groovy Ltd as at 30 September 20X8 are as follows.

	Kool Ltd £'000	Groovy Ltd £'000
Freehold properties	-	210
Other fixed assets	3,650	420
Net current assets	1,160	51
	4,810	681
Ordinary share capital (£1 shares)	2,000	300
Reserves at 1 October 20X7	2,600	221
Net profit reported for 20X7/X8	210	160
	4,810	681

Kool Ltd acquired the entire share capital of Groovy Ltd on 30 September 20X8 for £900,000. The consideration took the form of five newly issued ordinary shares in Kool Ltd for every three shares currently held in Groovy Ltd. This transaction has not yet been recorded in the books of Kool.

Groovy Ltd's freehold properties possessed a fair value of £325,000 on 30 September 20X8. There were no significant differences between the book value and fair value of Groovy's remaining assets at that time.

Required

(a) Prepare the consolidated balance sheet of Kool Ltd and its subsidiary Groovy Ltd at 30 September 20X8 in accordance with the acquisition method of accounting specified in FRS 2. (Ignore the requirement to amortise goodwill.)

(b) Prepare the consolidated balance sheet of Kool Ltd and its subsidiary Groovy Ltd at 30 September 20X8 in accordance with the merger method of accounting specified in FRS 6.

Notes

(i) Assume the criteria of FRS 6 *Acquisition and mergers* for a merger are met.

(ii) Show all workings.

(iii) Ignore taxation.

(iv) The balance sheet should be framed, as far as possible, in the format given in the question, so as to show the group net profit reported for 20X7/X8.

Guidance notes

1 Lay out pro forma balance sheets for both methods.
2 You need workings for share capital, goodwill and the merger adjustment.

47 HILL AND GLEN (12/97 part) *27 mins*

Hill plc is a small company that has recently achieved a listing on the Alternative Investment Market. The company's management are ambitious and intend to expand rapidly. On 1 April 20X7 Hill plc acquired all of the ordinary share capital of Glen Ltd by way of a share exchange. Hill plc issued four of its own shares for every three shares in Glen Ltd. The market value of Hill plc's shares on 1 April 20X7 was £5 each. The share issue has not yet been recorded in Hill plc's books. The summarised financial statements of both companies for the year to 30 September 20X7 are as follows.

PROFIT AND LOSS ACCOUNTS

	Hill plc		Glen Ltd	
	£'000	£'000	£'000	£'000
Turnover		1,000		1,000
Cost of sales		630		660
Gross profit		370		340
Operating expenses		120		100
Operating profit		250		240
Taxation		50		40
Profit after tax		200		200
Dividends: interim	40		-	
final (proposed)	40		60	
		80		60
Retained profit for the year		120		140

BALANCE SHEETS

	Hill plc		Glen Ltd	
	£'000	£'000	£'000	£'000
Fixed assets		440		670
Current assets				
Stock	240		280	
Debtors	170		210	
Bank	20		40	
	430		530	
Creditors: amounts falling due within one year				
Creditors	170		160	
Taxation	50		40	
Dividends	40		60	
	260		260	
Net current assets		170		270
		610		940
Debentures		-		150
Net assets		610		790
Capital and reserves				
Ordinary shares of £1 each		200		150
Profit and loss account		410		640
		610		790

The following information is relevant.

(a) The fair values of Glen Ltd's land and stock were in excess of their book values at the date of acquisition by £125,000 and £25,000 respectively. The fair values of other net assets were equal to their book values. All of the stock at the date of acquisition had been sold prior to 30 September 20X7.

(b) Consolidated goodwill is to be written off to cost of sales over five years. A full year's charge is made in the year of acquisition.

(c) Hill plc includes only post acquisition dividends, calculated on a time apportioned basis, in its consolidated reserves. It has not accounted for the proposed dividend of Glen Ltd. All profits accrue evenly throughout the year.

Required

Prepare the following for Hill plc.

(a) Using acquisition accounting:

(i) A consolidated profit and loss account for the year to 30 September 20X7

Note. You are not required to analyse the profit and loss account between continuing operations and acquisitions.

(ii) A consolidated balance sheet as at 30 September 20X7. (11 marks)

(b) Using merger accounting, the consolidated reserves at 30 September 20X7. (4 marks)

(15 marks)

48 HOLDING (12/99) *45 mins*

Holding plc acquired 18 million of Subside plc's ordinary shares on 1 January 20X9 at a cost of £10 per share. Holding plc's accounting year end is 30 September, the year end of Subside plc prior to its acquisition had been 30 June. In order to comply with the relevant requirement of FRS 2 *Accounting for subsidiary undertakings,* Subside plc has changed its year end to 30 September and prepared its financial statements for the 15 months period to 30 September 20X9. The following are the profit and loss accounts of both companies.

	Holding plc 12 months to 30 September 20X9	*Subside plc 15 months to 30 September 20X9*
	£m	£m
Turnover	350	280
Cost of sales	(200)	(170)
Gross profit	150	110
Operating expenses	(72)	(35)
Interest payable	(10)	(5)
Dividend from Subside plc	15	-
Profit before tax	83	70
Taxation	(22)	(10)
Profit after tax	61	60
Dividends: final proposed	(25)	
final paid (15 September 20X9)		(20)
Retained profit for the period	36	40

The share capital and reserves of Subside plc at 30 June 20X8 were:

	£m	£m
Ordinary shares of £1 each		24
Reserves		
Profit and loss reserve	64	
Revaluation reserve	20	
		84
		108

The following information is relevant:

(a) In the post acquisition period Holding plc sold goods to Subside plc at a price of £30 million. Holding plc had marked up the cost of these goods by 25%. One third of these goods were still held in stock by Subside plc at 30 September 20X9.

(b) The revaluation reserve of Subside plc relates to an investment property carried at its fair value. It was last revalued on 30 June 20X8. At the date of acquisition the value of the property had increased by a further £4 million.

(c) The only other fair value adjustment that is required in respect of the acquisition is in relation to the plant and equipment of Subside plc, the details of this are:

	Book value at 30 June 20X8
	£m
Cost on 1 July 20X6	100
Depreciation (2 years)	(40)
Net book value	60

The plant is being depreciated over a five-year life using the straight-line method. This is in line with group policy. The cost of sales expense of Subside plc contains an amount of £25 million in respect of depreciation on the plant for the 15 months to 30 September 20X9. The replacement cost of the type of plant used by Subside plc has increased dramatically since it was acquired and Holding plc estimated that the fair value of Subside plc's plant at the date of acquisition was £90 million. The estimate of its remaining life was unaltered.

(d) Subside plc's business activities are not seasonal in nature and therefore it can be assumed that profits, and the related dividend, accrued evenly throughout the 15 month period to 30 September 20X9. Dividends paid out of pre-acquisition profits should **not** be treated as income in the consolidated profit and loss account.

(e) Goodwill is to be amortised on a straight-line basis over six years using time apportionment in the year of acquisition. This should be treated as an operating expense.

Required

(a) Calculate the consolidated goodwill in respect of the acquisition of Subside plc. (8 marks)

(b) Prepare the consolidated profit and loss account of Holding plc for the year to 30 September 20X9. (17 marks)

(25 marks)

49 FRUIT AND VEGETABLES *36 mins*

On 1 January 20X4 Fruit plc acquired all of the issued share capital of Vegetables plc in exchange for shares in Fruit plc.

Shares in both companies have a nominal value of £1 each and a market value at 1 January 20X4 of £5 for a £1 Fruit plc share and £2.25 for a £1 Vegetables plc share. The agreed terms were 1 ordinary share in Fruit plc for every 2 ordinary shares in Vegetables plc.

At 31 December 20X4 the register of members of Fruit plc was correct but no entries had been made in the books of accounts of either company to record the exchange.

At 1 January 20X4 the balance sheet of Vegetables plc was as follows.

Fixed assets	£	£
Freehold premises		573,750
Plant and machinery at cost	316,965	
Less provision for depreciation	127,500	
		189,465
Quoted investments at cost		140,250
Net current assets		309,060
		1,212,525
Capital and reserves		
Ordinary shares of £1 each		765,000
Retained earnings		447,525
		1,212,525

At 1 January 20X4 the quoted investments had a market value of £318,750; the freehold premises a market value of £828,750; the plant and machinery (which had an expected unexpired useful life of four years) a market value of £300,000. Vegetables plc advised that it was their regular practice to invest surplus cash on a short-term basis in quoted investments. Draft accounts prepared for the two companies at the end of their financial year on 31 December 20X4 showed the following.

PROFIT AND LOSS ACCOUNTS
FOR THE YEAR ENDED 31 DECEMBER 20X4

	Fruit plc	*Vegetables plc*
	£	£
Profit before depreciation	568,310	437,070
Depreciation for the year	91,290	40,035
Trading profit	477,020	397,035
Profit on sale of investments	-	138,465
Profit before tax	477,020	535,500
Taxation	119,255	149,940
Profit after tax	357,765	385,560

BALANCE SHEETS AS AT 31 DECEMBER 20X4

Fixed assets		
Freehold premises	1,657,500	573,750
Plant and machinery at cost	653,055	316,965
Aggregate depreciation	(276,165)	(167,535)
Net current assets	249,390	874,905
	2,283,780	1,598,085
Capital and reserves		
Ordinary shares of £1 each	1,275,000	765,000
Retained earnings	1,008,780	833,085
	2,283,780	1,598,085

Required

(a) Prepare draft accounts for 20X4 for the consolidation on the following bases.

(i) The criteria for merger accounting under FRS 6 are met.

(ii) The criteria for merger accounting under FRS 6 are not met: assume a policy of amortisation over ten years for any goodwill that arises.

(Ignore any deferred taxation implications.) (12 marks)

(b) Discuss the bases for computing the asset values and reserves in the financial statements that appear under the two alternatives. (8 marks)

(20 marks)

50 BACUP (6/97) *45 mins*

The summarised balance sheets of Bacup plc, Townley plc and Rishworth plc as at 31 March 20X7 are as follows.

	Bacup	*Townley*	*Rishworth*
	£'000	£'000	£'000
Fixed assets			
Tangible fixed assets	3,820	4,425	500
Development expenditure	-	200	-
Investments	1,600	-	-
	5,420	4,625	500
Current assets			
Stock	2,740	1,280	250
Debtors	1,960	980	164
Cash at bank	1,260	-	86
	5,960	2,260	500

Creditors: amounts falling due within one year			
Trade creditors	1,620	2,870	142
Bank overdraft	-	2,260	-
Taxation	400	150	58
Proposed dividends	500	200	-
	2,520	5,480	200
Net current assets (liabilities)	3,440	(3,220)	300
Net assets	8,860	1,405	800
	£'000	£'000	£'000
Share capital and reserves			
Ordinary shares of 25p each	4,000	500	200
Reserves			
Share premium	800	125	
Profit and loss account at 31 March 20X6	2,300	380	450
Retained for year	1,760	400	150
	8,860	1,405	800

The following information is relevant.

(a) *Investments*

Bacup plc acquired 1.6 million shares in Townley plc on 1 April 20X6 paying 75p per share. On 1 October 20X6 Bacup plc acquired 40% of the share capital of Rishworth plc for £400,000.

(b) *Group accounting policies*

(i) Development expenditure should be written off as incurred. The development expenditure in the balance sheet of Townley plc relates to a project that was commenced on 1 April 20X5. At the date of acquisition the value of the capitalised expenditure was £80,000. No development expenditure of Townley plc has yet been depreciated.

(ii) All goodwill is written off on a straight-line basis over a five year life. Time apportionment is used where goodwill arises part way through an accounting period.

(c) *Intra group trading*

The stock of Bacup plc includes goods at a transfer price of £200,000 purchased from Townley plc after the acquisition. The stock of Rishworth plc includes goods at a transfer price of £125,000 purchased from Bacup plc. All stock transfers were at cost plus 25%.

The debtors of Bacup plc include an amount owing from Townley plc of £250,000. This does not agree with the corresponding amount in the books of Townley plc due to a cash payment of £50,000 made on 29 March 20X7, which had not been received by Bacup plc at the year end.

(d) *Share premium*

The share premium account of Townley plc arose prior to the acquisition by Bacup plc.

Required

(a) Prepare a consolidated balance sheet of the Bacup plc group as at 31 March 20X7.
(18 marks)

(b) Norden Manufacturing plc has been approached by Mr Long, a representative of Townley plc. Mr Long is negotiating for Norden plc to supply Townley plc with goods on six-month credit. Mr Long has pointed out that Townley plc is part of the Bacup plc group and provides the consolidated balance sheet to support the credit request.

Briefly discuss the usefulness of the group balance sheet for assessing the creditworthiness of Townley plc and describe the further investigations you would advise Norden Manufacturing plc to make. (7 marks)

(25 marks)

51 **REN (6/96)** *45 mins*

The following information relates to the balance sheets of Ren plc, its subsidiary Sino plc, and an associated company Malic Ltd at 31 May 20X6.

	Ren plc	*Sino plc*	*Malic Ltd*
	£'000	£'000	£'000
Tangible fixed assets	16,400	14,500	
Investments			5,000
Shares in Sino plc (at cost)	13,200		
Shares in Malic Ltd (at cost)	3,000		
	32,600	14,500	5,000
Current assets			
Stock	2,612	2,010	
Debtors	2,036	1,195	
Cash at bank and in hand	882	115	
	5,530	3,320	
Creditors: amounts falling due within one year	2,502	1,360	
Net current assets	3,028	1,960	
Total assets less current liabilities	35,628	16,460	
Creditors: amounts falling due after more than one year	5,350	1,470	
	30,278	14,990	

	Ren plc	*Sino plc*	*Malic Ltd*
Capital and reserves	£'000	£'000	£'000
Ordinary £1 shares	20,000	8,000	5,000
7% £1 preference shares		4,000	
Share premium account	4,950	350	
Profit and loss account	5,328	2,640	
	30,278	14,990	5,000

The following points are relevant to the preparation of the Ren plc group balance sheet.

(a) Ren plc owns 80% of the ordinary £1 shares and 30% of the 7% £1 preference shares of Sino plc.

(i) The preference shares of Sino plc were originally issued on 1 June 20X5 at par and are to be redeemed on 31 May 20Y5 (ten years after issue) at a premium of 10%.

(ii) Ren plc paid £13.2 million for the ordinary £1 shares and the 7% £1 preference shares on 1 June 20X5 when Sino plc's profit and loss account was £3 million (credit balance).

(iii) The share premium account of Sino plc comprises the original premium on the issue of the ordinary shares.

(iv) Any premium on the redemption of preference shares is to be dealt with, for the purposes of FRS 4 *Capital instruments*, by using the straight line method. The premium has not been dealt with in the accounting records of Sino plc.

(b) The fair value of the net assets of Sino plc were not materially different from their book value at the time of its acquisition by Ren plc.

(c) Sino plc has already paid its dividends for the current financial year and no other dividends are proposed. The company paid an ordinary dividend of 1p per share and the 7% preference dividend. Ren plc has included the dividends received in its profit and loss account. The auditors of Ren plc observed that the payment of the dividends by Sino plc was out of pre-acquisition profits and has contributed to an impairment of the holding company's investment. They feel that Ren plc should account for the dividends accordingly.

(d) Sino plc sold an item of stock to Ren plc on 1 July 20X5. Ren plc has treated this item correctly as plant and machinery in its financial statements. The item was sold at cost plus 20% and is shown in the fixed assets of Ren plc at £2.4 million. A full year's depreciation of 20% per annum has been charged on this amount in the financial statements of Ren plc. Ren plc has not fully paid the cost of the fixed asset to Sino plc. There is an amount of £500,000 outstanding.

(e) Ren plc bought 30% of the shares of Malic Ltd on 31 May 20X6. Malic Ltd is an investment company whose only asset is a portfolio of investments with a book value of £5 million. The market value of these investments on 31 May 20X6 was £9 million.

(f) Goodwill arising on acquisition is to be written off against the profit and loss account in the year of acquisition.

Required

(a) Prepare the consolidated balance sheet for the Ren Group plc as at 31 May 20X6. (21 marks)

(b) Describe, with reasons, the different ways in which a dividend paid by a subsidiary out of pre-acquisition profits may be treated in the accounting records of the holding company. (4 marks)

(25 marks)

52 **JASMIN (6/94)** *45 mins*

Relevant balance sheets as at 31 March 20X4 are set out below.

	Jasmin (Holdings) plc	*Kasbah plc*	*Fortran plc*
	£'000	£'000	£'000
Tangible fixed assets	289,400	91,800	7,600
Investments			
Shares in Kasbah (at cost)	97,600		
Shares in Fortran (at cost)	8,000		
	395,000		
Current assets			
Stock	285,600	151,400	2,600
Cash	319,000	500	6,800
	604,600	151,900	9,400
Creditors: amounts falling due within one year	289,600	238,500	2,200
Net current assets	315,000	(86,600)	7,200
Total assets less current liabilities	710,000	5,200	14,800

Capital and reserves			
Called up share capital			
Ordinary £1 shares	60,000	20,000	10,000
10% £1 preference shares		4,000	
Revaluation reserve	40,000		1,200
Profit and loss reserve	610,000	(18,800)	3,600
	710,000	5,200	14,800

You have recently been appointed chief accountant of Jasmin (Holdings) plc and are about to prepare the group balance sheet at 31 March 20X4.

The following points are relevant to the preparation of those accounts.

(a) Jasmin (Holdings) plc owns 90% of the ordinary £1 shares and 20% of the 10% £1 preference shares of Kasbah plc. On 1 April 20X3 Jasmin (Holdings) plc paid £96 million for the ordinary £1 shares and £1.6 million for the 10% £1 preference shares when Kasbah's reserves were a credit balance of £45 million.

(b) Jasmin (Holdings) plc sells part of its output to Kasbah plc. The stock of Kasbah plc on 31 March 20X4 includes £1.2 million of stock purchased from Jasmin (Holdings) plc at cost plus one third.

(c) The policy of the group is to revalue its tangible fixed assets on a yearly basis. However, the directors of Kasbah plc have always resisted this policy preferring to show tangible fixed assets at historical cost. The market value of the tangible fixed assets of Kasbah plc at 31 March 20X4 is £90 million. The directors of Jasmin (Holdings) plc wish you to follow the requirements of FRS 2 *Accounting for subsidiary undertakings* in respect of the value of tangible fixed assets to be included in the group accounts.

(d) The ordinary £1 shares of Fortran plc are split into 6 million 'A' ordinary £1 shares and 4 million 'B' ordinary £1 shares. Holders of 'A' shares are assigned 1 vote and holders of 'B' ordinary shares are assigned 2 votes per share. On 1 April 20X3 Jasmin (Holdings) plc acquired 80% of the 'A' ordinary shares and 10% of the 'B' ordinary shares when the profit and loss reserve of Fortran plc was £1.6 million and the revaluation reserve was £2 million. The 'A' ordinary shares and 'B' ordinary shares carry equal rights to share in the company's profit and losses.

(e) The fair values of Kasbah plc and Fortran plc were not materially different from their book values at the time of acquisition of their shares by Jasmin (Holdings) plc.

(f) Goodwill arising on acquisition is amortised over five years.

(g) Kasbah plc has paid its preference dividend for the current year but no other dividends are proposed by the group companies. The preference dividend was paid shortly after the interim results of Kasbah plc were announced and was deemed to be a legal dividend by the auditors.

(h) Because of its substantial losses during the period, the directors of Jasmin (Holdings) plc wish to exclude the financial statements of Kasbah plc from the group accounts on the grounds that Kasbah plc's output is not similar to that of Jasmin (Holdings) plc and that the resultant accounts therefore would be misleading. Jasmin (Holdings) plc produces synthetic yarn and Kasbah plc produces garments.

Required

(a) List the conditions for exclusion of subsidiaries from consolidation for the directors of Jasmin (Holdings) plc and state whether Kasbah plc may be excluded on these grounds. (4 marks)

(b) Prepare a consolidated balance sheet for Jasmin (Holdings) Group plc for the year ending 31 March 20X4. (All calculations should be made to the nearest thousand pounds.) (18 marks)

(c) Comment briefly on the possible implications of the size of Kasbah plc's losses for the year for the group accounts and the individual accounts of Jasmin (Holdings) plc. (3 marks)

(25 marks)

53 AUGMENT (12/98)

45 mins

Augment plc, a medium sized listed company, entered into an expansion programme on 1 October 20X7. On that date the company purchased from Bagshot plc two investments:

(i) The entire share capital of Caldershaw Ltd
(ii) 50% of the share capital of Debut Ltd.

Both investments were previously wholly owned by Bagshot plc. Debut Ltd is to be run by Augment plc and Bagshot plc as a joint venture. Augment plc makes up its financial statements to 30 September each year. The terms of the acquisitions were as follows.

Caldershaw Ltd

The total consideration was based on a price earnings (PE) multiple of 12 applied to the reported profit of £2 million of Caldershaw Ltd for the year to 30 September 20X7. The consideration was settled by Augment plc issuing £14m 8% debentures (at par) and the balance by a new issue of £1 ordinary shares, based on a market value of £2.50 each.

Debut Ltd

The value of Debut Ltd at 1 October 20X7 was mutually agreed as £37.5m. Augment plc satisfied its share (50%) of this amount by issuing 7.5m £1 ordinary shares (market value £2.50 each) to Bagshot plc.

Note. Augment plc has *not* recorded the acquisition of the above investments nor the issuing of the consideration.

The summarised balance sheets of the three entities at 30 September 20X8 are as follows.

	Augment plc		*Caldershaw Ltd*		*Debut Ltd*	
	£'000	£'000	£'000	£'000	£'000	£'000
Fixed assets						
Tangible assets		34,260		27,000		21,060
Current assets						
Stocks	9,640		7,200		18,640	
Trade and other debtors	11,200		5,060		4,620	
Cash	-		3,410		40	
	20,840		15,670		23,300	
Creditors: amounts falling due within one year						
Trade and other creditors	13,120		5,270		14,100	
Operating overdraft	1,540		-		-	
Taxation	5,640		2,400		760	
Proposed dividends	4,000		-		-	
	(24,300)		(7,670)		(14,860)	
Net current assets (liabilities)		(3,460)		8,000		8,440
Net assets		30,800		35,000		29,500
Capital and reserves						
Ordinary shares £1 each		10,000		20,000		25,000
Reserves						
Profit and loss account		20,800		15,000		4,500
		30,800		35,000		29,500

The following information is relevant.

(i) The book values of the net assets of Caldershaw Ltd and Debut Ltd at the date of acquisition were considered to be a reasonable approximation of their fair values. Caldershaw Ltd's tangible fixed assets are all non-monetary and had a fair value of £24m and a remaining useful life of five years at the date of acquisition (straight-line depreciation is used). At this date Caldershaw Ltd's only other non-monetary asset was its stock which had a fair value of £6m. All of this stock had been sold by the company's year end.

(ii) In September 20X8, Augment plc sold goods to Caldershaw Ltd at a price of £1,250,000. This included a mark-up on cost of 25%. Caldershaw Ltd has not yet sold any of these goods, but it paid for them on 28 September 20X8. Augment plc had not received this payment at the balance sheet date. This has been the only intra-group trading.

(iii) The profits of Caldershaw Ltd and Debut Ltd for the year to 30 September 20X8 were £8m and £2m respectively. No dividends have been paid by any of the entities during the year.

(iv) Goodwill is to be amortised on a straight-line basis over 10 years. Negative goodwill is to be treated in accordance with FRS 10 *Goodwill and intangible assets.*

Required

(a) Prepare the journal entries (ignoring narratives) to record the acquisition of Caldershaw Ltd and Debut Ltd in the accounting records of Augment plc as at 1 October 20X7. Show your workings. (4 marks)

(b) Prepare the consolidated balance sheet of Augment plc as at 30 September 20X8.

Note. Ignore the additional disclosures relating to joint ventures at 15% and 25% thresholds. (16 marks)

(c) Explain the circumstances in which negative goodwill may arise, and describe its accounting treatment in FRS 10 *Goodwill and intangible assets.* (5 marks)

(25 marks)

THE THEORETICAL FRAMEWORK OF ACCOUNTING

Questions 54 to 56 cover the theoretical framework of accounting, the subject of Part D of the BPP Study Text for Paper 2.5.

54 PREPARATION QUESTION: CHANGING PRICES

The following information has been extracted from the accounts of Epsilon plc prepared under the historical cost convention for 20X6.

PROFIT AND LOSS ACCOUNT EXTRACTS 20X6

	£m
Turnover	200
Operating profit	15
Less interest payable	3
Net profit	12

SUMMARISED BALANCE SHEET AT 31 DECEMBER 20X6

	£m	£m
Fixed assets at cost less depreciation		60
Current assets		
Stocks	20	
Debtors	30	
Bank	2	
	52	
Current liabilities	30	
Net current assets		22
Total assets less current liabilities		82
Less 15% debentures		20
		62
Capital and reserves		62

The company's accountant has prepared the following current cost data.

	£m
Current cost adjustments for 20X6	
Depreciation adjustment	3
Cost of sales adjustment	5
Replacement cost at 31 December 20X6	
Fixed assets, net of depreciation	85
Stocks	21

Required

(a) Calculate the current cost operating profit of Epsilon plc for 20X6 and the summarised current cost balance sheet of the company at 31 December 20X6, so far as the information permits.

(b) Calculate the following ratios from both the historical cost accounts and current cost accounts:

(i) Interest cover
(ii) Rate of return on shareholders' equity
(iii) Debt/equity ratio.

(c) Discuss the significance of the ratios calculated under (b) and of the reasons for differences between them.

Note. Ignore taxation.

55 RECOST (12/98) *45 mins*

For over 20 years the accounting professions in the UK and other countries have attempted to formulate a method of preparing financial statements that takes account of the effects of price increases (inflation). It seems that no proposed method of reflecting the effects of changing prices has gained acceptance. The most recent advice, as far back as 1986, from the Accounting Standards Committee is that no form of accounting for price changes should be made compulsory, but companies are encouraged to present such information.

There have been two main methods put forward by the ASC for reporting the effects of price changes. One method is based on the movements in general price inflation (as measured by the Retail Price Index – RPI) and is referred to as current purchasing power accounting (CPP); the other method is based on specific price changes of goods and is generally referred to as current cost accounting (CCA). A later pronouncement on the subject also suggested an approach which combines features of each method.

Required

(a) Explain the limitations of (pure) historic cost accounts when used as a basis for assessing the performance of an enterprise. You should give an example of how each of three different user groups may be misled by such information. (10 marks)

(b) Describe the advantages and criticisms of CPP and CCA accounting. (8 marks)

(c) Recost plc assembles computer equipment from bought-in components and then retails them under their own brand name. Performance measures highlighted in a report issued by their stockbrokers on the historic cost accounts for the year to 30 September 20X8 are:

(i) Turnover up by 9.7% (turnover in 20X7 was £18.2m)

(ii) Earnings per share (EPS) are 8p

(iii) Return (profit before interest and tax) on capital employed (ROCE) is 18.5% ((3,500 + 200)/20,000)

The summarised financial statements of the company for the year ended 30 September 20X8 are as follows.

PROFIT AND LOSS ACCOUNT

	£'000	£'000
Turnover		19,965
Cost of sales		(13,100)
Gross profit		6,865
Operating expenses	1,665	
Depreciation	1,500	
Interest	200	
		(3,365)
Profit before tax		3,500
Taxation		(300)
Net profit for the period		3,200

BALANCE SHEET

	£'000	£'000
Tangible fixed assets		15,000
Current assets	10,000	
Current liabilities	(5,000)	
Net current assets		5,000
10% debentures		(2,000)
Net assets		18,000
Share capital and reserves		
Ordinary shares 25p each		10,000
Profit and loss account reserve		8,000
		18,000

Additional information

(i) The government's retail price index (RPI) has increased by 10% during the year to 30 September 20X8, but despite higher component and labour costs, the selling price of the computer equipment that Recost plc deals in has fallen by 5% due to competition from cheaper foreign imports.

(ii) The company's computerised stock program has calculated that the replacement cost of sales for the year ended 30 September 20X8 would have amounted to £14.7m, and the replacement cost of stock at 30 September 20X8 would be £500,000 higher than its historical cost.

(iii) The current cost of the tangible fixed assets at 30 September 20X8 would have been £20m after charging depreciation (based on current cost) of £2m for the year.

Required

In relation to the figures highlighted in the stockbroker's report, and adjusting for the above information, recalculate:

(i) The percentage changes in turnover based on general and specific price measures
(ii) The current cost earnings per share
(iii) The current cost return on capital employed (7 marks)

Note. You are not required to prepare price adjusted financial statements.

(25 marks)

56 ACCOUNTING THEORIES (12/95) *45 mins*

The Accounting Standards Board's *Statement of Principles* is a set of theoretical principles which are designed to influence the drafting of future accounting standards. However, it can be argued that accountancy research and accounting theory have no place in the standard setting process and are of little practical relevance to the accountant. Such terms as 'agency theory' and 'positive accounting theory' are meaningless to the practising accountant, and their underlying principles will never have an impact upon accounting practice.

Required

(a) Explain what you understand by the terms 'agency theory' and 'positive accounting theory', discussing whether these theoretical concepts can help explain why a company chooses a particular accounting policy and why accounting standards change over time. (13 marks)

(b) Discuss why accountancy research may appear to have little relevance to the practising accountant. (5 marks)

(c) Discuss the advantages of the Accounting Standards Board's *Statement of Principles* and whether the statement is too theoretical for use in the standard setting process.

(7 marks)

(25 marks)

ANALYSIS AND INTERPRETATION OF FINANCIAL STATEMENTS AND RELATED INFORMATION

Questions 57 to 60 cover analysis and interpretation of financial statements and related information, the subject of Part E of the BPP Study Text for Paper 2.5.

57 PREPARATION QUESTION: ANALYTICAL REVIEW

As internal auditor of Signomi plc you are conducting an investigation of the company's trading results. Your directors believe a further issue of debenture stock is needed to fund both the repayment of the 10% stock due for repayment in 20X9 and for investment in new plant and machinery. The industry in which Signomi plc operates is, and is likely to remain, highly competitive.

Note. 'Now' is November 20X8.

The following financial information has been provided.

BALANCE SHEETS AS AT 31 DECEMBER

	20X7	*20X6*	*20X5*	*20X4*	*20X3*
Net fixed assets	£m	£m	£m	£m	£m
Land and buildings	3.0	2.5	2.4	1.6	1.5
Plant and machinery	3.2	2.0	1.2	0.8	0.6
	6.2	4.5	3.6	2.4	2.1
Current assets					
Stocks	5.0	4.7	3.0	2.4	1.9
Debtors	2.6	2.0	1.9	1.5	1.4
Total assets	13.8	11.2	8.5	6.3	5.4
Creditors: amounts falling due within one year	4.3	4.0	3.5	2.2	2.0
*Total assets less current liabilities**	9.5	7.2	5.0	4.1	3.4
Creditors: amounts falling due after more than one year					
10% debenture stock 20X9	1.5	1.5	1.5	1.5	1.5
12% debenture stock 20Y5	2.0	2.0	-	-	-
Net capital employed	6.0	3.7	3.5	2.6	1.9
Capital and reserves					
Authorised and issued £1 shares fully paid	1.5	1.5	1.5	1.5	1.0
Retained profit	4.5	2.2	2.0	1.1	0.9
Shareholders' interest	6.0	3.7	3.5	2.6	1.9
*Includes bank overdraft	1.9	1.3	0.6	0.8	0.9

EXTRACTS FROM PROFIT AND LOSS ACCOUNT

Net sales	16.4	13.5	10.0	8.5	7.3
Cost of sales	8.9	7.1	6.1	5.5	4.8
Net profit before tax	3.0	1.5	1.4	0.8	0.5

Some average statistics for the industry as a whole in 20X7 are given as follows.

Net profit before tax: sales	14%
Net profit before tax: total assets less current liabilities	18%
Working capital (current) ratio	2.2:1
Liquidity ratio	0.75:1
Sales: fixed assets	3.0
Turnover of stock	2.8
Debtors collection period (based on average debtors)	45 days
Age of stock	120 days

Required

(a) Present a schedule of data derived from the financial information provided for AB plc which would be used as the basis of an analytical review.

(b) Use the data from (a) above:

(i) To analyse the financing proposals

(ii) To assess the reasonableness of the figures in the five-year statement of results

58 HEYWOOD BOTTLES (6/97 part) *27 mins*

Below are the summarised financial statements for the year to 31 March 20X6 and 20X7 of Heywood Bottles plc, a company which manufactures bottles for many different drinks companies.

Note. The statements for the year to 31 March 20X7 have not been audited.

PROFIT AND LOSS ACCOUNTS
FOR THE YEARS TO 31 MARCH

	20X6		*20X7*	
	£m	£m	£m	£m
Sales		120		300
Manufacturing costs	83		261	
Depreciation	7		9	
		90		270
Gross profit		30		30
Other expenses	10		28	
Interest	2		10	
		12		38
Profit/(loss) before tax		18		(8)
Tax		6		4
Profit/(loss) after tax		12		(12)
Dividends: interim paid	4		4	
final proposed	4		4	
		8		8
		4		(20)

BALANCE SHEETS AS AT 31 MARCH

	20X6		20X7	
	£m	£m	£m	£m
Fixed assets				
Land and buildings		5		5
Plant and equipment		38		58
		43		63
Current assets				
Stock	12		18	
Debtors	25		94	
Deferred expenditure	-		6	
Bank	8		-	
	45		118	
Creditors: amounts falling due within one year				
Trade creditors	15		80	
Others	10		12	
Bank	-		34	
	25		126	
Net assets (liabilities)		20		(8)
Total assets less current liabilities		63		55
Creditors amounts falling due after more than one year		19		32
Net assets		44		23
Share capital and reserves				
Ordinary shares		25		25
Reserves				
Capital reserves	11		10	
Profit and loss account	8		(12)	
		19		(2)
		44		23

Notes

1 Plant and equipment is made up as follows.

At 31 March	*20X6*	*20X7*
	£m	£m
Owned plant	10	18
Leased plant	28	40

2 Creditors falling due after more than one year are leasing obligations.

The directors were disappointed in the profit for the year to 31 March 20X6 and held a board meeting in April 20X6 to discuss future strategy. The Managing Director was insistent that the way to improve the company's results was to increase sales and market share. As a result the following actions were implemented.

(a) An aggressive marketing campaign through trade journals costing £12 million was undertaken. Due to expected long-term benefits £6 million of this has been included as a current asset in the balance sheet at 31 March 20X7.

(b) A 'price promise' to undercut any other supplier's price was announced in the advertising campaign.

(c) A major contract with Koola Drinks plc was signed that accounted for a substantial proportion of the company's output. This contract was obtained through very competitive tendering.

(d) The credit period for debtors was extended from two to three months.

A preliminary review by the board of the accounts to 31 March 20X7 concluded that the company's performance had deteriorated rather than improved. There was particular concern over the prospect of renewing the bank overdraft facility because the maximum agreed level of £30 million had been exceeded. The board decided that it was time to seek independent professional advice on the company's situation.

Required

In the capacity of a business consultant, prepare a report for the board of Heywood Bottles plc analysing the company's performance for the year to 31 March 20X7 in comparison with the previous year. Particular emphasis should be given to the effects of the implementation of the actions referred to in points (a) to (d) above. **(15 marks)**

59 CURRENT COST ACCOUNTING AND RATIOS (6/95) *45 mins*

It has been stated that: 'Current cost accounts allow for the impact of specific price changes on the net operating assets and thus the operating capability of the business The same tools of analysis as those applied to historical cost accounts are generally appropriate. The ratios derived from current cost accounts ... will often differ substantially from those revealed in historical cost accounts but should be more realistic indicators when assessing an entity or making comparisons between entities'.

Required

(a) Explain, with reasons, whether the value of the following ratios might differ if calculated using current cost accounts rather than the historical cost accounts.

(i) Return on capital employed (ROCE)
(ii) Stock turnover ratio (utilising the year end stock value)
(iii) Debtors turnover ratio
(iv) Gearing ratio (in the balance sheet) (8 marks)

(b) Explain the principal limitations of the specific historical cost ratios set out in part (a) when utilising them for the purpose of inter-firm comparison. (11 marks)

(c) Briefly discuss whether you feel that current cost based ratios are more realistic indicators of a company's performance than those ratios based upon historical cost accounts. (6 marks)

(25 marks)

66 OMEGAR *54 mins*

Omegar plc is a rapidly expanding trading and manufacturing company. It is currently seeking to extend its product range in new markets. To achieve this growth it needs to raise £800,000. The directors are considering two sources of funds.

(a) A rights issue at £2.00 per share. The shares are trading at £2.50 (20X0: £2.20) per share.

(b) A bank loan at an interest rate of 15% and repayable by instalments after two years. The bank would want to secure the loan with a charge over the company's property.

The following are extracts from the draft financial statements.

OMEGAR PLC
DRAFT PROFIT AND LOSS ACCOUNT EXTRACT
YEAR ENDED 31 DECEMBER

	20X1	20X0
	£'000	£'000
Turnover	1,991	1,967
Operating profit	698	636
Interest payable	(55)	(45)
Profit before taxation	643	591
Taxation	(190)	(140)
Profit after taxation	453	451
Extraordinary item	-	(90)
Profit for the year	453	361

OMEGAR PLC
DRAFT BALANCE SHEET EXTRACT AS AT 31 DECEMBER

	20X1	20X0
	£'000	£'000
Fixed assets		
Tangible	1,504	1,132
Intangible	298	247
	1,802	1,379
Current assets		
Stocks	679	684
Debtors	511	471
Cash in hand and at bank	117	80
Creditors: due within one year		
Trade	(308)	(336)
Taxation	(190)	(140)
Dividends	(80)	(80)
Creditors: due after more than one year		
10% debentures, repayable 20Y4	(450)	(450)
Finance lease	(100)	-
	1,981	1,608
Capital and reserves		
Ordinary share capital £1 shares	800	800
Revaluation reserve	144	144
Profit and loss	1,037	664
	1,981	1,608

Operating profit

Operating profit has been arrived at after charging or crediting the following.

	20X1	20X0
	£'000	£'000
Depreciation	150	110
Gain on disposal of property (as part of a sale and leaseback transaction)	95	-

Extraordinary item

The extraordinary loss consists of reorganisation costs in a branch where a reduction in activity involved various measures including redundancies. Attributable tax credit is £38,000. (Do not assume that this classification is correct.)

Deferred taxation

Deferred taxation has not been provided because it is not considered probable that a liability will crystallise. If deferred taxation had been provided in full then a liability for the year of £7,000 would have arisen (20X0: £8,000). (The accounts were drawn up before the introduction of FRS 19.)

Contingent liability

There is a contingent liability of £85,000 (20X0: £80,000) in respect of bills of exchange discounted with bankers.

Further investigation has revealed that stock includes items subject to reservation of title of £40,000 (20X0: £40,000) and obsolete or slow moving items of £28,000 (20X0: £28,000). An age analysis of debtors has revealed that debts overdue by more than one year amount to £40,000 (20X0 £40,000).

The auditors are yet to report and there is some discussion as to the classification of reorganisation costs in the light of FRS 3 *Reporting financial performance.*

The directors forecast that the new funds will generate an operating profit of £300,000, and that the 20X1 operating profit will be repeated. If new shares are issued the dividend will increase to £150,000.

Required

(a) Analyse the accounts based on the following ratios, from the separate points of view of potential equity holders and debt holders:

(i) Current ratio
(ii) Interest cover
(iii) Debt/equity ratio
(iv) Earnings per share
(v) After tax return on equity
(vi) Price/earnings ratio.

Two different versions of each of these ratios should be calculated and used in your analysis where the input to the ratio calculation can be variously defined or where the data suggests uncertainty as to accounting treatment in the draft accounts.

Your analysis should clearly indicate which parts of it are of particular relevance to potential equity holders and which are of particular relevance to potential debt holders. It should also comment on the limitations of each of the ratios as an evaluative tool.

(20 marks)

(b) Assuming that either funding scheme becomes effective on 1 January 20X2, recalculate, for each scheme, the following ratios:

(i) Debt/equity ratio
(ii) Interest cover
(iii) After tax return on equity.

For ratios (ii) and (iii), adopt the directors' forecasts.

Advise the directors, with reasons, which scheme to adopt. List other factors the directors should consider. (10 marks)

Note. You should work to the nearest £'000. The corporation tax rate is 35%.

(30 marks)

Answers

1 ACCOUNTING TERMINOLOGY

> **Tutor's hint**. Sensible use of relevant examples will help you to keep your answers concise and to the point. It would be difficult, however, to produce a good answer to this question if you had never given any thought to the topic before.
>
> You must make time in your studies to think carefully about the assumptions underlying accountancy, as the difficulties in establishing a coherent conceptual framework for accountancy are at the heart of many of the problems currently challenging the profession.
>
> For example, if you can't define an asset how can you justify exclusion or non-exclusion of brands from the balance sheet? How can you decide the most appropriate basis of valuation for assets?
>
> Candidates often find difficulty writing in terms of abstract concepts and, consequently bring in examples which are not relevant, but the Paper 2.5 examiner is obviously keen to ask questions on these issues.
>
> Use headings and sub-headings to help the person making your script and maximise your marks.

(a) **Nature of an expense**

An expense is incurred when a business contracts to purchase goods or accept services which will not constitute a resource for the future from which economic benefits can be expected to flow. In other words, an expense is a cost which is not classified as an asset to the business.

FRS 5 defines an **asset** as a right or other access to **future economic benefits** controlled by an entity as a result of **past transactions or events**. A resource may be

- Tangible (eg plant and machinery), or
- Intangible (eg patents and copyrights)

In either event, it is not the underlying item which is recognised in financial statements but the fact that the item is able to generate economic benefits for the enterprise.

Without the ability to generate future economic benefits, an item such as plant and machinery would effectively be worthless scrap, and not an asset. In other words, the expenditure would be classified as of a **revenue** nature rather than **capital**. It would be written off against profit rather than **deferred**, the write off becoming necessary as soon as the item ceased to be thought of as an asset.

In practice, some businesses might write off all items of capital expenditure costing below a **predetermined limit** on the basis of immateriality. This is done to minimise record keeping. In consequence, some expenditure that should be classified as assets are in fact expensed through the profit and loss account. Care needs to be exercised to ensure that when all the **individual items** of capital items written off are **aggregated**, their **combined impact** does not constitute a **material misstatement**.

Illustrative example

The difference between an expense and an asset can best be illustrated via an example comparing the benefits to the business which arise from:

- Expenditure on the annual audit
- The purchase of three months worth of stationery, and
- The purchase of accounting software.

All three of the above examples give benefits. However, the audit will not generate future economic benefits (whatever the auditors may claim!) whereas the other two will. However, a large purchase of stationery is treated as an asset because it is really a

deferred expense whereas software will be in place for a much longer period. The former is therefore treated as a **current asset** and the latter as a **fixed asset.**

Accruals concept

Application of the **accruals concept,** in accordance with FRS 18 and CA 1985, requires that the **non-cash impact of transactions** and other events be reflected, as far as is possible, in the financial statements of the accounting **period in which they occur** and not, for example, in the period any cash involved is received or paid. However, under the new FRS 18 regime, in **conditions of uncertainty,** more **confirmatory evidence** will be required to support the **recognition** of **assets or a gain** as opposed to that required for the **recognition** of a **liability** or **loss.**

Hence, in practice, if in a given accounting period a business makes a hundred sales, then it should account for the costs of making all those sales, whether paid for yet or not. The expenses to be taken into account include overheads as well as direct costs.

In the above example, an audit fee is never payable in full until after the end of an accounting period. However, a company has an obligation at the end of each accounting period to have an audit. Therefore the audit fee must be accrued as an expense of the period whose accounts are to be audited.

Stationery stocks not used in an accounting period, if material, should not be treated as a charge to profit and loss account for that period. Instead the expenditure should be **deferred** and accounted for in the next period.

The above involves the same principle which is applied in accounting for stocks of components, goods for resale and so on, as assets at the end of an accounting period, if they are **expected** to be of **economic benefit** thereafter. However, where there is **uncertainty** regarding the likelihood of **future economic benefits** the items involved must not be treated as deferred expenses (or assets) but as **expenses** of **the current period.**

Benefits are derived from fixed assets over **several accounting periods** but in most cases the expected economic life of the asset is limited. It is therefore argued that **fixed assets** should be **written off** over their **economic lives** in **proportion** to the **benefit derived in each period.**

The writing off process is called **depreciation** (or amortisation, in the case of an asset with a predetermined life, such as a patent or a leasehold). Depreciation is in keeping with the accruals concept to ensure that financial statements reflect the **non-cash impacts of transactions** in the **relevant accounting period.**

The approach enshrined in FRS 18 facilitates the simultaneous recognition of revenues and costs that result from the same transactions.

Meaning of liability

A liability may be defined as 'an entity's **obligation** to **transfer economic benefits** as a result of **past transactions** or events' (which is in accordance with the definition used in FRS 5 and the Statement of Principles).

FRS 12 provides the following examples of liabilities.

(i) **Trade creditors.** These are liabilities to pay for goods or services that have been **received** or **supplied** and have been invoiced or formally agreed with the supplier; and

(ii) **Accruals.** These are liabilities to pay for goods or services that have been received or supplied but have **not been paid, invoiced or formally agreed** with the supplier, including amounts due to employees (for example amounts relating to accrued holiday pay). Although it is **sometimes necessary to estimate** the amount or timing of accruals, the **uncertainty is generally much less than for provisions.**

(iii) **Provisions.** An important point is **the distinction between liabilities and provisions**. Per FRS 12, a **provision is a liability of uncertain timing or amount** of expenditure required in settlement.

In practice, the terms accruals and provisions are sometimes used in confusion. Strictly these terms should not be used interchangeably. Accruals should be reported as trade and other creditors, whereas provisions are reported separately.

The Companies Act also **defines capital** (ie the amount due to the owners of a business) **as a liability,** but this is of a **special kind** as in normal circumstances **capital is not expected to be repaid.**

(b) **Conceptual tensions**

There are several possible sources of conceptual tension in classifying costs as either expenses or assets.

(i) There is an obvious tension, touched on above, between the **accruals** and **prudence** concepts.

(ii) **Materiality** also restricts the full application of the accruals concept.

(iii) When the **going concern concept is not met**, there will be many costs which should be treated as expenses rather than assets, because the business no longer expects to continue in operational existence for the foreseeable future.

There are several accounting standards which are concerned with cost classification.

Stocks and long-term contracts

SSAP 9 requires the application of the matching concept in determining what value to place on stock and work in progress. The explanatory note to SSAP 9 says that:

> 'the cost of unsold or unconsumed stocks will have been incurred in the expectation of future revenue, and when this will not arise until a later year it is appropriate to carry forward this cost to be matched with the revenue when it arises; the applicable concept is the matching of cost and revenue in the year in which the revenue arises rather than in the year in which the cost is incurred.'

However, SSAP 9 goes on to recognise the need to exercise **prudence** in stock valuation:

> 'if there is no reasonable expectation of sufficient future revenue to cover cost incurred ... the irrecoverable cost should be charged to revenue in the year under review. Thus, stocks normally need to be stated at cost, or, if lower, at net realisable value.'

In discussing long-term contract valuation, SSAP 9 takes the view that to defer recognition of profit on such contracts until they end 'may result in the profit and loss account reflecting not so much a fair view of the results of the activity of the company during the year but rather the results relating to contracts that have been completed in the year'.

Acknowledging again that a strict application of the matching concept may be imprudent, SSAP 9 requires that until the outcome of the contract is **reasonably certain,** no profit should be accounted for (although to help in showing activity for the period, turnover may be recorded as long as cost of sales recorded for the period is the same amount). FRS 18 specifies that profits should be treated as realised only when realised in the form of cash, or in the form of other assets, the ultimate cash realisation of which can **be assessed with reasonable certainty**. This certainty relates to both

existence and **measurement reliability**. Furthermore, although profits are not anticipated, a **foreseeable loss** must be accounted for in the period when it is first foreseen.

The above confirms the revised approach to prudence adopted by FRS 18. Under FRS 18 prudence is now a **desirable quality** of financial statements rather than part of the bedrock of accounting. There is no need to enforce prudence where **uncertainty** does not exist – it should not be used as an argument for overstating liabilities or losses, otherwise the financial statements are **not neutral** and therefore **not reliable**.

Accounting for research and development

SSAP 13 deals with the criteria for deferring development expenditure (that is, capitalising it and treating it as an intangible asset).

The explanatory note to SSAP 13 still explicitly refers to the need for accounting policies on research and development expenditure to be formulated with regard to both the **accruals and prudence concepts**. It concludes that research and development expenditure may prudently only be deferred if it is established that such expenditure can be linked with the revenue of a future period with reasonable certainty.

Expenditure on **pure and applied research** cannot be directly linked to future revenue:

> 'in general, no one particular period rather than any other will be expected to benefit and therefore it is appropriate that these costs should be written off as they are incurred.'

However, expenditure on the **development of new products and services**:

> 'is normally with a reasonable expectation of specific commercial success and of future benefits arising from the work, either from increased revenue and related products or from reduced costs. On these grounds it may be argued that such expenditure, to the extent that it is recoverable, should be deferred to be matched against the future revenue.'

The use of **future economic benefit** as the criteria for deferring expenditure and therefore creating an asset minimises the conceptual conflict between the accruals and prudence concepts. If the future benefit to be expected from an item of expenditure is **uncertain**, it is prudent to write it off now as well as fulfilling the requirement to ensure that the **non-cash impacts of transactions** are **reflected in the period to which they relate (occur) rather than when payment is made.**

2 ACCOUNTING STANDARDS

> **Tutor's hint**. This should be a very familiar subject matter by now, even old hat as it is now over ten years since the ASB was established. However, you will impress the examiner if you can mention very recent matters or cases, which you should have gleaned from the accountancy press.
>
> **Examiner's comment**. This question was satisfactorily answered on the whole. However, some candidates assumed, wrongly, that they would gain marks by writing everything they knew about the standard-setting process (part (b)).

(a) The **users of financial information** - creditors, management, employees, business contacts, financial specialists, government and the general public - are entitled to information about a business entity to a greater or lesser degree. However, the needs and expectations of these groups will vary.

The **preparers of the financial information** often find themselves in the position of having to reconcile the **interests of different groups** in the best way for the business entity. For example whilst shareholders are looking for increased profits to support higher dividends, employees will expect higher wage increases. However higher profits without corresponding higher tax allowances (increased capital allowances for example) is likely to result in a larger corporation tax bill.

Without accounting standards to prescribe how certain transactions should be treated, preparers might be tempted to produce financial information which meets the **expectations of the favoured user group**. For example **creative accounting methods,** such as off balance sheet finance might be used to enhance a company's balance sheet to make it more attractive to investors/lenders.

The **aim of accounting standards** is that they should **regulate financial information** in order that it shows the following characteristics.

(i) Relevance
(ii) Reliability
(iii) Comparability
(iv) Understandability

(b) (i) **Failure to develop an agreed conceptual framework and to specify user needs**

In the past, UK accounting standards have developed haphazardly and in response to perceived problems. The lack of a **conceptual framework** resulted in fundamental principles being tackled more than once in different standards. This produced **contradictions** and **inconsistencies** in **basic concepts** such as those of prudence and accruals.

Towards the end of the ASC's life, it realised the need for a conceptual framework and recognised the IASC's **Framework** as an appropriate set of guidelines.

In contrast, the ASB identified a need for a conceptual framework at an early stage in its work. In July 1991, the ASB issued a Statement of aims that announced it intention to achieve its aims by 'developing principles to guide it in establishing standards and to provide a framework within which others can **exercise judgement in resolving accounting issues**'.

The conceptual framework was fleshed out in the ASB'S **Statement of Principles for Financial Reporting,** which consists of eight chapters covering the fundamental principles of accounting and the content of accounts. The ASB has used the IASC **Framework** to a large extent as the basis for the *Statement of Principles*, adding material where necessary.

Direct consultation of users was not practised under the ASC regime. Users were merely asked to comment on exposure drafts. A variety of user groups are now represented on the Financial Reporting Council (FRC) which controls the work of the ASB.

(ii) **Composition of the ASC and ASB**

The **ASB membership** is drawn from the accounting profession who act on a voluntary part-time basis, but the Board also has a full-time chairman and technical director.

It could be argued that the structure of the ASB reflects very little change from the ASC. However, unlike the ASC, which was controlled by the CCAB and hence the accounting profession, the **ASB is controlled by the FRC** which has 25 members drawn from a **wider sphere** and includes users, preparers and auditors of accounts.

(iii) **Inadequate enforcement of standards**

The enforcement of accounting standards, particularly for the large public companies has been enhanced in two ways.

(1) CA 1989 now requires that financial statements must state that they have been prepared in accordance with accounting standards. Where there are any **significant departures** these must be **explained and justified.**

(2) The **Review Panel** was established under the control of the FRC. Its brief is to examine the accounts of large companies and **question the departure** from **accounting standards**. The Panel has the power, as its ultimate weapon, to apply to the court for **revision** of the **accounts**. The experience to date however is that most companies prefer to resolve any issues by discussion.

(iv) **ASC too open to pressure**

The ASC was open to political pressure in two ways.

(1) Its members, all being from the accounting profession, were perceived as reluctant to produce standards that would act to the detriment of their **clients.**

(2) The ASC was pressurised via the government, which was subject to lobbying by large companies with **vested interests**.

(v) **Emerging issues**

The ASC could only react to emerging issues by going through the **long- drawn out process** of producing an **exposure draft** which in **due course** and after some **amendment** would become an accounting standard. The **effective date** of the standard coming in to force was usually **some months after its publication**.

Under the new regime the **Urgent Issues Task Force** was set up as an offshoot of the ASB. It deals with urgent issues not covered by existing standards. Its pronouncements, called **abstracts**, are intended to **come into effect quickly,** usually within **one month of publication**.

UITF abstracts sometimes later become incorporated into accounting standards, but in some cases a standard is not necessary.

3 PREPARATION QUESTION: COMPANY REPORTS

> **Tutor's hint**. Make sure you consider the importance of user needs and bring out the distinction between *communicating* information and merely *reporting* it.
>
> You will fail to gain marks in the examination if you select only some of the issues raised in the statement in the question.
>
> Help your marker by the use of headings and subheadings which show that you have answered the question.

Communication objectives

Dealing with the first half of the question, it should be said that the **value** of financial reporting is **maximised** only if it **communicates** effectively with the **recipients** of the report but moreover the communication is of little value unless the recipients can **understand** the information.

Most shareholders are unlikely to be specialists in accounting and will not be familiar with the conventions adopted or all the terminology used. This point has been put forward as an argument in favour of **simplified financial statements** and will be developed below.

However, whether or not one is in favour of simplified accounts, a clear presentation and the absence of unnecessary technical jargon will always be desirable.

Content of financial reports

Turning now to the second part of the statement, a number of factors have contributed to the increasing length and complexity of companies' financial statements.

(a) **Implementation of EU requirements**. The Companies Acts 1981 and 1989 introduced much more prescriptive regulations on the form and content of company accounts, in order to comply with EU directives, which are now embodied in the Companies Act 1985.

(b) **Changes in the business environment**. Increased overseas activities and fluctuating exchange rates have reinforced the need for disclosure of policies adopted in respect of foreign currency translation. Inflation has prompted disclosure of information relating to the effects of price changes.

(c) **Publication of accounting standards**, which are published partly in response to the changing business environment. For example, the factors noted in (b) above helped prompt the publication of SSAP 20 and SSAP 16 although neither received unanimous approval and the latter had to be withdrawn. As more standards are published, more information is required in company accounts.

Factors contributing to complexity

Much of the information published is complex in itself. For example, it is **difficult** for the non-specialist to **understand** information on deferred taxation or finance leases.

The **volume** of information may itself be a **source of obscurity**.

Different opinions may be held on which items are **essential** and which **peripheral**. Some companies put forward their own view on this by highlighting what they consider to be the principal features either on a separate highlights page or in the chairman's report.

Users' needs

Until recently, companies legislation required the circulation of full statutory accounts to all shareholders who wished to receive them. The shareholders' varying abilities to understand and digest the content of those accounts were not taken into consideration.

The problem was already widely acknowledged, though more often in the context of employees' information needs than in the case of shareholders. Many companies already produce employee reports, providing financial and employment information to employees in a form they are likely to understand.

The increasing use of **value added statements** is partly accounted for by the fact that they are usually a great deal **simpler to understand** than the profit and loss account. At the very least, it is essential to ensure that the statutory accounts are no more complicated than they need to be; clear presentation and **avoidance of accounting jargon** can both **contribute to easier understanding.**

Summary financial statements

The Companies Act 1985 was amended by the Companies Act 1989 to allow listed companies to send a **summary financial statement** (SFS) to those shareholders who do not want (or are indifferent about) full accounts. This measure was not, however, introduced to make the accounts easier to understand but to reduce the costs of printing and posting the full glossy report to millions of small shareholders, as recently privatised companies such as British Telecom had been forced to do.

The mandatory contents of the SFS are few and the main exclusions are from the notes. The SFS is in fact required to include a **warning** that it does **not contain enough information** to allow a **full understanding** of the results and state of affairs of the company.

Commenting on the introduction of the SFS, Ernst & Young said 'this approach could merely exacerbate the common misunderstanding that the results and financial position of a **highly complex organisation** can be encapsulated in simple measures such as EPS and gearing'.

It seems therefore, that instead of making accounts more understandable, the introduction of the SFS indicates that the government and **many large companies do not think that most shareholders are really interested in the accounts.**

The annual reports of many large companies now relegate the accounts to the back or to a relatively unattractive supplement, leaving the optimistic words of the chairman and the photographs, pie charts and so on to take pride of place.

Equity investment perspective

Equity investment will only be a sensible option for the average investor when he is in a position to pick up a set of accounts with a **good chance of understanding** its **contents.** Ignorance about financial reporting tends to reinforce the feeling amongst investors that equity investment is too risky, in most cases, to be undertaken directly.

Arguments against the publication of simplified accounts

(a) **Accounting information** is by its nature **complex.** Companies operate in a complicated and rapidly changing business environment. To gloss over the complexities may present a misleading picture.

(b) Shareholders need to satisfy themselves that the directors have **carried out** their **stewardship function satisfactorily.** Simplified accounts may not provide sufficient information for them to do so.

(c) Statute insists that financial statements should give a **true and fair view** and the work of the Accounting Standards Board is also directed towards ensuring that they do. The publication of simplified accounts might be regarded as a lowering of professional standards.

(d) There is a danger that simplified accounts might be used for **purposes for which they are not suitable.** For example, shareholders or potential investors might be tempted to base investment decisions on them. To an extent, the same difficulty applies with full statutory accounts which also are **not designed primarily to aid investment decisions**; but the problem is aggravated in the case of simplified accounts.

(e) Shareholders who find difficulty in understanding full accounts may have recourse to a **professional adviser** to assist them.

Company law review

This issue of the content of financial statements is being addressed once again in the Company Law Review currently underway, managed by the Department of Trade and Industry. The Department of Trade and Industry published recommendations for comment late in 2002.

4 WINGER

> **Tutor's hint.** As with consolidated accounts questions, a question on the preparation of a single company's accounts needs a methodical approach. Lay out proformas and fill the numbers in gradually by systematically working through the question.

(a) WINGER PLC
PROFIT AND LOSS ACCOUNT
FOR THE YEAR ENDED 31 MARCH 20X1

	£'000	£'000
Turnover (358,450 – 27,000)		331,450
Cost of sales (W1)		(208,550)
Gross profit		122,900
Distribution expenses		(28,700)
Administration expenses		(15,000)
Operating profit		79,200
Exceptional items		
Profit on disposal of land and buildings (95,000 - 80,000)		15,000
Loss on abandonment of research project		(30,000)
Profit on ordinary activities before interest		64,200
Interest expense (W3)		(11,200)
Profit before tax		53,000
Taxation (15,000 - 2,200)		(12,800)
Profit after tax		40,200
Dividends: interim	12,000	
final (W4)	18,000	
		(30,000)
Retained profit for the period		10,200
Retained profit b/f (71,600 + 30,000)		101,600
Profit and loss account reserve		111,800

(b) BALANCE SHEET AS AT 31 MARCH 20X1

	£'000	£'000
Fixed assets: tangible		
Land and buildings (200,000 - 6,000 (W2))		194,000
Plant and machinery (W5)		160,000
		354,000
Current assets		
Stock (28,240 + 22,500 (W1))	50,740	
Debtors (55,000 – 27,000 (W1))	28,000	
Cash	10,660	
	89,400	
Creditors due within one year		
Trade and other creditors (W6)	51,400	
Taxation	15,000	
Proposed dividends (W4)	18,000	
	84,400	
Net current assets		5,000
Total assets less current liabilities		359,000
Creditors due after one year		
Lease creditor (W7)		(47,200)
8% debentures		(50,000)
Net assets		261,800
		£'000
Capital and reserves		
Ordinary shares 25p each		150,000
Profit and loss account (see (a))		111,800
Shareholders' funds		261,800

Workings

1 *Cost of sales*

	£'000
Per question	185,050
Less sale/return goods (27,000 × 100/120)	(22,500)
Add depreciation (W2)	46,000
	208,550

2 *Depreciation*

	£'000
Building (100,000 ÷ 50)	2,000
Heating system (20,000 ÷ 10)	2,000
Lifts (30,000 ÷ 15)	2,000
	6,000
Leased plant (80,000 × 20%)	16,000
Owned plant (154,800 - 34,800) × 20%	24,000
	46,000

3 *Interest expense*

	£'000
Debenture interest (50,000 × 8%)	4,000
Finance lease (80,000 - 20,000) × 12%	7,200
	11,200

4 *Final dividend*

	£'000
Total dividend required £1.25 × 4% × (150,000 × 4)	30,000
Interim dividend paid	(12,000)
Final dividend required	18,000

5 *Plant and machinery*

		£'000
Cost:	owned plant	154,800
	leased plant	80,000
		234,800
Depreciation:	owned plant (34,800 + 24,000 (W2))	(58,800)
	leased plant (80,000 × 20%)	(16,000)
		160,000

6 *Trade and other creditors*

	£'000
Trial balance	29,400
Lease creditor (W7)	20,000
Accrued debenture interest	2,000
	51,400

7 *Lease creditor*

	£'000
Total payments due	80,000
Less amount paid	(20,000)
	60,000
Add accrued interest (60,000 × 12%)	7,200
Total creditor	67,200
Due within one year	20,000
Due after one year	47,200

(c) **Policy on depreciation of buildings**

Prior to the issue of FRS 15 *Tangible fixed assets*, companies often used to justify the non-depreciation of buildings on several grounds, including:

(i) That the current value of the buildings was **higher than cost**.

(ii) That the level of **maintenance** meant that no deterioration or consumption had taken place.

(iii) That the depreciation charge would **not be material**.

FRS 15 dismisses the first two of them as being **insufficient grounds** for a policy of non-depreciation. Depreciation is **not** a **valuation model**; rather it is a means of **allocating the depreciable amount** of the asset to accounting periods.

However, it is **still permissible not to charge depreciation** on the grounds of **non-materiality**, but only when **both**:

(i) The **depreciation charge** for the period **and**

(ii) The **accumulated depreciation** that would have been charged against the value of the asset at that point in time,

are immaterial.

Thus assets with very long lives and/or high residual values may meet the criteria not to be depreciated. For depreciation to be classed as immaterial FRS 15 specifies certain conditions:

(i) There must be a policy of **regular maintenance**.

(ii) The asset is unlikely to **suffer obsolescence**.

(iii) There is a policy **and** practice of disposing of similar assets long **before** the **end of their useful lives** at proceeds not materially less than their carrying amounts.

An annual **test for impairment** is also required (except for land).

On the facts given, Winger's policy may have complied with FRS 15.

			Marks
(a)	Profit and loss account:		
	Turnover		1
	Cost of sales		5
	Distribution and administration		1
	Profit on sale of property		1
	Finance costs		2
	Taxation		1
	Dividends		1
		Available	12
		Maximum	9
(b)	Balance sheet		
	Land and buildings		2
	Plant and equipment		3
	Stocks		1
	Debtors		1
	Creditors		2
	Income tax provision		1
	Dividends		1
	Profit and loss account reserve		1
	Creditors over one year		2
		Available	14
		Maximum	11
(c)	One mark per valid point to max		5
		Maximum	5
		Maximum for question	**25**

5 LARCHER

Tutor's hint. This question is designed to give you a taste of the kind of accounts preparation issues the examiner is likely to set. It covers some of the specific topics dealt with in later questions in this Practice & Revision Kit. Make sure you get your proformas down first. Answer all parts of the question.

Examiner's comments. Some candidates missed out on marks by failing to prepare the STRGL. Problem areas included the finance lease and debt factoring.

(a) PROFIT AND LOSS ACCOUNT FOR THE YEAR ENDED 30 SEPTEMBER 20X8

	£'000
Turnover	247,450
Cost of sales (165,050 + 13,500 + 2,500 + 600)	(181,650)
Gross profit	65,800
Distribution expenses	(14,200)
Administration expenses (12,300 – 500) (W2)	(11,800)
Financing costs (1,500 + 1,500 + 300)	(3,300)
Profit before taxation	36,500
Taxation	(9,000)
Net profit from ordinary activities for the year	27,500
Dividends	(13,500)
Retained profit for the year	14,000

(b) STATEMENT OF TOTAL RECOGNISED GAINS AND LOSSES FOR THE YEAR ENDED 30 SEPTEMBER 20X8

	£'000
Profit for the year	27,500
Unrealised surplus on the revaluation of land and buildings	44,000
Total recognised gains and losses	71,500

(c) BALANCE SHEET AS AT 30 SEPTEMBER 20X8

	£'000	£'000
Tangible fixed assets		
Land and buildings (120,000 – 2,500) (W1)		117,500
Plant and equipment (124,740 – 34,740 – 13,500 + 2,400) (W1)		78,900
		196,400
Current assets		
Stocks	16,240	
Trade debtors (W2)	35,500	
Cash in hand and at bank	4,640	
	56,380	
Creditors: amounts falling due within one year		
Trade and other creditors		
(8,540 + 1,500 + 550 + 9,500) (W2)/(W3)	20,090	
Taxation	9,000	
Proposed dividends (13,500 – 3,200)	10,300	
	39,390	
Net current assets		16,990
Creditors: amounts falling due after one year		
(30,000 + 1,950) (W3)		(31,950)
Net assets		181,440
Share capital and reserves		
Ordinary shares of £1 each		100,000
Revaluation reserve (W1)		43,100
Profit and loss account (23,440 + 14,000 + 900)		38,340
		181,440

Workings

1 *Fixed assets*

	Land	*Buildings*
	£'000	£'000
Original cost	12,000	80,000
Accumulated depreciation	-	(16,000)
Net book value	12,000	64,000
Revaluation	20,000	100,000
Revaluation reserve	8,000	36,000

Total revaluation reserve 8,000 + 36,000 – 900 (see below) = £43,100

Depreciation of buildings $\frac{\pounds 100{,}000}{40}$ = £2,500 cost of sales,

previously, $\frac{\pounds 80{,}000}{50}$ = £1,600

Difference to transfer from revaluation reserve £2,500 – £1,600 = £900

Depreciation of plant and equipment (124,740 – 34,740) × 15% = £13,500

Depreciation of lease asset (see (W3)) £3m × 20% = £600 - cost of sales

Leased asset in fixed assets at £3,000 – 600 = £2,400.

2 *Debtors*

According to the factoring agreement Larcher bears the risk on the bad debts. Therefore under FRS 5 *Reporting the substance of transactions* the full amount of debtors should be disclosed (£35.5m). The loan provided by the factor should be disclosed under trade and other creditors (£9.5m) and £0.5m should be credited to administration expenses.

3 *Lease creditors*

	£'000
Cost of lease asset	3,000
Depreciation for the year (£3m × 20%)	(600)
Net book value	2,400
Lease rental for the year	800
Less interest (£3m × 10%)	(300)
Capital element of repayment	500
Liabilities	
At 1.10.97	3,000
Capital element repaid	(500)
	2,500
Due in one year (800 – [2,500 × 10%])	(550)
Due after one year	1,950

4 *Dividends*

	£'000
Interim dividend	3,200
Less: total dividend (£2.25 × 6% × 100,000)	(13,500)
Proposed dividend	10,300

6 ACCOUNTING POLICIES AND ESTIMATION TECHNIQUES

Tutor's hint. The situations in (b) are taken directly from the Standard, which has a short checklist to determine whether the change is due to an accounting policy or just an estimation technique. To summarise the results of this for each part of (b):

Does this involve a change to:	(i)	(ii)	(iii)	(iv) (1)	(iv) (2)	(v)	(vi) (1)	(vi) (2)	(vii)
Recognition?	✓	×	×	×	×	×	×	×	×
Presentation?	✓	×	✓	×	✓	×	×	×	×
Measurement basis?	×	×	×	×	×	✓	✓	×	✓

(a) **Accounting policies** are defined by FRS 18 as those principles, bases, conventions, rules and practices applied by an entity that specify how the effects of transactions and other events are to be reflected in its financial statements through recognising, selecting measurement bases for, and presenting assets, liabilities, gains, losses and changes to shareholders' funds. Accounting policies by definition do not include estimation techniques.

Accounting policies define the **process** whereby transactions and other events are reflected in financial statements. For example, an accounting policy for a particular type of expenditure may specify whether an asset or a loss is to be recognised; the basis on which it is to be measured; and where in the profit and loss account or balance sheet it is to be presented.

Estimation techniques are the methods adopted by an entity to arrive at estimated monetary amounts, corresponding to the **measurement bases** selected, for assets, liabilities, gains, losses and changes to shareholders' funds.

Estimation techniques implement the measurement aspects of accounting policies. An accounting policy will specify the basis on which an item is to be measured; where there is uncertainty over the monetary amount corresponding to that basis, the amount will be arrived at by using an estimation technique.

The **distinction is important** because changes in accounting policy are accounted for as **prior period adjustments**, whereas the effects of changes in estimation techniques are taken through the current year profit and loss account.

(b) (i) The transaction whose effects are being reflected is the incurring of directly attributable finance costs. That transaction is still being measured in the same way, but there is a change to recognition, in that it is now being recognised as (part of) an asset rather than as an expense. (FRS 18 states that where accounting standards allow a choice over what is to be recognised, that choice is a matter of accounting policy.) There is also, consequently, a change to the presentation of the transaction in the balance sheet and the profit and loss account. This is a **change of accounting policy**.

(ii) This example has similarities with (i). Cost centre C may be contrasted with interest in that example. The key difference is that, in (i), FRS 15 allows the entity a choice of how to treat directly attributable interest – as an asset or as an expense. There is no such choice here; directly attributable costs, once estimated, must be treated as part of an asset. Accordingly there is no change to recognition. In addition, both stocks and overheads continue to be presented in the same way and measured on the same basis (stocks are measured at the amount of directly attributable historical costs). This is a **change of estimation technique**.

(iii) Although there is no change to the recognition and measurement of costs, they are being presented differently. This is therefore a **change of accounting policy**.

(iv) (1) Vehicles are being recognised and presented in the same way as before, and using the same, historical cost measurement basis. The only change is to the estimation technique used to measure the unexpired portion of each vehicle's economic benefits. This is **not a change of accounting policy**. (Note that this point is also made in FRS 15 *Tangible fixed assets*.)

(2) This accounting change involves both a change to presentation, as in (iii), and a change of estimation technique, as in (iv) (1) above. For the reasons set out in those examples, the former is a change of accounting policy but the latter is not. The two changes must therefore be **accounted for separately**. No change is made to the amount of depreciation charged in earlier periods, but the profit and loss account for the preceding period is restated to move the depreciation charge from cost of sales to administrative expenses.

(v) There is explicitly a change of measurement basis. This is therefore a **change of accounting policy**, and it should be disclosed. However, a prior period adjustment will be required only if the difference between weighted average and FIFO is **material**.

(vi) (1) FRS 19 allows entities to report deferred tax on either a discounted or an undiscounted basis. These are two different measurement bases, and it is a matter of accounting policy which an entity chooses to adopt. Therefore this is a **change of accounting** policy.

(2) FRS 12 requires entities to report provisions at the best estimate of the expenditure required to settle the present obligation at the balance sheet date. Where that estimate is based on future cash flows, it is permissible to use undiscounted amounts only where the effect of the time value of money is not material. In such circumstances, the use of undiscounted future cash flows is, in effect, an estimation technique for arriving at the present value. Therefore this is **not a change in accounting policy**.

7 PREPARATION QUESTION: DEPRECIATION

> **Tutor's hint**. Identify meaningful headings to help you plan and write your answer.

(a) (i) **Definition of tangible fixed assets**

FRS 15 defines tangible assets as follows.

'Assets that have physical substance and are held for use in the production or supply of goods or services, for rental to others, or for administrative purposes on a continuing basis in the reporting entity's activities.'

The two important aspects of this definition to consider are:

- Tangible assets **have physical substance**, and are thus distinguished from intangible fixed assets,
- Assets are **held for use on a continuing basis**, differentiating fixed assets from current assets.

(ii) **Initial measurement of tangible fixed assets**

FRS 15 requires that tangible fixed assets should initially be measured at **cost.** This applies whether the asset is purchased or whether it is constructed.

'Cost', broadly speaking, is purchase cost less any trade discounts plus any costs **directly attributable** to bringing it into working condition for its intended use.

Directly attributable costs are:

- The **incremental costs** to the entity that would have been avoided only if the tangible fixed asset had not been constructed or acquired
- The **labour costs of own employees** arising **directly** from the construction or acquisition of the tangible fixed asset

Administration and other general overhead costs would, logically, be excluded from the cost of a tangible fixed asset.

Directly attributable costs include:

- **Acquisition costs,** eg stamp duty, import duties
- Cost of **site preparation** and clearance
- Initial **delivery and handling** costs
- **Installation** costs
- **Professional fees,** eg legal fees
- The estimated cost of **dismantling and removing** the asset and restoring the site, to the extent that it is recognised as a provision under FRS 12 *Provisions, contingent liabilities and contingent assets*

The above costs should only be capitalised for the **period** in which the activities that are necessary to **get the asset ready for use** are **in progress**.

Abnormal costs, such as those arising from design error, industrial disputes or idle capacity are not directly attributable costs and therefore should not be capitalised as part of the cost of the asset.

The **capitalisation of finance costs,** including interest, is **optional**. However, if an entity does capitalise finance costs they must do so **consistently**. All finance costs that are **directly attributable** to the construction of a tangible fixed asset should be capitalised as part of the cost of the asset.

If finance costs are capitalised, capitalisation should start when:

- Finance costs are being incurred

- Expenditure on the asset is being incurred
- Activities necessary to get the asset ready for use are in progress

Capitalisation of finance costs should cease when the asset is ready for use.

The **overall amount to be capitalised** in accordance with the principles of FRS 12 would be the amount of **foreseeable expenditure**, discounted where appropriate.

(b) **Kabin Ltd – Review of company's proposals**

General approach

FRS 15 specifies that where a tangible fixed asset comprises two or more major components with substantially different useful economic lives, each component should be accounted for separately for depreciation purposes and depreciated over its individual useful economic life.

Land and buildings are separable components and are dealt with separately for accounting purposes, even when they are acquired together. With certain exceptions, land has an unlimited life and therefore is not depreciated. Buildings have a limited life and therefore are depreciated.

In this situation, Kabin Ltd is changing from not providing depreciation to providing depreciation on its properties. The company is correct in separating the property into different components with significantly different useful economic lives, as this is required by FRS 15. The question that now arises is whether the carrying amount of the components should be depreciated prospectively over their remaining useful economic lives or whether the change should be reflected as a prior year adjustment.

Prospective recognition v prior period adjustment

Generally FRS 15 states that revisions to useful economic lives, including those where assets are now being depreciated for the first time, should be treated as a **change in estimate**, rather than of accounting policy and **recognised prospectively**, ie the carrying amount of the tangible fixed asset at the date of the revision should be **depreciated** over the **revised remaining useful economic life**. No prior year adjustment would be involved.

However, there may be circumstances where assets are being split into different components with significantly different useful economic lives for depreciation purposes for the first time. In such cases changes should instead be treated as a **change in accounting policy**, in other words as a **prior year adjustment**.

Land v buildings

In the case of the split of the property between land and buildings, a case cannot be made for providing **backlog depreciation** as a prior year adjustment. FRS 15 states that land and buildings should be treated separately for the purposes of depreciation on the grounds that buildings have a limited useful life while land does not.

Splitting the property between land and buildings is **not identifying separate components for the first time**, and therefore the carrying amount of the building should be **depreciated prospectively** over its **remaining (revised) useful economic life**.

Shop facias

However, the shop facias of the retail stores represent a different scenario. In the past they have been treated as an integral part of the building of which they formed a part.

Under FRS 15 they are **separate components** because they have **substantially different useful economic lives.** Accordingly, where this asset is **separated out for the first time** and **depreciated over its (shorter) useful life**, there should be an adjustment for the accumulated depreciation that would have been charged if the **new policy** had always been in force. FRS 15 therefore allows a **prior year adjustment in this case.**

8 SSAP 19

> **Tutor's hint**. For part (a) you need to know the SSAP 19 definition of an investment property. Remember that associated companies are not group companies. Be clear that investment properties which have an unexpired lease of 20 years or less should be depreciated.

(a) **Identification of investment properties**

SSAP 19 defines an **investment property** as an interest in land and/or buildings:

(i) In respect of which **construction work and development** have been **completed**

(ii) Which is **held for its investment potential**, any rental income being negotiated at arm's length.

Excluded from the definition, however, are:

(i) Any property owned and occupied by a company for its own purposes

(ii) Any property let to and occupied by another group company.

These exceptions apply in the case of the properties North and South and neither is therefore an investment property.

The property East is let to an **associated company**. Associated companies are not group companies and the exclusion clause therefore does not apply. The property appears to be an **investment property** and the further information required for a final decision, assuming that construction work and development are complete, is whether Kumar charges the market rent to its associated company and hold the property for its investment potential.

The property West is presumably let at a full rental and is an investment property.

(b) **Appropriate depreciation policy**

FRS 15 requires that fixed assets, including buildings (though not land), should be **depreciated**. This applies even though the market value of the building may be rising, and is intended to reflect the finite useful lives of the buildings.

By contrast, **SSAP 19** emphasises the concept of '**current value**' in determining the balance sheet valuation of investment properties. Such fixed assets are not used up or consumed during a company's business operations in the way that plant and machines are.

Similarly, the disposal of investment properties would not materially affect the company's trading activities. In these circumstances, the provisions of FRS 15 are not properly applicable and SSAP 19 states that investment properties should not be subject to periodic depreciation charges, but should be disclosed in the balance sheet at their open market value. An exception is leasehold investment properties where the unexpired term is 20 years or less.

Applying these principles to Kumar's properties, we can reach the following conclusions.

(i) North and South are not investment properties and should be depreciated according to FRS 15. No depreciation should be provided on the land, but the cost or revalued amount of the buildings should be written off over their useful lives.

(ii) East, it is assumed, is an investment property and should not be depreciated. Balance sheet disclosure should be at open market value.

(iii) West is a leasehold property with an unexpired term of less than 20 years. Its cost or revalued amount should be depreciated in accordance with FRS 15 over the 15 years which the lease has to run.

9 DAWES

> **Tutor's hint**. Questions of this nature require a *broad* knowledge of examinable accounting standards. In this case SSAP 21, and FRSs 3, 4 and 15.
>
> **Examiner's comment**. Part (a) was straightforward and generally well answered. In part (b), administration costs were often (wrongly) treated as finance costs. In part (c), many failed to realise that the sale was beyond the FRS 3 three month limit.

(a) *Corrected schedule of movements in the cost and depreciation of plant*

	Working	*Cost*	*Depreciation*
		£m	£m
As at 1.10.20X6		81.20	32.50
Additions at cost	1	21.50	
Additions leased assets	2	16.00	
Disposals	3	(15.00)	(9.00)
Depreciation for year	4		20.74
As at 30.9.20X7		103.70	44.24

Workings

1 *Additions*

	£m
Cost	20.00
Installation	1.00
Testing	0.50
	21.50

VAT is excluded on the grounds that it will be reclaimed.

Government grants are treated according to SSAP 4 and the company accounting policy and therefore are excluded.

Insurance and maintenance must be revenue expense items chargeable to the profit and loss account.

2 *Fair value of lease commitments*

	£m
Balance b/f	21.40
Capital repaid	(8.40)
New leased assets acquired (bal fig)	16.00
Balance c/f	29.00

3 *Disposals*

At cost £15m (per question item 3)

Depreciation = 3 years × 20% × £15m = £9m

4 *Depreciation*

20% of adjusted cost of £103.7m = £20.74m

(b) *Profit and loss account extract*

	£m
Interest paid on loan stock (5% × £20m)	1.0
Financing charge accrual	0.7
	1.7

Balance sheet extract

	£m
Creditors: amounts falling due after more than one year	
5% loan stock (2006)	17.0
Accrued financing charge (W)	0.7
	17.7

Working: finance charge

	£m
The issue proceeds were £20m × 90%	18
Less deductible issue costs	1
Net proceeds	17
Interest payable over debt period = £20m × 5% × 10 years	10
Redemption cost (£20m × 1.2 (20% premium))	24
Total cost of debt	34

Therefore total finance cost = £34m – £17m = £17m

On a straight line basis finance cost = £1.7m per annum

Therefore an annual accrual of interest/finance charges is required of £1.7m – £1.0m = £0.7m

(c) (i) **Disposal of engineering division**

On 1 July 20X7 a binding decision was taken to sell the loss making operation. FRS 3 would require such material losses to be disclosed as an exceptional item under discontinued operations.

FRS 3 requires *all* the following criteria to be satisfied before an operation can be classified as discontinued.

- Permanent cessation of operations
- Material disposal
- Separately distinguishable results
- Completion of the disposal at the latest within three months of the year end

As the sale was completed more than three months after the year end (10 January 20X8) the disposal cannot be disclosed under discontinued operations (the other three criteria are satisfied).

Provisions must therefore be made under continuing operations in the year to 30 September 20X7 for the following.

	£m
Operating losses	4.5
Loss on sale £(46 – 30 + 2)m	18.0
Provision for damages	5.0
	27.5

(ii) **Claim for damages**

The provision for damages would, however, only be recognised if the company had an *obligation* to make a payment at 30 September 20X7 if the provisions of FRS 12 (on provision and contingencies) are applied. Otherwise, disclosure would be necessary as a contingency. Dawes plc is still liable in this case as the sale to Manulite is *not* of a legal entity, which would take such claims with it, but only of part of operations.

The contingent asset (£5m × 40% = £2m) regarding the counter claim must be treated as separate from the possible provision. It should *not* be recognised in the financial statements; disclosure only may be made if the success of the counter claim is probable.

(d) **Leasehold property – depreciation issue**

The directors' proposal demonstrates a basic misunderstanding of the purpose behind a depreciation charge (**allocating cost** to periods expected to derive economic benefits from the use of the asset).

Depreciation must be charged based on an **appropriate value** (cost or revalued amount). The valuation and depreciation issues must not be confused.

Note. Some companies have in the past avoided depreciation charges on the grounds of high levels of maintenance expenditure being a surrogate for the value of the asset consumed. Whilst this may have been acceptable in the past, the introduction of FRS 15 *Tangible fixed assets* prevents such treatment.

(i) *Where property is carried at cost*

Balance sheet

	£'000
Cost of lease	4,000
Amortisation £4m/25 years × 6 years	(960)
Net book value	3,040

Profit and loss account

Depreciation	160

(ii) *Where property is revalued*

Balance sheet

	£'000
Valuation	6,000
Depreciation (over 20 year remaining life)	(300)
Carrying value	5,700
Revaluation reserve (W1)	2,660

Profit and loss account

Depreciation	300

Statement of total recognised gains and losses

Unrealised revaluation surplus (W1)	2,800

Working: revaluation surplus

	£'000
Net book value of leasehold as at 1 October 20X6	
4,000 – (5 years × 160)	3,200
Revaluation	6,000
Revaluation surplus	2,800

A transfer from revaluation reserve to profit and loss reserve will be required (representing the difference between the depreciation based on the revalued sum and the depreciation based upon the original historical cost of the lease, ie 300 – 160 = 140) over the 20 year remaining life of the leasehold.

The revaluation reserve at 30 September 20X7 is therefore 2,800 – 140 = 2,660.

10 IMPAIRMENT OF ASSETS

Tutor's hint. This question covers some of the major aspects of impairment, a popular topic with the Paper 2.5 examiner.

(a) **Criterion and calculation of impairment**

An asset is impaired when its recoverable amount falls below its carrying value, where recoverable amount is the higher of the value in use of the asset or its net realisable value. This is the central rule of the standard.

(i) **Carrying amount** is the cost or revalued amount of the asset that is recognised in the balance sheet, less accumulated depreciation (or 'amortisation' for intangibles) and impairment losses to date.

(ii) **Value in use** is calculated by working out all the future cash flows expected to arise from both the asset's continued use and its eventual sale and then discounting all these to their present value.

(iii) **Net realisable value** is the estimated sales value of the asset now, less the costs of disposal, where the sale is between willing and knowledgeable parties (ie the sale is not forced, nor at an inflated value).

The **impairment loss** that must be **recognised** is therefore the **difference** between the **carrying value** and a **lower recoverable amount.**

(b) **Indicators of impairment**

Examples of events and changes in circumstances that indicate an impairment may have occurred include the following.

(i) A **current period operating loss** in the business in which the fixed asset or goodwill is involved or **net cash outflow** from the operating activities of that business, combined with either past operating losses/net cash outflows or expected continuing operating losses/net cash outflows.

(ii) A significant decline in a fixed asset's **market value** during the period.

(iii) Evidence of **obsolescence or physical damage** to the fixed asset.

(iv) A significant **adverse change** in:

(1) Either the **business or the market** in which the fixed asset or goodwill is involved, such as the entrance of a major competitor

(2) The **statutory** or other regulatory environment in which the business operates or

(3) Any 'indicator of value' (for example turnover) used to **measure the fair value** of a fixed asset on acquisition.

(v) A commitment by management to undertake a significant **reorganisation.**

(vi) A major loss of **key employees.**

(vii) A significant increase in market **interest rates** or other market rates of return that are likely to affect materially the fixed asset's recoverable amount.

(c) **Calculation of recoverable amount and impairment loss**

The net selling price of the machine is below its carrying value so it is definitely impaired. It is now necessary to find value in use in order to determine what the impairment loss is.

Year	*Long term growth rate*	*Projected future cash flows*	*PV factor at 10%*	*Discounted future cash flows*
		£'000		£'000
1		600	0.90909	545
2		660	0.82645	545
3		710	0.75131	533
4		755	0.68301	516
5		790	0.62092	491
6	+2%	806	0.56447	455
7	–1%	798	0.51316	409
8	–7%	742	0.46651	346
9	–16%	623	0.42410	264
10	–30%	436	0.38554	168
	Total			4,272

To calculate the impairment loss, compare the carrying value of £5m with the higher of value in use (£4.272m) and net selling cost (£3.2m). The impairment loss is therefore £5m – £4.272m = £728,000.

(d) (i) **Definition of IGU**

To determine whether impairment of a fixed asset has occurred, it is necessary to **compare** the **carrying amount** of the net asset with its **recoverable amount**. The recoverable amount is the higher of net realisable value and value in use.

In practice, it is not always easy to estimate value in use. In particular, it is not always practicable to identify cash flows arising from an individual fixed asset. If this is the case, value in use should be calculated at the level of **income generating units.**

An income generating unit is defined as a **group of assets, liabilities and associated goodwill** that generates income that is **largely independent** of the reporting **entity's other income streams.** The assets and liabilities include those already involved in generating the income and an appropriate portion of those used to generate more than one income stream.

(ii) **Identification of IGUs**

(1) The income-generating unit comprises **all the sites** at which the product can be made.

(2) **Each restaurant is an income-generating unit by itself.** However, any impairment of individual restaurants is unlikely to be material. A material impairment is likely to occur only when a number of restaurants are affected together by the same economic factors. It may therefore be acceptable to **consider groupings of restaurants** affected by the same economic factors rather than each individual restaurant.

11 PREPARATION QUESTION: SSAP 13

> **Tutor's hint**. Note that you are required to discuss the criteria, not just to state them.

SSAP 13 distinguishes between the activities of research and development.

(a) **Research activity** is directed towards the advancement of knowledge, sometimes with no commercial end in view (pure research), sometimes with a view to a specific practical objective (applied research).

(b) **Development activity** aims to exploit existing knowledge and techniques so as to introduce or improve specific products or processes.

Expenditure on pure or applied research does not relate to one accounting period more than another, but is part of a continuing operation to maintain a company's business or market position. It is therefore appropriate to write off such expenditure in the year in which it is incurred.

Expenditure on development, however, will, if successful, lead to increased revenue or reduced costs once the new products or processes are launched. It appears reasonable that such costs should be carried forward and matched with the related revenue or savings.

SSAP 13 lays down strict **criteria** to determine when carry forward is permissible.

(a) It must be possible to **isolate the work** done on a development project and the expenditure incurred on it. Such expenditure may include the cost of fixed assets purchased wholly for use on the project.

(b) It must be **reasonably clear that the project can be completed.** To this end estimates must have been made of the projected resources available to the company as a whole and the amounts which can be spared from trading activities for allocation to the project. Equally, an assessment must have been made of the **technical feasibility** of the work and of the costs to be incurred in completing it.

(c) The project's **ultimate success** must have been **predicted with reasonable probability.** This will involve consideration of the results of market research and, in some cases, of consumer and environmental legislation. Estimates will need to be made of quantities to be sold and the net revenue arising on sales. It must be reasonably clear that net revenue from the project will exceed not only costs incurred by the balance sheet date, but also the costs to be incurred in completing the project.

12 INVESTMENTS, GOODWILL AND INTANGIBLES

Tutor's hints. Take care here not to answer a question you would have liked to have been asked rather than the one given. Discounting is regularly examined at this level, so you must be able to perform calculations such as that to determine the fair value of the loan.

(a) **Treatment of movements in investments**

		Valuation as at	*Treatment*		*Valuation as at*	*Treatment*	
	Cost	*30.9.X7*	*P&L*	*Reserve*	*30.9.X8*	*P&L*	*Reserve*
	£'000	£'000	£'000	£'000	£'000	£'000	£'000
Alto	2,100	3,200	-	1,100	5,300	-	2,100
Bedo	8,600	9,000	-	400	7,600	(1,000)	(400)
Celtic	6,000	4,700	(1,300)	-	5,100	400	-
Dalmo	8,500	7,300	(1,200)	-	9,100	1,200	600
	25,200	24,200	(2,500)	1,500	27,100	600	2,300

In the year to 30 September 20X7 £2.5m would have been expensed through the profit and loss for the year and £1.5m (which is the reserve noted in the question) would have been credited to the revaluation reserve. For 30 September 20X8 an income of £600,000 will be credited to the profit and loss account for the year partly as a result of the reversing of previously expensed amounts on Celtic and Dalmo. The revaluation reserve will be credited by £2.3m.

(b) **Recognition criteria and accounting treatment**

FRS 10 *Goodwill and intangible assets* sets out guidelines for the initial recognition and subsequent accounting treatment of goodwill and intangible assets.

Purchased goodwill

Purchased goodwill should be recognised as an asset on the face of the balance sheet. The previous practice of writing off goodwill immediately to reserves is no longer allowed.

Negative goodwill should also be shown on the face of the balance sheet, immediately below any positive amount.

The value of purchased goodwill is calculated by deducting the fair values (governed by FRS 7 *Fair values in acquisition accounting*) of the assets and liabilities purchased during the acquisition of a business entity from the consideration paid over.

Non-purchased goodwill

Goodwill generated within the business entity cannot be capitalised due to the difficulties in establishing its value.

Intangible assets

This involves three different identifiable scenarios.

(i) **Internally developed**

FRS 10 allows companies to **capitalise non-purchased** ('internally-developed') **intangibles** but **only to the extent that they have a 'readily ascertainable market value'**. This is an important definition that **means that**:

- **The asset must be a member of a group of homogenous assets** (ie they are all of the same kind), which are equivalent in all material aspects.
- **There is an active market for that group of assets**, evidenced by frequent transactions.

FRS 10 goes on to suggest that it is not possible to determine a market value for unique intangible assets such as brands and publishing titles. However, certain entities that are regularly involved in the purchase and sale of unique intangible assets have developed techniques for estimating their values indirectly. Techniques used can be based, for example, on 'indicators of value' – such as multiples of turnover – or on estimating the present value of the royalties that would be payable to license the asset from a third party.

(ii) **Purchased separately**

An intangible asset purchased separately from a business should be capitalised at its cost.

(iii) **Purchased as part of business acquisition**

Where an intangible asset is acquired **as part of the acquisition of a business** the treatment depends on whether its value can be measured reliably on its initial recognition.

(1) If its value **can be measured reliably**, it should initially be **recorded at its fair value**. (The fair value should not create or increase any negative goodwill arising on the acquisition unless the asset has a readily ascertainable market value.)

(2) If the value of the asset **cannot be measured reliably,** the intangible asset must be **subsumed within the amount of the purchase price attributed to goodwill.**

Accounting treatment

Goodwill is assumed to have an estimated useful life of 20 years or less. Goodwill is therefore amortised over a period of 20 years or less.

This assumption applies to intangible assets as well.

If goodwill or an intangible asset have a demonstrably longer life than 20 years then it must be amortised over its estimated useful life. In some circumstances, an indefinite life may be demonstrated.

When an intangible asset or goodwill is not amortised then an annual impairment review as prescribed by FRS 11 *Impairment of fixed assets and goodwill* must be undertaken by the company.

(c) **Fast Trak intangibles**

Goodwill calculation.

			£m	£m
Consideration				
Cash				25
Redeemable loan note (25m @ 0.60)				15
Shares in Sunfil 20m @ £4				80
				120
Fast Trak's assets			64	
Intangibles	(i)	Kleenwash	12	
	(ii)	Government licences	-	
	(iii)	Fishing quota	16	
				(92)
Goodwill				28

Notes on intangible assets

(i) **Kleenwash**: this brand has been valued by an independent company which specialises in the valuation of brands. As the brand is being purchased it is permissible to disclose this asset separately.

(ii) **Government licence**: as the question states, it is difficult to place a value on this licence. The license is tied up with Fast Trak's mine and there does not appear to be an outside market for it. Fast Trak itself did not pay any money for the licence, so it would be held at a nil value on its own balance sheet.

It is unclear as to how the director's £9 million valuation was arrived at. It is likely that the licence's revenue generating capabilities cannot be separated from the mine and the extraction equipment owned by Fast Trak.

The licence cannot be shown as a separate intangible asset.

(iii) **Fishing quota**: this quota is a marketable item. Quotasales plc actively trades in this type of quota and so the fair value can be capitalised and disclosed in the consolidated accounts

(iv) **Goodwill**: this is purchased goodwill, the excess of the purchase consideration over the fair value of the net tangible and intangible assets.

Marking guide

			Marks	
(a)	General treatment of capitalisation		1	
	Concept of measured reliably		1	
	Separate acquisition		1	
	Part of a business combination		1	
	Internal goodwill cannot be recognised		1	
	Requirement to amortise over life - 20 years		1	
	Rebuttable presumption of 20 years max life		1	
	Requirement for an impairment review		1	
		Available	8	
		Maximum		7
(b)	Internally developed	– Condition for capitalisation	2	
		– Highlight unique v active market	2	
		– Examples, brands, titles etc	2	
	Separately purchased		2	
	Part of acquisition		2	
		Available	10	
		Maximum		9
(c)	Cash consideration		1	
	Redeemable loan note		2	
	Shares in Sunfil		2	
	Fast Trak's assets		1	
	Intangibles (½ each)		1½	
	Goodwill		1½	
	Notes (½ each)		2	
		Available	11	
		Maximum		9
				25

13 PREPARATION QUESTION: HIRE PURCHASE

Tutor's hint. This question allows you to practise the accounting treatment of both hire purchase agreements and finance leases. By producing the HP loan account you are half way towards the balance sheet extracts. Remember the HP creditor is only the capital element.

(a)

HIRE PURCHASE LOAN ACCOUNT

		£			£
20X7			*20X7*		
1.1	Bank	6,000	1.1	Machine	20,000
31.12	Bank	5,828	31.12	Loan interest	
	Balance c/d	9,852		(12% × £14,000)	1,680
		21,680			21,680
20X8			*20X8*		
31.12	Bank	5,828	1.1	Balance b/d	9,852
	Balance c/d	5,206	31.12	Loan interest	
				(12% × £9,852)	1,182
		11,034			11,034
20X9			*20X9*		
31.12	Bank	5,831	1.1	Balance b/d	5,206
			31.12	Loan interest	
				(12% × £5,206)	625
		5,831			5,831

(b) EXTRACTS FROM BALANCE SHEETS AS AT 31 DECEMBER

	20X7	*20X8*	*20X9*
	£	£	£
Fixed assets			
Machine at cost	20,000	20,000	20,000
Less accumulated depreciation	4,000	8,000	12,000
	16,000	12,000	8,000
Creditors: amounts falling due within one year			
Obligations under HP contract	4,646	5,206	-
Creditors: amounts falling due after more than one year			
Obligations under HP contract	5,206	-	-

14 TRACY

> **Tutor's hint**. There is a lot of disclosure required for finance leases and operating leases. Make sure that you have produced all 7 notes to the Financial Statements given in the answer.

PROFIT AND LOSS ACCOUNT EXTRACT

	20X3
	£
Operating profit (note 1)	X
Interest payable and similar charges (note 2)	1,171
Profit on ordinary activities before taxation	X

BALANCE SHEET EXTRACT

	20X3
	£
Fixed assets	
Tangible assets (note 3)	X
	X
Creditors: amounts falling due within one year (note 4)	X
Creditors: amounts falling due after more than one year (note 5)	X

Notes

1 *Operating profit*

Operating profit is arrived at after charging:

	20X3
	£
Depreciation of owned assets	X
Depreciation of assets held under finance leases	6,157
Hire of plant and machinery - operating leases	10,000

2 *Interest payable and similar charges*

	£
Finance charges payable - finance leases (W2)	1,171

3 *Tangible assets*

	£
Cost at 1 January 20X3	X
Additions	X
Cost at 31 December 20X3	X
Accumulated depreciation at 1 January 20X3	X
Charge for the year	X
Accumulated depreciation at 31 December 20X3	X
Net book value at 31 December 20X3	X
Net book value at 1 January 20X3	X

The net book value of fixed assets of £X includes an amount of £55,413 in respect of assets held under finance leases.

4 *Creditors: amounts falling due within one year*

	£
Trade creditors	X
Obligations under finance leases (note 6)	8,708
	X

5 *Creditors: amounts falling due after more than one year*

	£
Debenture loans	X
Obligations under finance leases (note 6)	51,033
	X

6 *Obligations under finance leases*

The minimum lease payments to which the company was committed at 31 December 20X3 are as follows.

	£	£
Under one year		12,000
Over one year		
In the second to fifth years inclusive	48,000	
Over five years	15,000	
		63,000
		75,000
Less: Interest allocated to future periods (W4)		15,259
	(W2)	59,741
Due within one year (W3)		8,708
Due after more than one year (W3)		51,033
	(W2)	59,741

7 *Commitments under operating leases*

At 31 December 20X3 the company had an annual commitment of £10,000 under a non-cancellable operating lease, in respect of plant and machinery, which expires after more than five years from the balance sheet date.

Workings

1 *Depreciation charge for the year*

	£
Cost of asset	61,570
Useful life	10 years
Depreciation charge	£6,157

2 *Obligation to date*

	£
Cash price	61,570
Instalment 1 October 20X3	(3,000)
	58,570
Interest October – December 20X3 (2%)	1,171
Balance 31 December 20X3 (c/d)	59,741

3 *Obligation under one year*

	Balance	*Interest*	*Payments*
Balance 31 December 20X3 (b/d)	59,741		
Instalment 1 January 20X4	(3,000)		3,000
	56,741		
Interest January - March 20X4 (2%)	1,135	1,135	
Balance 31 March 20X4	57,876		
Instalment 1 April 20X4	(3,000)		3,000
	54,876		
Interest April - June 20X4 (2%)	1,098	1,098	
Balance 30 June 20X4	55,974		
Instalment 1 July 20X4	(3,000)		3,000
	52,974		
Interest July - September 20X4 (2%)	1,059	1,059	
Balance 30 September 20X4	54,033		
Instalment 1 October 20X4	(3,000)		3,000
	51,033		
Instalments due under one year			12,000
Interest for next year		3,292	(3,292)
Obligation due within one year			8,708

4 *Interest analysis*

	£
Total payments (£300 × 26)	76,000
Cash price	(61,570)
Total interest	16,430
Interest to date (W1)	(1,171)
Interest in respect of future periods	15,259

15 PREPARATION QUESTION: STOCKS AND WIP

Tutor's hint. This question revises your earlier studies of SSAP 9. It requires some thought about issues rather than simple implementation, something you are likely to face at this level.

(a) **Principle v practice**

The **general principle** underlying SSAP 9 is that stocks should be shown in financial statements at the **lower of cost and net realisable value**. This principle accords with the accounting concepts envisaged by FRS 18:

(i) The accruals basis of accounting specifies that the non-cash impacts of transactions are reflected in financial statements for the period in which they occur, rather than in the period of payment

(ii) The going concern basis assumes that the business is likely to continue into the foreseeable future rather than have account balances recognised on break-up value.

The above general principle is one that commands wide acceptance, at least within the historical cost convention. As the quotation from the standard indicates, most of the problems relating to accounting for stocks involve practical considerations of what expenditure is included in 'cost' for the purpose of the standard.

Cost

Cost clearly includes, but is **not limited to**, the amount that the enterprise has **paid to third parties** to acquire the stock. The difficulties arise when an enterprise incurs ***internal*** **costs** in connection with the production, storage and processing of stock. The issue arises as to whether these should be charged to profit and loss account in the period of payment or whether an element should be carried forward into future periods.

In practice, neither approach would provide information regarding income and financial position that is as useful as that provided by a compromise solution. The **practical compromise solution** usually involves the inclusion of direct acquisition costs, direct stockholding costs and production overhead based on a **normal level of activity**. General overheads are excluded.

Direct acquisition costs such as freight, insurance or the direct costs of producing own-manufactured stock are included on the grounds that they are **truly incremental**. If the stock had not been acquired or manufactured, such costs would not have arisen. They are therefore a valid part of the 'cost' of the stock.

Production overheads are usually incurred on a time basis and not in relation to the quantities of stock produced. In the short run, therefore, they **cannot be regarded as truly incremental**. However, most businesses are assumed to continue operating in the medium term and production overheads are part of the inevitable cost of providing production facilities in the medium term. Therefore, provided the scale of the overheads is not distorted by unusual **levels of activity**, it is reasonable to **include** production overheads in the 'cost' of stock produced in the period to which they relate.

General overheads are less likely to be related to the production of the stock. **Conventionally**, therefore, general overheads are **excluded** from stock valuation.

Allocation of overheads procedures may, in practice, not be sufficiently sophisticated to provide a fair allocation between production and general overheads. Typical examples are the allocation of the costs of technical departments, distribution, purchasing and supervisory management costs. Identifying a **'normal' level of activity**, particularly when the business of a company and its level of stockholding is seasonal, may cause **practical problems**.

Net realisable value

The establishment of NRV also poses a number of practical problems. For many intermediate products, and even for finished items, there may be a limited market and the stock volumes may represent a significant proportion of the market especially if disposed of under distress conditions. This is particularly true of long-term work in progress or such items as ships, aircraft, heavy vehicles and military equipment.

Where a well-developed and liquid market does not exist, it is usually appropriate to base NRV on an orderly disposal after allowing for the reasonable additional costs of marketing and distribution.

(b) **Unfinished goods**

The accounts of a business are intended to show

- The **financial performance** of that business for a particular period
- The **financial condition** of the business at the end of that period.

To achieve this, a number of **concepts** have been developed, one of which is the accruals concept.

The accruals basis of accounting requires the **non-cash impacts** of transactions to be reflected in the financial statements of the **accounting period to which they relate** (occur), rather than the period any cash involved is paid or received.

The recording of cash received as revenues and cash expended as costs is difficult for two reasons.

(i) Firstly, such receipts and expenditures will often relate to capital items, the effects of which need to be recognised over several accounting periods, such as the acquisition of fixed assets.

(ii) Expenditure on items such as stock are retained in the balance sheet at the period end to be matched against the proceeds from selling the stock in the following period.

In order to calculate the **real profit earned** in an accounting period **rather than** simply the **net cash movement, recognition** must be taken of the **value attributable** to **opening** and **closing stocks** of raw material, work in progress and finished stocks. The value attributed to these items are usually based on their cost, which may not be the price which they would fetch in the open market. So long as it is probable that, after the additional costs that must be incurred to prepare them for sale, these items will at least fetch an amount equivalent to at least all associated costs, this is the proper basis for including them in the accounts.

This reflects another basic accounting concept, known as the '**going concern basis**'. This means that accounts should normally be prepared on the assumption that the business is expected to continue in operational existence for the foreseeable future. The values attributed to assets in the balance sheet should be on the basis that they are to be disposed of in the normal course of business. If, however, there is any real doubt about the continuation of the business, it would be appropriate to value the assets on a break-up basis, which would normally be considerably lower than on a going concern basis.

Contracts

The accounting treatment of **long-term contracts** reflects **both the accruals and the going concern concepts**.

A long-term contract is one that extends beyond the end of an accounting period. While the amount of profit made on a long-term contract can only be known with certainty at or some time after the completion of a long-term contract, this does not mean that the profit is not made until it is completed.

It is generally considered that profit is earned proportionally as the contract progresses and that the recognition of profit only in the year that a contact is completed would hinder rather than assist in the assessment of the profitability of companies undertaking them in comparison with each other and over time.

Consequently, an assessment needs to be made at the end of an accounting period of the amount of profit earned on each long-term contract. In the absence of a better measure, the estimated final profit on a contract may be assumed to accrue evenly over the expected duration of the contract subject to two provisos.

(i) The first is that the contract should be sufficiently well advanced for a reasonable assessment to be possible of the likely outcome.

(ii) The second is that, in order to comply with the principle that accounts should be prepared on a prudent basis, any expected losses on long-term contracts should be provided for in full as soon as they become apparent.

This approach, reflected in an old standard, is somewhat at odds with the asset and liability recognition approach in the ASB's *Statement of Principles* and FRS 18. These reflect a **balance sheet values driven approach** rather than a matching approach, preferring instead to require **assets and liabilities** to be **measured** and **recognised** at **balance sheet date**, with **earnings following** as a **consequence**.

16 SHIPRIGHT

> **Tutor's hint.** Accounting for long term contracts is the most likely aspect of SSAP 9 to be examined at this level.
>
> **Examiner's comment.** In (a) candidates found it easier to determine the costs but failed to follow the question requirements that revenues should be determined on a cost basis. Another common error was the use of cumulative rather than annual figures in the profit and loss account. Most alarmingly a few candidates failed entirely to answer this and the computational parts of other questions.

(a) SHIPRIGHT PLC
PROFIT AND LOSS ACCOUNTS FOR THE YEARS ENDING

	31 March 20X6	*31 March 20X7*	*31 March 20X8*	*31 March 20X9*
	£m	£m	£m	£m
Sales	160	160	373	209
Cost of sales	(128)	(136)	(317)	(213)
Profit	32	24	56	(4)

Workings

20X6: $\frac{128}{640} = 20\%. \ 20\% \times £800\text{m} = £160\text{m}$

20X7: $\frac{264}{660} = 40\%. \ (40\% \times £800\text{m}) - £160\text{m} = £160\text{m}$

Costs: £264m – £128m = £136m

20X8: $\frac{507 + 48}{660 + 80} = 75\%$

	£m
Sales: ((800 + 100) × 75%) – 320	355
Incentive payment (2% × 800)× 75%	12
Labour cost escalation	6
	373
Sales	
Costs: 507 + 20 + 48 – 264 + 6	317

20X9: $\frac{680 + 84}{680 + 84} = 100\%$

	£m
Sales: 800 + 100	900
Less previously stated sales (373 + 320)	(693)
Less penalty clause (1% of 800)	(8)
Labour cost escalation	10
	209

Sales	
Costs: 680 + 84 + 4 – (507 + 48)	213

(b) **Alternative measure of contract completion**

	20X6	*20X7*	*20X8*	*20X9*
$\frac{\text{Value of work certified}}{\text{Contract price}}$	$\frac{136}{800} = 17\%$	$\frac{280}{800} = 35\%$	$\frac{570 + 60}{800 + 100} = 70\%$	$\frac{900}{900} = 100\%$

SSAP 9 *Stocks and long term contracts* does not stipulate any one method of allocating the proportion of the contract completed in each year. The main point is that Shipright plc **consistently applies** the **same** methods to each of its contracts.

If the alternative method had been used then the first year would have seen no profit recognised as Shipright recognises no profits until the contract is at least 20% complete.

The alternative method is more prudent in each year, recognising a lower proportion of the contract. This is because sales value is used instead of costs incurred.

17 MULTIPLEX

> **Tutor's hint**. The type of calculation in (a) comes up quite often in this level of exam paper. Impairment, covered in (b), is a difficult subject – make sure you understand where you went wrong (if at all!)

(a) (i) **Finance charge – year to 31 March 20X1**

	£'000	£'000
Total proceeds £80m × 90%		72,000
Total payments made		
Interest (£80m × 8% × 5 years)	32,000	
Redemption (£80m × 112%)	89,600	
Issue costs: direct only	400	
		122,000
Total finance cost		50,000

This is apportioned (straight line per the question) over 5 years of the loan stock life:

Profit and loss charge = £10m

(ii) **Balance sheet extract**

	£'000
Proceeds received	72,000
Less issue costs	(400)
Less payments made £80m × 8%	(6,400)
Add finance charge	10,000
Balance at 31 March 20X1	75,200

Shown in creditors due after more than one year.

(b) **Carrying value of assets**

The impairment losses are allocated as required by FRS 11 *Impairment of fixed assets and goodwill*.

	Asset at 1.1.20X1	*1st provision*	*Assets at 1.2.20X1*	*2nd provision*	*Revised asset*
	£'000	£'000	£'000	£'000	£'000
Goodwill	200	(200)	-	-	-
Operating licence	1,000	(300)	700	(100)	600
Property: stations/land	250	-	250	(50)	200
Rail track/coaches	250	-	250	(50)	200
Steam engines	1,000	(500)	500	-	500
Other net assets	300	-	300	-	300
	3,000	(1,000)	2,000	(200)	1,800

Workings

1 *First provision*

£500,000 relates directly to an engine and its recoverable amount can be assessed directly (ie zero).

FRS 11 then requires goodwill to be written off. Any further impairment must be written off intangible assets.

2 *Second provision*

The first £100,000 of the impairment loss is applied to the operating licence to write it down to NRV.

The remainder is applied pro rata to assets carried at other than their net selling prices.

(c) **Correct accounting treatment – closure of engineering division**

At the year end of 31 March 20X1, the company has committed itself to a **binding decision** to close the engineering operation. The expected losses on closure **must** therefore **be provided** for and, as they are **material,** they will be classed as **exceptional.** FRS 3 *Reporting financial performance* requires **separate disclosure** of losses on the closure of an operation on the face of the profit and loss account.

However, again under FRS 3, the closure of the division appears to meet **only three** of the four criteria for it to be treated as a discontinued operation, ie:

(i) The activities have **ceased permanently.**

(ii) The closure has a **material effect** on the nature and focus of Multiplex's operations.

(iii) The results are **separately distinguishable.**

(iv) But the closure will *not* be completed **within three months** of the year end.

The provision must therefore be shown as part of **continuing operations,** although the circumstances may be explained in the notes to the financial statements.

The amount will be:		£m
Loss on sale of net assets (46 – 30)		16.0
Other costs:	redundancies	2.0
	Professional costs	1.5
	Penalty costs	3.0
		22.5

The treatment of the future operating losses of £4.5 million is less clear.

The company is 'demonstrably committed' to the sale, and therefore FRS 3 requires it to make a provision for losses up to the date of sale. However, FRS 12 *Provisions, contingent liabilities and contingent assets* does not allow any future operating losses to be recognised as a provision unless they relate to 'onerous contracts' (which is not indicated in this question). FRS 12 excludes provisions covered by another accounting standard and this presumably includes FRS 3. Commentators have pointed out this apparent conflict between the two standards.

There is a case for recognising a provision on the grounds that FRS 3 appears to require it. The pertinent question is: does the company have an obligation to incur the losses? In other words, has it any alternative to operating the business at a loss until the date of sale? If not, the spirit of FRS 12 suggests that a provision should not be recognised.

(d) **Accounts extracts**

Profit and loss account	£m
Turnover (W2)	18.0
Cost of sales (balancing figure)	(14.1)
Profit (W3)	3.9

Balance sheet:	£m
Current assets	
Long-term contract balances (W5)	6.0
Debtors: amounts recoverable on long-term contracts (W6)	5.0

Workings

1 *Percentage completion*

$$\text{Percentage completion} = \frac{\text{Work certified}}{\text{Contract price}}$$

20X0 *20X1 (including variation)*

$$\frac{£12\text{m}}{£40\text{m}} = 30\% \qquad \frac{£30\text{m}}{£45\text{m}} = 66.7\% \text{ (ie } ^2/_3 \text{)}$$

2 *Turnover*

Accumulated turnover to 31 March 20X1 = £45m × $^2/_3$ = £30m

In 20X1 turnover = £30m – £12m (20X0) = £18m

3 *Profit*

Revised estimated total profit = £45m – £30m = £15m

Accumulated to 31 March 20X1 = £15m × $^2/_3$ = £10m

Total profit for year ended 31 March 20X1:

	£m
Accumulated to date	10.0
Less 20X0 profit taken (W4)	(3.6)
Less rectification costs	(2.5)
	3.9

4 *Profit for 20X0*

	£m
Turnover	12.0
Cost of sales (bal fig)	(8.4)
Profit = (£40m – £28m) × 30%	3.6

5 *Long-term contract balance*

		£m
Costs incurred to 31 March 20X1		28.5
Cost of sales charged:	20X0 (W4)	(8.4)
	20X1	(14.1))
		6.0

6 *Debtors: amounts recoverable*

	£m
Value of work certified 31 March 20X1	30.0
Payments on account	(25.0)
Amounts due	5.0

			Marks
(a)	Proceeds of issue		1
	Interest for five years		1
	Redemption costs (above items give total finance cost)		1
	Finance cost accrual in P&L a/c		1
	Balance sheet liability		1
		Available	5
		Maximum	5
(b)	First provision - engine		1
	- goodwill		1
	- balance to licence		1
	Second provision - licence at selling price		1
	- balance pro rata to other assets		2
		Available	6
		Maximum	6
(c)	Satisfies most of discontinuing operation criteria, but		2
	not a discontinuing operation in current period (3 month rule)		1
	Must provide for losses in current period		1
	Loss on sale of net assets		1
	Associated costs (redundancy, professionally and penalty)		1
	Future operating losses cannot be provided for		1
		Available	7
		Maximum	5
(d)	Turnover in 20X0		1
	Turnover in 20X1		2
	Profit for 20X1 (including correct treatment of rectification work)		3
	Long-term contract balance		2
	Amount recoverable on contract		2
		Available	10
		Maximum	9
		Maximum for question	**25**

18 DEFERRED TAXATION

Tutors hint. Part (b) is a good illustration of how in this paper it is just as important to understand the reasons for the rules as it is to be able to apply the rules to numerical examples. Review your answer carefully, noting particularly the method of scheduling reversals when discounting deferred tax provisions.

(a) **Nature and purpose of deferred taxation**

Accounting profits and taxable profits are not the same. There are several reasons for this but they may conveniently be considered under two headings: permanent differences and timing differences.

(i) **Permanent differences** arise because certain expenditure, such as entertainment of UK customers, is not allowed as a deduction for tax purposes although it is quite properly deducted in arriving at accounting profit. Similarly, certain income (such as franked investment income) is not subject to corporation tax, although it forms part of accounting profit.

(ii) **Timing differences** arise because certain items are included in the accounts in a period different from that in which they are dealt with for taxation purposes.

Deferred taxation is a means of ironing out the tax inequalities arising from timing differences. In years when corporation tax is saved by timing differences such as **accelerated capital allowances,** a charge for **deferred taxation** is made in the profit and loss account and a provision set up in the balance sheet; in years when timing **differences reverse,** because the depreciation charge exceeds the capital allowances available, a **deferred tax credit** is made in the profit and loss account and the balance sheet provision is reduced.

The tax actually payable to the Inland Revenue is the **corporation tax liability**. The credit balance on the deferred taxation account represents an estimate of tax saved because of timing differences but expected ultimately to become payable when those differences reverse.

The main categories in which timing differences can occur are as follows.

(i) **Short-term timing differences**. These arise because taxable profits are calculated on a receipts and payments basis, whereas accounting profits are calculated on an accruals basis.

For example, general provisions for bad debts in the financial accounts are not allowable for tax purposes until they crystallise into specific bad debts.

(ii) **Accelerated capital allowances**. When new assets are purchased, capital allowances may be available against taxable profits which exceed the amount of depreciation chargeable on the assets in the financial accounts for the year of purchase. These can be very large now, with 100% first year allowances available for 'small' companies on computers and software.

(iii) **Revaluation surpluses on fixed assets** for which a taxation charge does not arise until the fixed assets are eventually realised.

(iv) **Surpluses on disposals of fixed assets** which are subject to rollover relief.

Deferred taxation is therefore an accounting convention which is introduced in order to apply the **accruals concept to income reporting** where **timing differences** occur.

A comprehensive tax allocation system would be one in which deferred taxation is computed for every instance of timing differences **(full provision)**. The opposite extreme would be the *nil provision* approach, where only the tax payable in the period would be charged to that period.

The old accounting standard, SSAP 15 *Accounting for deferred tax*, rejected both these approaches and prescribed a middle course, called **partial provision**. Under partial provision, tax deferred or accelerated by the effect of timing differences is accounted for to the extent that it is probable that a liability or asset will crystallise. Tax deferred or accelerated by the effect of timing differences is not accounted for to the extent that it is probable that a liability or asset will not crystallise.'

However, the new standard, FRS 19 *Deferred tax*, requires a full provision for deferred tax, in line with the international approach.

(b) (i) The future depreciation of the existing pool of fixed assets is compared with the future writing-down allowances available on the pool to determine the years of reversal of the capital allowances.

When forecasting capital allowances for future periods, it is assumed that allowances will be claimed as early as possible and that the residual values of the assets will equal those forecast for depreciation purposes.

Year ended 31 March	*Depreciation* (a)	*Capital allowances* (b)	*Reversal of timing difference* ((a) – (b))	*Deferred tax Liability @ 30% (undiscounted)* ((a) – (b)) × 30%
	£'000	£'000	£'000	£'000
20X2	300	278	22	7
20X3	300	209	91	27
20X4	300	157	143	43
20X5	300	93	207	62
20X6	200	69	131	39
20X7	200	52	148	44
20X8	200	14	186	56
20X9	100	11	89	27
20Y0	100	(69)	169	51
Total	2,000 (W1)	814 (W2)	1,186	356

These detailed calculations have been carried out to assist in part (ii) of this question. With no discounting the deferred tax liability under full provision ie simply the timing difference at the year end multiplied by the tax rates 1,186 × 30% = £356,000.

(ii)

Year ending 31 March	*Deferred tax liability (undiscounted)*	*Discount Factor*	*Deferred tax liability (discounted)*
	£'000		£'000
20X2	7	0.962	7
20X3	27	0.925	25
20X4	43	0.889	38
20X5	62	0.855	53
20X6	39	0.822	32
20X7	44	0.790	35
20X8	56	0.760	43
20X9	27	0.731	20
20Y0	51	0.703	36
Total	356		289

Workings

1 *Depreciation*

For each asset, annual depreciation is £(1,100,000 – 100,000)/10 = £100,000 pa. The residual value of £100,000 is £1,100,000/11. Each asset has a life of 10 years and is then assumed to be sold for residual value.

For the years ended 20X2, 20X3, 20X4, 20X5, depreciation = £100,000 × 3
= £300,000

At the end of 20X5, asset 1 has been depreciated to residual value and is assumed to be sold for that value.

For the years ended 20X6, 20X7, 20X8, depreciation = £100,000 × 2
= £200,000.

At the end of 20X8, asset 2 is assumed to be sold for residual value.

For the years ended 20X9, 20Y0, deprecation = £100,000 × 1
= £100,000.

At the end of 20Y0, asset 3 is assumed to be sold for residual value.

2 *Capital allowances*

		£'000	
Tax written down value at 31.3.X1		1,114	
20X2:	Capital allowances at 25%	(278)	278
		836	
20X3:	Capital allowances at 25%	(209)	209
		627	
20X4:	Capital allowances at 25%	(157)	157
		470	
20X5:	Sales proceeds for asset 1	(100)	
		370	
	Capital allowances at 25%	(93)	93
		277	
20X6:	Capital allowances at 25%	(69)	69
		208	
20X7:	Capital allowances at 25%	(52)	52
		156	
20X8:	Sales proceeds for asset 2	(100)	
		56	
	Capital allowances at 25%	(14)	14
		42	
20X9:	Capital allowances at 25%	(11)	11
		31	
20Y0:	Sales proceeds for asset 3	(100)	
	Balancing charge	(69)	69

19 ABROAD LTD

Tutor's hint. The accounting part of this question requires knowledge of a wide range of accounting standards. However, none is examined in a particularly complicated fashion. New standards, like that on deferred tax covered here, are prime candidates for the examination in the next two or three sittings.

(a) ABROAD LIMITED
PROFIT AND LOSS ACCOUNT
FOR THE YEAR ENDED 31 OCTOBER 20X6

	£'000	£'000
Turnover		
Continuing operations		8,900
Cost of sales (W1)		(7,844)
Gross profit		1,056
Distribution costs (633 + 32)	665	
Administrative expenses	541	
		(1,206)
Operating loss: continuing operations		(150)
Provision for withdrawal from contract	(50)	
Profit on sale of factory (W2)	58	
		8
		(142)
Interest receivable	161	
Interest payable (W3)	(163)	
		(2)
Loss on ordinary activities before taxation		(144)
Tax on ordinary activities (W5)		(109)
		(253)
Dividends		(52)
Retained loss for the year		(305)

Workings

1 *Cost of sales*

	£'000
Per profit and loss account	7,094
Add consignment stock in closing stock	2,000
Deduct consignment stock in opening stock	(1,250)
	7,844

Note. FRS 5 *Reporting the substance of transactions* requires that stocks held on consignment in the circumstances outlined in this question should be excluded. A deduction from opening stock reduces cost of sales and a deduction from closing stock increases it.

2 *Exceptional items*

	£'000
Provision for cost of withdrawal from contract	50
Sale of factory	
Sale proceeds (103 + 50 + 85)	238
Less carrying value	(180)
Profit on disposal	58

Note. **FRS 3** requires that the '**extraordinary items**' be **reclassified** as **exceptional.** It also requires that the **profit on disposal** be **calculated** as the **sale proceeds less the carrying value,** which in this case is based on a **revalued amount.** The sale proceeds are calculated by taking the extraordinary profit of £103,000 and adding back the provision for the cost of withdrawal from the contract and the cost of the factory.

3 *Interest payable*

		£'000
Interest on debentures (2,000 × 8%)		160
Issue costs amortised on straight-line basis	$\frac{12,000}{4}$	3
		163

4 *Deferred taxation*

FRS 19 states that deferred tax should not be provided on revaluation gains when there is no commitment to sell it. The provision in relation to this part of deferred tax should be reduced:

£37,500 × 32% = £12,000

Timing differences

5 *Taxation charge*

	£'000
Charge in p & l	88
Decrease in deferred tax provision	(12)
Tax on exceptional items (49,000 – (32% × 50,000)	33
	109

(b) **Main requirements of FRS 19**

FRS 19 *Deferred tax* requires **full provision** to be made for deferred tax assets and liabilities arising from **timing differences** between the recognition of gains and losses in the financial statements and their recognition in a tax computation.

The general principle underlying the requirement is that deferred tax should be recognised as a liability or asset if the transactions or events that give the entity an obligation to pay more tax in future or a right to pay less tax in future have occurred by the balance sheet date.

(i) Deferred tax is recognised on most types of timing difference, including those attributable to:

(1) **Accelerated capital allowances**

(2) **Accruals** for **pension costs** and other **post-retirement benefits** that will be deductible for tax purposes only when paid

(3) Elimination of **unrealised intragroup profits** on consolidation

(4) **Unrelieved tax losses**

(5) Other sources of **short-term timing differences**

(ii) The FRS prohibits the recognition of deferred tax on timing differences arising when:

(1) A **non-monetary asset** is **revalued without** there being any **commitment** to **sell** the asset (subject to one exception outlined below)

(2) The gain on sale of an asset is **rolled over** onto replacement assets

(3) A **non-monetary asset** is **adjusted** to its **fair value** on the acquisition of a business

(4) The **remittance** of a subsidiary, associate or joint venture's earnings would cause tax to be payable, but **no commitment** has been made to the **remittance of the earnings.**

(iii) **Deferred tax assets are recognised to the extent that it is regarded as more likely than not that they will be recovered.**

As an **exception** to the general requirement not to recognise deferred tax on revaluation gains and losses, the FRS requires deferred tax to be recognised when assets are **continuously revalued to fair value,** with changes in fair value being recognised in the profit and loss account.

The FRS permits but does not require entities to adopt a policy of discounting deferred tax assets and liabilities.

The FRS includes other requirements regarding the measurement and presentation of deferred tax assets and liabilities. These include requirements for the deferred tax to be:

(1) Measured using **tax rates** that have been **enacted** or **substantively enacted**

(2) **Presented separately** on the face of the balance sheet if the amounts are so **material** that, in the absence of such disclosure, readers may misinterpret the accounts.

The FRS requires information to be disclosed about **factors affecting current** and **future tax charges.** A key element of this is a requirement to disclose a **reconciliation** of the **current tax charge** for the period to the **charge** that would arise if the **profits reported** in the accounts were **charged at a standard rate of tax.**

The FRS **amends FRS** 7 *Fair values in acquisition accounting*. The amendment requires deferred tax recognised in a fair value exercise to be measured in the same way as it would have been if the **adjustment** to **fair values** had been **gains** and **losses** reflected in the **acquired entity's own financial statements.**

(c) **Reasons for introduction of full provision approach**

The changes introduced by FRS 19 reflect an acceptance of the need to **harmonise** the way in which deferred tax is accounted for in the UK with the way in which it is accounted for in **other countries.** The new standard replaced SSAP 15 *Accounting for deferred tax*.

In recent years, the partial provision method of accounting for deferred tax required by **SSAP 15 has lost favour internationally,** primarily because it is **subjective** (relying heavily on management expectations about future events) and inconsistent with other areas of accounting. Other major standard-setters and IAS 12 (revised 1996), now require deferred tax to be provided for in full. Whilst the ASB could see the merits of the partial provision method, it accepted some of the arguments against it and concluded that deferred tax was not an area where a good case could be made for taking a stand against the direction of international opinion.

The approach developed by FRS 19 has similar objectives to the 'temporary difference' approach on which IAS 12 is based. However, it is framed differently and does not require exceptions to its basic principles to avoid some of the more controversial consequences of the temporary difference approach.

In summary then, SSAP 15 was replaced for the following reasons.

(i) The UK needed to be brought into line with **international practice** which favours the **full provision approach.**

(ii) The partial provision method enables deferred tax *not* to be provided for if management assess the tax liabilities as being unlikely to crystallise. This involves subjectivity.

(iii) The estimates of capital allowances and depreciation under partial provision are unreliable.

(iv) Under **full provision the maximum tax liability** is provided so profit after tax is seen as a **more realistic measure**.

However, when the full provision method is used, deferred tax balances may build up which will **reduce equity** and **increase gearing**. The amounts provided will not be payable for some time (if at all); the revised standard does permit the use of discounting of liabilities to present values, which mitigates some of these effects.

Marking guide

				Marks	
(a)	Cost of sales			2	
	Distribution costs			1	
	Administration expense			1	
	Exceptional items -	property		2	
		fixed assets		3	
	Interest payable			3	
	Taxation			3	
	Format			2	
			Available	16	
			Maximum		14
(b)	Full provision			1	
	General explanation			1	
	Timing differences, examples			2	
	Prohibitions			2	
	Deferred tax assets			1	
	Revaluation exceptions			1	
	Rates used			1	
	Discounting			1	
	FRS 7			1	
			Available	11	
			Maximum		10
(c)	International practice			1	
	Problems with partial provision				
	- management subjectivity			1	
	- unreliability			1	
	IAS 12/differences			2	
	Eventual payment of tax			1	
			Available	7	
			Maximum		6
			Total maximum		30

20 PREPARATION QUESTION: EARNINGS PER SHARE

Tutor's hint. This question covers some of the basic requirements of FRS 14. You must be able to explain EPS as well as calculate it. You must also be familiar with P/E ratio, earnings yield and diluted EPS.

(a) **Calculation of basic EPS**

Basic EPS should be calculated by dividing the net profit or loss attributable to ordinary shareholders by the weighted average number of ordinary shares outstanding during the period. (*Note.* Shares are 'outstanding' as soon as the consideration for their issue is receivable.)

In the most straightforward case, an **issue of shares for cash**, those shares would be 'outstanding' as soon as the cash was receivable. As another example, if a company makes an acquisition and **deferred consideration** is payable in the form of shares, those shares will be included in the calculation of basic EPS from the acquisition date, since that is when the consideration for their issue - ie the benefits to be received from the acquired business - is receivable.

(b) (i) **Contingently issuable shares**

These are ordinary shares that are issuable once certain conditions are satisfied. Once all the necessary conditions are met, including the consideration being receivable, and there are no circumstances in which the shares will not be issued, they are included in the calculation of basic EPS.

(ii) **Shares included in calculation of EPS**

$20,000 \times 9/12 = 15,000$ shares would be included in the calculation of basic EPS for 20X8.

(c) **The P/E ratio** is calculated by dividing the market price by the EPS. It has the effect of comparing the market price of a share with its current earnings. It indicates how long an investor would have to hold a share, assuming earnings were unchanged and distributed in full, in order to recoup the original purchase price. A high P/E ratio relative to other comparable companies indicates that the market has confidence in the company's growth potential or regards it as low risk; a low P/E ratio has the opposite implications. The P/E ratio has the advantage of being based on earnings rather than dividends, and hence will not be affected by the company's distribution policy.

Earnings yield is the inverse of the P/E ratio (ie earnings ÷ price) and measures the rate of return. It gives useful information not provided by dividend yield because it allows for the element in the market price attributable to the worth of *retained* earnings. However, one of an investor's primary concerns will always be the cash flow expected from a share investment and so dividend levels (and ratios based thereon) are of great importance.

(d) **Diluted earnings per share** is calculated by adjusting the figures used to calculate basic EPS. The earnings figure and the number of shares are adjusted for the effects of all **dilutive** potential ordinary shares. Potential ordinary shares include share warrants and options, convertible preference shares or debentures and so on. It is useful for current holders of ordinary shares to be able to assess how their per share earnings will, in future, be **diluted** by these new shares. It is not possible to tell what earnings will be in the period in which such shares might come into existence, so instead the calculation is carried out using **current earnings** as if the dilutive potential ordinary shares were in existence in the current period.

Diluted EPS thus may act as an **indicator** to current ordinary shareholders that the company is **promising part of future earnings to others**, perhaps in recompense for current services (eg share options for directors that may be exercised in the future).

21 ABC

Tutor's hint. The calculations involved in this question are not particularly complicated. However, a large number of marks are available for explanations and understanding. Part (a), particularly requires you to think very carefully about the implications of merger accounting for EPS. Note that FRS 14 has changed the calculation of basic EPS very little.

Examiner's comment. Answers to part (a) were very variable. Many had problems with the theoretical ex-rights price. The merger accounting aspect was handled surprisingly well. Parts (b) and (c) were well answered, although many did not mention that it is possible to overemphasise the importance of earnings per share.

(a) (i) **20X2**

Earnings		£200,000
Number of shares		
In issue for full year		250,000
In issue 1.1.X2 - 31.3.X2		
$50,000 \times {}^{3}/_{12} \times 75\%$	9,375	
In issue 1.4.X2 - 31.12.X2		
$50,000 \times {}^{9}/_{12} \times 100\%$	37,500	
		46,875
		296,875

$$\text{Earnings per share for 20X2} = \frac{£200{,}000}{296{,}875} = 67.4\text{p}$$

Note. There is no information given for a 20X1 comparative.

(ii) **20X3**

Theoretical ex-rights price per share

	£
Value of 2 shares before rights issue (2 × £1.80)	3.60
Value of 1 rights issue share	1.20
Value of 3 shares after rights issue	4.80

$$\text{Theoretical ex rights price} = \frac{£4.80}{3} = £1.60$$

Earnings		£250,000
Number of shares in issue		
1.1.X3 - 31.8.X3		
$300{,}000 \times {}^{8}/_{12} \times \frac{£1.80}{£1.60} =$	225,000	
1.9.X3 - 31.12.X3		
$450{,}000 \times {}^{4}/_{12}$	150,000	
		375,000

$$\text{EPS} = \frac{250{,}000}{375{,}000} = 66.7\text{p}$$

Revised EPS calculation for 20X2

$$67.4\text{p} \times \frac{1.60}{1.80} = 59.9\text{p}$$

ABC GROUP
EARNINGS PER SHARE FOR THE YEAR ENDED 31 DECEMBER

	20X3	*20X2*
	66.7p	59.9p

(iii) **20X4**

Earnings		£450,000
Number of shares		
As at 1 1.X4	450,000	
2 XYZ for 1 ABC	× 2	900,000

$$\text{EPS} = \frac{£450{,}000}{900{,}000} = 50\text{p}$$

Note. We are told in the question that the principles of merger accounting have been adopted. This means that the shares in issue at the end of the year are assumed to have been in issue for the whole of the year. There is therefore no need to time apportion as we had to with the rights issue. The previous year's EPS figure will have to be adjusted to reflect the number of shares deemed to have been in issue in that year, ie twice as many as were in fact in issue.

Previous year

EPS = 66.7p × ½ = 33.3p

XYZ GROUP

EARNINGS PER SHARE FOR THE YEAR ENDED 31 DECEMBER

20X4	20X3
50p	33.3p

(b) A **rights issue** is a popular method through which public companies are able to access the stock market for further capital. Under the terms of such an issue, existing shareholders are given the opportunity to acquire further shares in the company on a pro-rata basis to their existing shareholdings.

The 'rights' shares will usually be offered at a discount to the market price. In such cases, the issue is equivalent to a bonus issue combined with an issue at full market price. **Bonus issues** are treated as though they have been in issue for the whole year and are also taken into account in the previous year's EPS calculation to give a comparable result. FRS 14 states that it is necessary to adjust the number of shares in issue before the rights issue to reflect the bonus element inherent in the issue. The notes to the financial statements should preferably refer to the adjustments made to the comparative EPS figure to reflect the bonus element of the rights issue.

The bonus element of the rights issue is given by the following fraction, sometimes referred to as the **bonus fraction.**

$$\frac{\text{Fair value per share immediately before the exercise of rights}}{\text{Theoretical ex rights fair value per share}}$$

The fair value before the exercise of rights is the **actual** price at which the shares are quoted inclusive of the right to take up the future shares under the rights issue.

The ex rights fair value per share is the **theoretical** price at which the shares would be quoted, other stock market factors apart, after the rights issue shares have been issued.

In order to calculate earnings per share with a rights issue, the shares are time apportioned before and after the date of the rights issue. The number of shares is calculated in two stages as follows.

Before rights issue:

Number of shares before rights issue × Bonus fraction × Fraction of year before rights issue

After rights issue:

Number of shares after rights issue × Fraction of year after rights issue

The two figures produced by the above calculations are added together to give the denominator for the fraction required in calculating earnings per share.

When calculating the revised earnings per share for the previous year, the latter has to be adjusted to take account of the bonus element by multiplying it by the following.

$$\frac{\text{Theoretical ex rights fair value}}{\text{Actual cum rights fair value}}$$

This makes the previous year's figure comparable with that of the current year.

(c) **Earnings per share** (EPS) is one of the most frequently quoted statistics in financial analysis. Because of the widespread use of the price earnings **(P/E) ratio** as a yardstick for investment decisions, it became increasingly important.

It seems that reported and forecast EPS can, through the P/E ratio, have a significant effect on a company's share price. Thus, a share price might fall if it looks as if EPS is going to be low. This is not very rational, as EPS can depend on many, often subjective, assumptions used in preparing a historical statement, namely the profit and loss account. It does not necessarily bear any relation to the value of a company, and of its shares. Nevertheless, the **market is sensitive to EPS**.

EPS has also served as a means of **assessing the stewardship** and management role performed by company directors and managers. Remuneration packages might be linked to EPS growth, thereby increasing the pressure on management to improve EPS. The danger of this, however, is that management effort goes into distorting results to produce a favourable EPS.

The ASB believed that undue emphasis was being placed on EPS, and that this led to simplistic interpretations of financial performance. Consequently, in issuing FRS 3 *Reporting financial performance*, the ASB attempted to de-emphasise EPS by requiring it to be calculated after extraordinary items (carried on into FRS 14). Because of this, and other changes, **EPS is now very volatile** and, arguably less useful for analysis; many companies are providing additional EPS figures, prepared on what they see as a more meaningful basis.

22 PERFORMANCE REPORTING

> **Tutor's hint**. FRS 3 introduced some radical ways of reporting financial performance which are very important to users of accounts. Questions on FRS 3 are very popular with the examiner.
>
> **Examiner's comment**. Answers were very disappointing; this is an important topic and similar questions have been asked before. Exam technique was lacking; candidates often knew the requirements of FRS 3, but failed to apply this to the specific question set.

(a) **Comprehensive income approach**

FRS 3 *Reporting financial performance* advocates the 'comprehensive income' approach described in the question. It was the first standard to take such a radical approach, although other national standard setters have followed suit (including the USA).

The main problem for the ASB in taking this approach was that, although certain **unrealised gains and losses** are recognised in accounts under current standards or legislation (eg revaluation gains and losses on fixed assets), only **realised gains and losses** may be reported in the profit and loss account under UK company law.

The ASB overcame this problem by introducing a 'statement of total recognised gains and losses' or **STRGL**. In this statement, all gains and losses recognised during the period must be shown (including, as a summary item, the net profit or loss for the period).

This was an important step forward in reporting financial performance. If nothing else, it tended to **highlight** certain items of financial performance, for example translation gains and losses on the net investment in a foreign entity, that had previously been **'lost' in the notes to the accounts** dealing with reserves.

The ASB did not seek to justify its approach in any detailed conceptual manner. It did state, however, that the STRGL would:

'contribute further to the purposes of financial reporting by:

(a) combining information about operating and related performance with other aspects of a reporting entity's financial performance; and

(b) providing information (jointly with the other primary statements) that is useful for assessing the return on investment in a reporting entity'.

(b) **Role in improving information content**

(i) **Continuing v discontinued operations**

This analysis allows users to focus on the **likely trends** of performance which will continue in the future by disregarding discontinued activities. (Past period results can be adjusted to exclude current period discontinued activities as well.)

(ii) **Extraordinary and exceptional items**

Extraordinary items were effectively **banned** by FRS 3 because of the very tight definitions of both **ordinary activities** and extraordinary items. This was mainly because the ASB felt it was not justifiable to maintain a completely separate category for all sorts of different items not deemed by the management to be part of ordinary activities in a particular period.

For company law reasons, however, the notion of extraordinary items had to remain.

In the past, extraordinary items were not included in the EPS calculation. In the event that they do occur, they must now be included in earnings for the EPS calculation.

Exceptional items fall into two categories under FRS 3.

(1) Those **required** to be disclosed by FRS 3 ('super-exceptionals'), ie:

- Profits/losses on termination of an operation
- Costs of restructuring
- profits/losses on sales of fixed assets.

(2) All others warranting disclosure (such as an abnormal bad debt charge).

This latter category must be kept with the line item to which they relate, thus showing that they are **part of the operating activities** of the entity. When any such item is sufficiently material, in order to show a true and fair view, it must be disclosed on the face of the profit and loss account.

(iii) **Disposals**

Profits or losses on disposal of fixed assets were often treated in an inconsistent manner prior to FRS 3. When an asset has been revalued, FRS 3 requires the reported profit to be calculated as cost less depreciated revalued amount.

Previously, recognised revaluation surpluses or deficits became realised on sale and were included by a **transfer** between revaluation and the profit and loss account reserves. This transfer still takes place, FRS 3 prevents transfer to the profit and loss for the year.

Under the approach taken by FRS 3 (described in (a) above), gains and losses **should not be recognised twice** (eg a holding gain recognised when a fixed asset is revalued should not be recognised a second time when the revalued asset is sold).

(iv) **STRGL**

Gains and losses which, although not realised, nevertheless increase shareholders interests as they are recognised are reported in the STRGL (as discussed in part (a) above).

(v) **Historical cost profits and losses**

This note reconciles the **reported profit** figure to that which would have appeared if the company used 'pure' **historical cost reporting methods** and will include adjustments arising from excess depreciation on revalued assets and the realisation of revaluation gains or losses. This note aids comparisons between those companies which do and those which do not revalue fixed assets.

(c) **Criticisms** could include the following.

(i) Inconsistent treatment of 'discontinued activities' despite the criteria set out in FRS 3.

(ii) Lack of consistency with the definition of business segments in SSAP 25.

(iii) Confusing messages arising from companies reporting multiple EPS figures.

(iv) The STRGL has been thought of as a confusing statement, bringing together realised and unrealised items.

(v) The continuing support for the historic cost model as shown by the requirement to produce the 'note of historical cost profits and losses' seems incongruous with current thinking which seems to prefer 'current value' reporting.

23 FRESNO

> **Tutor's hint**. Questions on FRS 3 or aspects of it are likely to be *very* common in this exam. You need to learn the formats of the statements and notes required, including the revised profit and loss account and *understand* the contents and purpose of each one.
>
> **Examiner's comment**. This was the least popular question with candidates displaying a disappointing ignorance of this very important standard. In part (b) many candidates could not tell the difference between a discontinued and a discontinuing operation.

(a) (i) FRESNO GROUP PLC
STATEMENT OF TOTAL RECOGNISED GAINS AND LOSSES

	£m
Profit for the financial year (W)	140
Other recognised gains and losses for the year	
Unrealised surplus on revaluations of fixed assets	375
Total recognised gains and losses for the year	515

(ii) RECONCILIATION OF MOVEMENTS IN SHAREHOLDERS' FUNDS

	£m
Profit for the financial year (W)	140
Dividends	15
	125
Other recognised gains and losses for the year after dividends	375
Issue of new share capital (150 + 450)	600
Net addition to shareholders' funds	1,100
Opening shareholders' funds	1,395
Closing shareholders' funds	2,495

(iii) ANALYSIS OF MOVEMENTS ON RESERVES

	Merger reserve	*Revaluation reserve*	*Profit and loss*	*Total*
	£m	£m	£m	£m
Opening balance	55	215	775	1,045
Profit for financial year			140	140
Property revaluation		375		375
Total recognised gains and losses for the year		375	140	515
Transfer of previous revaluation surplus realised in the year		(54)	54	-
Depreciation on revalued assets less historical cost depreciation		(9)	9	-
Adjustments to reported profit to give profit on a historical cost basis		(63)	63	-
Issue of shares	450			450
Dividend for year			(15)	(15)
Closing balance	505	527	963	1,995

(iv) NOTE OF HISTORICAL COST PROFITS AND LOSSES

	£m
Reported profit on ordinary activities before taxation (W)	230
Realisation of property revaluation gains of prior years	54
Difference between historical cost depreciation and depreciation calculated on the revalued amounts (16 – 7)	9
Historical cost profit on ordinary activities before tax	293

Working: P & L account

	£m
Profit before taxation: continuing operations	300
Provision for loss on operations to be discontinued (30 + 15)	(45)
Amortisation of goodwill (250 ÷ 10)	(25)
Profit before tax	230
Tax	(90)
Profit after tax	140
Dividends	(15)
Retained profit for the year	125

(b) (i) **Accounts for year to 31 January 20X4**

The decision to close Reno plc was made before the year end, but closure did not take place until after the year end. In this case, the results of Reno plc should be included in continuing operations, but a provision for losses on operations to be discontinued should be made. This will comprise any costs of closure and any operating losses to the date of closure. In this case operating losses of £30m and the redundancy costs, stock and plant write downs of £15m give a total of £45m, which should be disclosed as an exceptional item.

The company might also decide to disclose the results of Reno plc separately in a note to the accounts under 'results of operations due for discontinuation'.

(ii) **Accounts for the year to 31 January 20X5**

In the year to 31 January 1995 Reno plc is actually closed down. The results up to closure will therefore appear in the group financial statements as follows.

	£m	£m
Turnover: discontinued operations		175
Cost of sales		(195)
Gross loss		(20)
Administrative expenses	15	
Selling and distribution expenses	30	
		(45)
Operating loss		(65)
Release of provision		30
Operating loss: discontinued operations		(35)
Loss on disposal of discontinued operations	(12)	
Release of provision	15	
		3
Loss on ordinary activities before tax		(32)

The effects of the financial statements would thus be:

(1) An actual loss of £65m, with an offset of the part of the £45m provision relating to operating losses (£30m)

(2) The turnover and operating loss would be classified as discontinued in the financial statements

(3) The provision of £15m should be set off against the loss on disposal of discontinued operations.

24 VENTNOR

Tutor's hint. In this question only 6 marks are for numerical calculations with 19 marks for discussion. Allocate your time accordingly.

Examiner's comment. Answers to the written element of the question were very basic, few candidates provided in-depth answers.

Part (b) was well answered, but few candidates calculated the comparatives correctly. The discussions about whether the change of focus was a discontinuance ranged from non-existent to underdeveloped. Candidates should seek to provide a well measured argument, not a yes or no answer.

(a) (i) **Classification criteria – discontinued operations**

The criteria for classification of discontinued operations as laid out by FRS 3 are:

- The operation must have discontinued within the reporting period or within three months after the year end (or when the financial statements were approved, if earlier)
- The activity must have ceased permanently
- The discontinuance must be material. It must represent a material reduction in the entity's operating facilities either because the entity has withdrawn from a market or experienced significantly reduced turnover in continuing markets
- The results can be clearly identified both on a physical and operational basis.

All these criteria must be fulfilled.

The operation must be discontinued on or around the period end. This means that only the costs in the final period of the discontinued segment's existence can be disclosed separately. **Costs incurred earlier** than this will be classed as part of the **continuing operations**.

The first and second criteria both establish that events are such that a reversal of the decision to discontinue the operation is remote. This prevents business segments being classed as discontinued based purely on management decisions, which can more easily be reversed.

The third and fourth points prevent time being wasted on unnecessary and confusing disclosure.

They help **prevent** any **creative accounting**. The discontinued operation must be a **discrete** and **identifiable entity**. This means that a general slump in overall turnover cannot be attributed to a business segment to which it does not actually relate. Whereas, the **rationalisation** of a business segment or the **closure** of a **branch** can be **disclosed** under **discontinued operations** if the **nature and focus** of the business have been **affected**.

(ii) **Relevance of comparative information**

Comparative information is used to assess the financial performance of the entity. **Discontinued activities** are **disclosed separately** so that the continuing activities can be compared and trends identified.

Newly acquired business in the current period is also **separately disclosed** so that the users can compare the relevant continuing operations.

(iii) **Usefulness of information**

The information stipulated by FRS 3 is designed to help users of the accounts assess the profitability and financial performance of an entity.

The information relating to discontinued operations allows the user to analyse the continuing and newly acquired operations of the business in order to assess the future prospects of the entity.

However, FRS 3 has helped bring the emphasis away from the bottom line profit figure and the earnings per share. The ASB has been concerned with investors and other interested parties being too focused on these figures and has stressed that other elements of the financial statements are equally important.

FRS 3 disclosure requirements reflect an '**information set**' **approach** that highlights a range of important aspects of performance. This is intended to provide a **framework** that will facilitate the **analysis and interpretation** of the various aspects of **performance**

The **statement of total recognised gains and losses** (STRGL) includes gains and losses which may not have affected the profit and loss account.

- Revaluation gains
- Foreign exchange gains/losses
- Prior period adjustments

This statement highlights movements that may previously only have gone through reserves. Certain users of the accounts may be more interested in this information than the other information presented in the accounts. Finance providers may look at the revaluation gains as they have loans secured on the assets of the business, for instance.

The **reconciliation of the movement on shareholders' funds** also highlights information not supplied in the profit and loss account or the STRGL, such as the issue or redemption of new shares.

(b) (i) VENTNOR PLC

PROFIT AND LOSS ACCOUNT FOR THE YEARS

	31 March 20X9				*31 March 20X8*		
	Continuing	*Acquisitions*	*Discontinuing*	*Total*	*Continuing*	*Discontinuing*	*Total*
	£'000	£'000	£'000	£'000	£'000	£'000	£'000
Turnover	610	70	70	750	460	260	720
Cost of sales	(287)	(49)	(84)	(420)	(204)	(244)	(448)
Gross profit	323	21	(14)	330	256	16	272
Other operating expenses	(56)	(12)	(12)	(80)	(42)	(30)	(72)
Profit before tax	267	9	(26)	250	214	(14)	200

Tutor's hint. The continuing figures are balancing figures. You start with the total columns and work out the discontinued and acquisition figures. The comparative discontinued figure includes the existing discontinued engineering business. The comparative continuing figure includes acquisitions as this is now continuing business.

(ii) **Assessment of accounting treatment – hotel division**

The application of FRS 3 requires a **degree of judgement**. The directors are changing the focus of their hotel business from the business market to the tourist and holiday market.

Judgement needs to be exercised as to whether this **change in focus** has **materially affected** the **nature and scope of the business.**

From the information in the question it would appear that a number of hotels have been sold or refurbished and others have been acquired.

We have information as to how the new and existing parts of the business have performed so this would suggest that the results can be clearly identified and they are certainly material.

It also appears that the activities were discontinued by the year end.

The above information leads to the conclusion that the treatment of the hotel business is correct.

Marking guide

					Marks
(a)	(i)	Definition/criteria for discontinuance		3	
		Comments on the usefulness of the information and problems relating to it		4	
	(ii)	Importance of comparative and the adjustments required		3	
	(iii)	Usefulness – of STRG/reconciliation of shareholders' funds			
		1 mark per point up to	Available	5	
			Maximum		15
(b)	(i)	2 marks each for continuing, acquisitions, discontinued operations for each year	Available	10	
			Maximum		6
	(ii)	1 mark per point up to	Maximum		4
					25

25 PREPARATION QUESTION: CASH FLOWS

> **Tutor's hint.** Make sure that you know the FRS 1 format and set out a pro forma cash flow statement and notes. Begin with the reconciliation of operating profit to net cash flow from operating activities. This gives you the first figure in the cash flow statement. Cross reference all of your workings.

JENNY LIMITED
CASH FLOW STATEMENT
FOR THE YEAR ENDED 31 DECEMBER 20X2

Reconciliation of operating profit to net cash inflow from operating activities

	£'000
Operating profit	350
Depreciation charge (W1)	90
Loss on sale of tangible fixed assets (45 – 32)	13
Profit on sale of fixed asset investments	(5)
Increase/decrease in stocks	(48)
Increase/decrease in debtors	(75)
Increase/decrease in creditors	8
Net cash inflow from operating activities	333

CASH FLOW STATEMENT

	£'000
Net cash inflow from operating activities	333
Returns on investments and servicing of finance (note 1)	((50)
Taxation (W2)	(110)
Capital expenditure	(189)
	(16)
Equity dividends paid	(80)
	(96)
Management of liquid resources (note 1)	(50)
Financing (note 1)	160
Increase in cash	14

Reconciliation of net cash flow to movement in net debt (note 2)

	£'000	£'000
Increase in cash in the period	14	
Cash received from long-term loan	(100)	
Cash used to increase liquid resources	50	
Change in net debt		(36)
Net debt at 1.1.X2		(97)
Net debt at 31.12.X2		(133)

NOTES TO THE CASH FLOW STATEMENT

1 *Gross cash flows*

	£'000	£'000
Returns on investments and servicing of finance		
Interest received	25	
Interest paid	(75)	
		50
Capital expenditure		
Payments to acquire intangible fixed assets	(50)	
Payments to acquire tangible fixed assets (W3)	(201)	
Receipts from sale of tangible fixed assets	32	
Receipts from sale of fixed asset investments	30	
		(189)

	£'000	£'000
Management of liquid resources		
Purchase of short-term investments		(50)
Financing		
Issue of ordinary share capital	60	
Issue of long-term loan	100	
		160

2 *Analysis of changes in net debt*

	At 1 Jan 20X2	*Cash flows*	*At 31 Dec 20X2*
	£'000	£'000	£'000
Cash in hand, at bank	1	1	2
Overdraft	(98)	13	(85)
		14	
Debt due within 1 year	-	-	-
Debt due after 1 year	-	(100)	(100)
Current asset investments	-	50	50
Total	(97)	(36)	(133)

Workings

1 *Depreciation charge*

	£'000	£'000
Depreciation at 31 December 20X2		340
Depreciation 31 December 20X1	290	
Depreciation on assets sold (85 – 45)	40	
		250
Charge for the year		90

2 *Tax paid*

CORPORATION TAX

	£'000		£'000
Tax paid	110	1.1.X2 balance b/d	110
		Profit and loss	
		140 – (70 – 50)*	120
31.12.X2 balance c/d	120		
	230		230

**Note.* The taxation charge in the profit and loss account includes the increase in deferred taxation provision. This must be excluded when calculating the amount of corporation tax paid.

3 *Purchase of tangible fixed assets*

TANGIBLE FIXED ASSETS

	£'000		£'000
1.1.X2 Balance b/d	595	Disposals	85
Revaluation (100 – 91)	9		
Purchases (bal fig)	201	31.12.X2 Balance c/d	720
	805		805

26 OZAC

> **Tutor's hint.** Cash flow statements questions often require the indirect method to be used – but not always, as this question demonstrates!
>
> **Examiner's comment.** Many candidates prepared the operating cash flows using the indirect method or a combination of the direct and indirect method; candidates must be able to use the direct method. Other errors included treating the barter transaction as a cash flow, treating the government grant as a credit adjustment, incorrect treatment of the amortisation of the discount and premium on the debenture, and failure to consider the deferred tax account.

CASH FLOW STATEMENT FOR THE YEAR ENDED 30 SEPTEMBER 20X9

	£'000	£'000
Operating activities		
Receipts from customers (W1)		3,170
Payments to suppliers (W1)		(928)
Payments to employees (W3)		(718)
Other cash operating expenses (W4)		(786)
Cash flow from operating activities		738
Returns on investment and servicing of finance (Note 1)		(58)
Taxation (W1)		(52)
Capital expenditure (Note 1)		(1,338)
		(710)
Equity dividends paid (W1)		(330)
		(1,040)
Management of liquid resources		-
Financing (Note 1)		1,090
Increase in cash		50

Note

1 *Gross cash flows*

	£'000
Returns on investments and servicing of finance	
Investment income (60 × 14%)	9
Interest paid (W4)	(67)
	58
Capital expenditure	
Payments to acquire tangible fixed assets(W2)	728
Payments to acquire investments (W2)	800
Receipts on government grants (W1)	(190)
	1,338
Financing	
Issue of new shares, including share premium	140
Issue of new debentures	950
	1,090

Workings

> **Tutor's hint**. Many of the following workings are done using a columnar approach for reduction of repetition and to save time. However, if you feel more comfortable using T accounts, please do use them for your own peace of mind.

1

	B/F	Charge	Cash/transfer	C/F
	£'000	£'000	£'000	£'000
Debtors/sales	194	3,536	3,170	(260)
		(300)*		
Stock/materials	628	1,209#	(1,079)**	(758)
Creditors/purchases	(253)	(1,209)#	928	234
Deferred taxation	141	(111)T	-	252
Taxation	204	111T	52	251
		(210)		
Dividends	(180)	(350)	330	200
Government grants				
≤ 1 year	(75)			125
> 1 year	(160)			220
	(235)	80	(190)	345

* non-cash payment from Petrov

** consumed per profit and loss account

\# purchases

T transfer

2

	B/F	Additions/ (charge)	Disposals	C/F
	£'000	£'000	£'000	£'000
Tangible fixed assets	2,640	728	-	3,368
Accumulated depreciation	(1,055)	(220)	-	1,275
Investments	-	800	-	800

3 *Payments to employees*

	£'000
Labour	758
Share issue [10,000 @ (5 – 1)]	(40)
	718

4 *Other cash operating expenses*

Production overheads	453
Selling and distribution	221
Administration	252
Government grant amortisation (W1)	80
Depreciation (W2)	(220)
	786

Note. Remember that the government grant amortisation is a *credit*.

5 *Interest paid*

Interest payable	85
Amortisation of debenture:	
Discount (5% of 1m) ÷ 5 years	(10)
Premium (4% of 1m) ÷ 5 years	(8)
	67

6 *Capital expenditure*

Fixed assets (W2)	728
Investment (W2)	800
Government grants (W1)	(190)
	1,338

7 *Financing*

Debenture issue: 1m @ 5% discount	950
New share issue	100
Share premium: (80 less 40 related to employee share scheme)	40
	1,090

27 BLUE TING

Tutor's hint. The most difficult part is the reconciliation of net cash flow to movement in net debt. Study our solution carefully if you had trouble with this.

Examiner's comment. In general this question was well answered. However, the treatment of the finance lease was less than satisfactory, with candidates showing the figures for net obligations under finance leases and additions to finance leases rather than simply the capital repayments and the interest element.

(a) BLUE TING PLC
CASH FLOW STATEMENT
FOR THE YEAR ENDED 31 MAY 20X5

Reconciliation of operating profit to net cash inflow from operating activities

	£m
Operating profit	100
Depreciation	37
Development expenditure amortisation	1
Profit on sales of fixed assets (21 – 19)	(2)
Decrease in stocks (155 – 140)	15
Increase in debtors (130 – 110)	(20)
Increase in creditors (220 – 131)	89
Net cash inflow from operating activities	220

Cash flow statement

	£m
Net cash inflow from operating activities	220
Returns on investments and servicing of finance (note 1)	(4)
Taxation (W1)	(16)
Capital expenditure (note 1)	(83)
	117
Equity dividends paid (W2)	(20)
	97
Management of liquid resources (note 1)	(75)
	17
Financing (note 1)	(6)
Increase in cash	16

Reconciliation of net cash flow to movement in net debt (note 2)

	£m	£m
Increase in cash in the period	16	
Cash inflow from decrease in finance lease	7	
Cash used to increase liquid resources	75	
Change in net debt resulting from cash flows		98
New finance lease		(28)
Conversion of debentures		29
Movement in net debt in the period		99
Net debt at 1 June 20X4		(90)
Net funds at 31 May 20X5		9

NOTES TO THE CASH FLOW STATEMENT

1 *Gross cash flows*

	£m	£m
Returns on investments and servicing of finance		
Interest received	3	
Interest paid	(4)	
Finance lease rental (interest element)	(3)	
		(4)
Capital expenditure		
Payments to acquire tangible fixed assets	(104)	
Receipts from sales of tangible fixed assets	21	
		(83)
Management of liquid resources		
Purchase of 12.5% Treasury Stock	(80)	
Decrease in loan notes	5	
		(75)
Financing		
Issue of share capital	10	
Share premium	4	
Cost of share issue	(1)	
Purchase of own shares	(12)	
Finance lease rental (capital element)(W3)	(7)	
		(6)

2 *Analysis of changes in net debt*

	At 1 June 20X4 £m	*Cash flows* £m	*Other changes* £m	*At 31 May 20X5* £m
Cash at bank and in hand	3	4	-	7
Overdraft	(20)	12	-	(8)
		16		
Debt due within one year	-	-	-	-
Debt due after one year*				
Debentures	(60)	-	29	(31)
Obligations under finance leases*	(33)	7	(28)	(54)
Loan notes repayable on demand (20 – 15)	20	(5)		15
Current asset investments		80		80
Total	(90)	98	1	9

**Note.* As stated in the question, the obligations under finance leases are listed separately from other debts. The information on the capital element of the repayment and the additions can be seen in W3.

Workings

1 *Taxation*

TAX

	£m		£m
Tax paid (bal fig)	16	Bal b/d	10
Bal c/d	16	P & L	22
	32		32

2 *Dividends paid*

DIVIDENDS

	£m		£m
Dividend paid (bal fig)	20	Bal b/d	8
Bal c/d	-	P & L	12
	20		20

3 *Finance lease rental (capital element)*

OBLIGATIONS UNDER FINANCE LEASES

	£m		£m
Capital repayment (bal fig)	7	Bal 1.4.X4	33
C/d 31.5.X5	54	Additions	28
	61		61

(b) The **advantages** of published cash flow forecasts are as follows.

(i) They provide an early warning of liquidity problems by estimating:

(1) How much cash is required
(2) When it is required
(3) How long it is required for
(4) Whether it will be available from anticipated sources.

(ii) This liquidity information is of help to creditors and investors as well as to management, as it assists them in assessing the ability of the company to pay its way.

(iii) Cash flow forecasts can help a bank monitor the progress of a company to which it has lent money, and to control its lending more effectively.

(iv) Many businesses fail because of cash flow problems. Forecasts focus the mind of management on going concern issues.

However, published cash flow forecasts have certain **disadvantages**, which are as follows.

(i) The information contained in them may be manipulated by unscrupulous managers wishing to show a favourable impression.

(ii) They are only as good as the assumptions on which they are based. Clearly there is an element of subjectivity and uncertainty involved in preparing them. However, users of cash flow statements should be aware of their limitations.

(iii) Cash flow forecasts are very difficult to audit, because they are based on subjective predictions. However, auditors can assess the accounting principles adopted and the consistency with which they are applied.

(iv) It is possible that competitors could make use of the information disclosed in a cash flow forecast, although if they were compulsory for all companies no single company would benefit from this advantage.

28 LADWAY PLC

Tutor's hint. Part (a) was the preparation of a cashflow statement for a single company. If you got the proforma down and worked through the question you should have got the majority of marks.

Part (b) is a short written question on the net debt reconciliation. Ensure you specifically describe and discuss the net debt reconciliation. Answers about the cashflow in general will gain few (if any) marks.

(a) LADWAY PLC
CASHFLOW STATEMENT FOR THE YEAR ENDED 31 MARCH 20X8

Reconciliation of operating profit to the net cash inflow from operating activities

	£m
Operating profit	583
Depreciation (366 + 36)	402
(Profit) on disposal of fixed assets (14 – 11)	(3)
Environmental provision (24 – 76)	52
Government grant released to profit and loss	(50)
Increase in stocks	(157)
Increase in debtors	(170)
Increase in creditors	162
Net cash inflow from operating activities	819

Cashflow statement

	£m
Net cash inflow from operating activities	819
Returns on investments and servicing of finance (note 1)	(43)
Taxation (185 + 177 – 176 + 30 – 52)	(164)
Capital expenditure (note 1)	(689)
	(77)
Equity dividends (40 + 180)	(220)
	(297)
Management of liquid resources	-
Financing (note 1)	200
Decrease in cash over the year	(97)

Notes

1 *Gross cash flows*

	£m	£m
Returns on investments and servicing of finance		
Preference dividend (350 × 10%)	(35)	
Interest paid (12 – 4)	(8)	
		(43)
Capital expenditure		
Payments to acquire intangible fixed assets (450 – 410 + 36)	(76)	
Payments to acquire tangible fixed assets (W2)	(723)	
Government grants (W1)	110	
		(689)
Financing		
Issue of ordinary share capital (W3)	120	
Issue of debenture loans (200 – 120)	80	
		200

2 *Reconciliation of net cashflow to movement in net debt (Note 3)*

	£m
Net cash outflow for the period	(97)
Cash received from debenture issue	(80)
Cash outflow from decrease in finance leases	-
Cash inflow from movement in liquid resources	-
Change in net debt as a result of cashflows	(177)
Debentures issued in exchange for fixed assets	(120)
Additional finance leases	-
Translation differences	-
Net debt as at 1 April 20X7	34
Net debt as at 31 March 20X8	(263)

Note. The detail shown above is to help answer part (b) of this question

3 *Analysis of changes in net debt*

	As at 1 April X7	*Cash-flows*	*Other changes*	*As at 31 March X8*
	£m	£m	£m	£m
Cash in hand and at bank	34	(34)		-
Overdraft	-	(63)		(63)
		(97)		
Debt due after one year	-	(80)	(120)	(200)
	34	(177)	120	(263)

Workings

1 *Government grants*

	£m
20X8 in one year	50
20X8 after one year	210
Charged to the profit and loss account	50
Less: 20X7 in one year	(40)
20X7 after one year	(160)
	110

2 *Tangible fixed assets*

	£m
20X8 balance sheet figure	2,480
less: revaluation	(170)
trade in allowance	(14)
debenture consideration	(120)
add: depreciation for the year	366
NBV of disposal	11
Less 20X7 balance sheet figure	(1,830)
	723

3 *Share issue*

	£m
20X8 share capital figure	500
20X8 share premium figure	90
less: 20X7 share capital	(400)
20X7 share premium	(70)
	120

Note. A bonus issue is a non-cash transaction. Share capital would increase in the year by £40m but this nets off with the subsequent decrease of share premium.

(b) **Reconciliation to net debt**

Please refer to the reconciliation of net cashflow to movement in net debt in part (a) for the composition of the reconciliation.

The reconciliation to net debt reconciles the increase (or decrease) of cash in the cashflow to the net debt figure shown in the analysis of changes in net debt note.

The nature of the debt included in the net debt figure is included, showing items such as debentures or liquid resources. The **reconciliation** also gives **more detail** on the nature of other **changes** which have not affected the cashflow but have **affected net debt**.

The reconciliation links the cashflow with the net debt analysis in order that the user of the accounts **can look** at the **liquid resources** of an organisation and the **quality of the cashflows** in **relation** to the **debt** of the entity. This should help them **assess** the **financial adaptability** of the business.

Marking guide

			Marks	
(a)	Net profit before interest and tax		1	
	Non-cash adjustments 1 per point maximum of		5	
	Working capital 1 per item		3	
	Interest/preference dividend		2	
	Tax		2	
	Equity dividend		1	
	Purchase of tangible fixed assets		4	
	Receipt of government grant		11	
	Purchase of goodwill		11	
	Share issue		22	
	Debenture issue		1	
	Decrease in cash		1	
		Available	24	
		Maximum		20
(b)	Description, 1 mark per point to maximum of		3	
	1 mark per item of composition maximum of		3	
		Available	6	
		Maximum		5
		Total maximum		25

29 PREPARATION QUESTION: SSAP 17

Tutor's hint. If you have a thorough knowledge of SSAP 17 you should find this question very straightforward as the SSAP contains examples of adjusting and non-adjusting events.

(a) **Post balance sheet events** are those events that occur between the date to which the balance sheet is drawn up and the date on which the accounts are approved by the board of directors.

Adjusting events are post balance sheet events that provide additional evidence about conditions that existed at the date of the balance sheet. The financial effects of adjusting events are incorporated into the accounts before they are approved (subject to the usual materiality conditions). Non-adjusting events are post balance sheet events that concern conditions that did not exist at the balance sheet date.

Examples of adjusting events might include:

(i) The subsequent determination of the price of an asset sold before the balance sheet date

(ii) The valuation of a property that confirms a permanent diminution in value

(iii) The receipt of evidence that a previous estimate of the accrued value of a long-term contract was inaccurate

(iv) The insolvency of a debtor

(v) The receipt of information regarding the applicable rates of taxation

(vi) The amounts received or receivable in respect of insurance claims that were in the course of negotiation at the balance sheet date

(vii) The discovery of errors or frauds that show the accounts were materially incorrect.

A conventional adjusting event is the subsequent declaration of a dividend out of the profits of the accounting period in question.

Examples of non-adjusting events might include:

(i) Mergers, acquisitions and reconstructions

(ii) The issue of shares or debentures

(iii) Purchases and sales of fixed assets and investments

(iv) Losses due to fires, floods and so on

(v) Changes in foreign exchange rates

(vi) Government action, such as nationalisation

(vii) Strikes and other labour disputes

(viii) Closing a significant part of the trading activities that has not been anticipated at the balance sheet date

(ix) Declines in the values of assets that occurred after the balance sheet date.

(b) An accounting standard is needed to **regulate the disclosure and accounting** for post balance sheet events in order to **remove subjectivity** from this area of financial reporting. Any set of accounts is based on a number of accounting estimates, in order that they may be issued within a reasonable period after the year end. In order to show the required true and fair view, it is clearly necessary to adjust for any material estimates which are seen to be inaccurate by the time the accounts are approved. However, the accounts are intended to represent the position at the year end and it would be misleading if they were adjusted to include transactions and events which occurred wholly after the accounting period had ended.

(c) The **financial effect of adjusting events** should be incorporated into the accounts and only disclosed separately if required under another SSAP or to provide a true and fair view. SSAP 17, however, does require disclosure of:

(i) A non-adjusting event of such materiality that its non-disclosure would affect the ability of the users of the accounts to reach a proper understanding of its financial results or condition

(ii) If it is the reversal or maturity after the balance sheet date of a transaction entered into before the balance sheet date the substance of which was primarily to alter the appearance of the balance sheet ('window dressing').

Where disclosure is required, the nature of the event and an estimate, if possible, of the financial effect of the event should be stated.

30 SUBSTANCE OVER FORM

> **Tutor's hint**. You must understand the principles of FRS 5 and be able to deal with scenarios such as consignment stock, sale and repurchase agreements and debt factoring.

(a) **Reasons for omitting assets and liabilities**

Companies may wish to **omit assets and liabilities from their balance sheet** for a number of reasons but the primary aim in all cases is to ensure that the **readers' expectations as to the position of the balance sheet is not undermined.**

Transactions are devised therefore that in strict legal form do not need to be reported in the financial statements and so any assets or liabilities arising from them can also be omitted. In most cases, the use of such transactions is not intended to deceive the user but is instead undertaken in the **best commercial interests** of the **company.**

They usually involve some limitation as to the risks and rewards accruing to the company which is the basis for their omission from the financial statements. The reasons why companies may wish to omit assets and liabilities from their balance sheets include the following.

(i) The need to **maintain low levels** of **gearing** in order to satisfy the **expectations** of users. For example, high levels of borrowing may lead analysts to expect a **rights issue.** Failure to make one may compromise the company's **share price.**

(ii) The need to maintain an **acceptable level of return on capital employed** may lead to **assets under development** being **excluded** from the **balance sheet.** These assets are **not producing** any **income** and hence will tend to **distort this ratio.**

(iii) **Group companies** with markedly **different activities** from other companies in the group would cause **ratios** to be **distorted** if included in the **group consolidation.** Hence the investment in such companies by the group is made in such a way that they are excluded from the consolidated financial statements.

(b) **Reasons for introducing FRS 5**

The reasons why the ASB felt it necessary to introduce FRS 5 *Reporting the substance of transactions* are as follows.

(i) The **increase in the number of transactions** over the past few years in which the **legal form of a transaction** was such that it **did not require disclosure** in the financial statements. The market in **financing products** has become **increasingly sophisticated and complex,** allowing companies to undertake a variety of transactions without showing them in the accounts.

(ii) The exclusion of these transactions meant that their **commercial effect** was **not recognised** in the financial statements so **undermining the true and fair view.** Only the most sophisticated users could appreciate the effects of such transactions.

(iii) Most seriously, the use of such transactions by some companies to **actively mislead** readers of the financial statements and the **subsequent failure** of some of these companies led to **criticism** of the **accounting profession** and its standard-setting procedures.

(iv) The very reason for and nature of **financial statements** was being **undermined**: comparability, consistency and truth and fairness were overridden by the use of such schemes.

(c) **Discussion of proposed treatments**

(i) Beak plc has sold the land to Wings plc at a price well under current market value for no discernible reason. It is **able to repurchase that land** at cost at any time in the next five years but **cannot be forced to do so**.

Unless the land value falls significantly it can be assumed that Beak plc will repurchase the land. Wings plc will not use the building or the land for redevelopment in that period otherwise on repurchase they would lose any investment they had made.

The **commercial effect** of this transaction, assuming land values do not fall significantly, is that of **a loan** to Beak plc secured on the land. The **commission is in effect interest** on the loan, **payment** being **deferred** until the **repurchase** takes place.

Beak plc should not treat this transaction as a sale. The land should continue to be shown as an asset in the balance sheet and a loan of £20m should be recorded. The profit and loss account should be charged annually with the commission charge and the accrual shown as a liability in the balance sheet.

(ii) The **substance** of this transaction appears to be that the **cars are part** of the **stock of Sparks Ltd** from the time they take delivery of them from Gocar plc.

(1) Sparks Ltd bears the risks and rewards of ownership, ie it has to insure the cars, but only pays the wholesale price in force on the date the cars were first supplied, so avoiding subsequent price rises.

(2) The monthly rental is a form of interest charged by Gocar plc, varying with the length of time Sparks Ltd holds the stock.

This interpretation of the transaction is also supported by the fact that Gocar plc cannot demand the return of the cars from Sparks Ltd.

The cars unsold for less than four months should be treated as stock in the financial statements and the liability to Gocar plc for them recognised.

31 ATOMIC POWER

> **Tutor's hint.** FRS 12 is an important 'anti-abuse' standard in the ASB repertoire. The definitions and recognition criteria you are required to discuss in (a) are fundamental to the standard. You must learn them thoroughly to be able to apply FRS 12 effectively in the exam.
>
> Again, use headings and sub-headings to help both yourself and the marker.

(a) TECHNICAL NOTE
FRS 12 PROVISIONS, CONTINGENT LIABILITIES AND CONTINGENT ASSETS

(i) **The need for issuing FRS 12**

The overall objective of FRS 12 is to obviate the practice of 'smoothing' results.

The use of provisions has created substantial opportunities for the **manipulation** of **reported profits**. One reason for this is that provisions are **pervasive**; they may arise in relation to almost all areas of a company's operations.

The **recognition** and **measurement** of provisions both rely greatly on the **judgement** of management. There is thus substantial scope for adjustment of provisions.

A particular issue is the way management use provisions to **'smooth' profits**; provisions are created for future expenditure in years when profits are healthy and then released to the profit and loss account as the expenditure arises, thus **reducing the volatility of reported profits** over time. FRS 12 is designed to prevent this.

Another difficult area is the use of provisions for future losses when one business acquires another. By **creating provisions for restructuring on acquisition** as part of the **fair value exercise**, the acquiring business can **increase** the **future profitability** of the **acquired entity**, again by releasing the provisions in future periods against the expenditure.

This practice has the perverse effect of increasing goodwill the greater the restructuring charges! This has been largely prevented, not only by FRS 12, but also by FRS 10 *Goodwill and intangibles* and FRS 7 *Fair values in acquisition accounting.*

(ii) **Main principles of FRS 12**

The definitions in FRS 12 are vital, because these determine initially the extent to which an obligation exists and hence a provision should be made.

Definition

Two of the fundamental definitions are liabilities and provisions, and these make clear the relationships between the two:

(1) **Liabilities** are obligations of an entity to transfer economic benefits as a result of past transactions or events.

(2) A **provision** is a liability of uncertain timing or amount, to be settled by the transfer of economic benefits.

Reliability requires that under conditions of **uncertainty, prudence** is exercised. However, it is not necessary to exercise prudence where there is no uncertainty. Prudence should not be used to create **excessive provisions** or overstated liabilities. That would meant the financial statements are not **neutral** and therefore not reliable.

Recognition

A **central tenet** of FRS 12 is that a provision should be recognised only when a **period end liability** exists that can be **measured reliably**.

In order to be clear when a liability or provision has actually arisen, FRS 12 makes it very clear what it means by an 'obligating event', which is part of the liability definition:

- An **obligating event** is an event that creates a **legal or constructive obligation** that results in an entity having no realistic alternative to settling that obligation.

Most people would readily accept that a legal obligation gives rise to a liability. FRS 12 nevertheless defines a legal obligation for the sake of clarity:

A **legal obligation** is an obligation that derives from:

(1) A contract (through its explicit or implicit terms)
(2) Legislation
(3) Other operation of law

However, the notion of a 'constructive obligation' may appear strange. FRS 12 is here trying to capture the notion that, although a company may have no legal obligation to transfer economic benefits, it may, by its past actions and stated policies, have created an obligation itself:

A **constructive obligation** is an obligation that derives from an entity's actions where:

(1) By an **established pattern** of **past practice, published policies** or a sufficiently specific **current statement**, the entity has **indicated** to other parties that it will **accept certain responsibilities.**

(2) As a result, the entity has created a **valid expectation** on the part of those other parties that it **will discharge** those responsibilities.

Even if the definitions given above are met, the standard also specifies certain **recognition criteria.** These also have to be satisfied in order for a provision to be recorded. FRS 12 states that a provision should be recognised when:

(1) An entity has a **present obligation** (legal or constructive) as a result of a past event

(2) It is **probable** that a transfer of economic benefits will be required to settle the obligation

(3) A **reliable estimate** can be made of the amount of the obligation

If these conditions are not met, no provision should be recorded.

Note the emphasis on a 'present obligation'; it is not sufficient to determine there may or will be some obligation in the future. Where it is unclear as to whether there is a present obligation, FRS 12 states that it should be assumed that there is one if, on the **available evidence**, it is **more likely than not** that one exists.

Measurement

Assuming the above definitions and recognition criteria are met, FRS 12 has rules regarding **measurement** of a provision. The amount recognised as a provision should be the **best estimate** of the expenditure required to settle the present obligation at the balance sheet date. It is necessary to incorporate this notion because of the uncertainties surrounding the outcome of provisions.

(b) **Advice on present accounting policy on provisions**

Atomic Power's current accounting policies regarding accounting for provisions is no longer acceptable under FRS 12. Where an entity has a present obligation that will (probably) lead to a transfer of economic benefits as a result of a past transaction or event, then a provision should be made of the full amount of the expected liability.

Where that amount is expressed in **future prices** then these must be **discounted back** at a **nominal rate**. Atomic Power should thus recognise £360m as a liability, not £540m, for environmental costs on 1 July 20X1.

The credit side of the accounting entry is thus to the balance sheet heading 'Provisions for liabilities and charges'. The treatment of the corresponding debit entry required by FRS 12 is controversial; it must be added to the cost of the asset, to be released as the asset is depreciated over its useful life. This effectively 'grosses up' the assets and liabilities of the balance sheet and has called into question the nature of the assets recognised in this way in relation to how assets are defined in the ASB's *Statement of Principles*.

In Atomic Power's case, the effect of all this (barring the error in using £540m instead of £360m), on profits will not be much different under FRS 12 than the previous policy. The value of the power station plus the provision for environmental costs will be written off over its 12 year life.

The treatment of the possible costs of contamination leaks is more problematic. The main issue is whether a 'past event' has taken place. Is the past event the leak itself, or is it the generation of the electricity that could lead to a leak? There is also the question of the probability of a leak. Generally, if there is a greater than 50% chance of a liability occurring, it should be provided for, but if below 50%, then presumably the liability would be classed as contingent only, and disclosed in the notes rather than provided.

The probability of a leak is only 30% in any year and indeed one did not occur this year. Over 12 years of generation of electricity, it seems that a leak will occur about four times (ie one year in three). The cost of each leak is £60m-£120m; so taking the mid-cost, the cost of three leaks will be £90m × 4 = £360m. Over 12 years, therefore, the company would provide £30m per year.

Applying the above, the revised accounts extracts are as follows.

PROFIT AND LOSS ACCOUNT (EXTRACTS)

	£m
Fixed asset depreciation: power station: 1/12 × (600 +360)	80
Provision for clean-up costs: 1/12 × (90 × 4)	30
	110

BALANCE SHEET (EXTRACTS)

	£m
Fixed assets	
Power station at cost	960
Depreciation (as above)	(80)
	880
Provisions for liabilities and charges	
Provision for environmental and clean-up costs (360 + 30)	390

(c) **Impact of alternative national scenarios**

Where there is no statutory requirement to clean up environmental damage, one might expect FRS 12 not to require a provision because there is no obligation to transfer economic benefits. However, FRS 12 also includes the notion of a 'constructive obligation'. A constructive obligation arises from the company's own actions and behaviour, either as a pattern of past practice, or statements of intention or policy.

In Atomic Power's case, the company has a track record for cleaning up environmental damage or pollution, or if it has stated its intention to do so in terms of specific or general commitment, then the provisions should be made as in (b) above. However, if the company has not raised any expectations that it will clean up environmental damage, then no provisions would be required and the power station would simply be recorded at a cost of £600m and depreciated by £50m a year over 12 years.

32 PREPARATION QUESTION: FRS 4

Tutor's hint. This question only asks for the basic disclosure requirements. FRS 4 could be examined as a question in its own right or may be one aspect of a larger question.

(a) The disclosure requirements of FRS 4 in relation to debt can be summarised as follows.

(i) The **amount of convertible debt** should be **shown separately** from other liabilities.

(ii) In respect of convertible debt, details of the **dates of possible redemption** and the amount payable on redemption should be disclosed.

(iii) In respect of convertible debt, the notes should state the **number and class** of shares into which the debt can be converted and the dates at which or periods in which the conversion can take place.

(iv) In respect of convertible debt, **whether conversion is at the option of the issuer or the holder** of the debt.

(v) Debt should be **analysed** between amounts falling due:

(1) In one year or less, or on demand
(2) Between one and two years
(3) Between two and five years
(4) In five years or more.

(vi) Where the maturity of debt has been assessed by taking into account **refinancing under committed facilities** then the amount of the debt treated in this way, analysed by the earliest date on which the lender could demand repayment in the absence of the facilities, should be disclosed.

(vii) A brief description should be given of the **legal nature** of any instrument included in debt where it is different from that normally associated with debt, for example where the debt is subordinated or where the obligation to repay is conditional.

(viii) Where amounts are included within debt which have very different claims in a winding up from the amounts shown in the financial statements, then a statement of the **amount of the claim in a winding up** should be stated.

(ix) **Gains and losses on the repurchase or early settlement** of debt should be disclosed in the profit and loss account (or notes) either within or adjacent to 'interest payable and similar charges'.

(b) The **disclosure** requirements relating to **shareholders' funds** are as follows.

(i) The **total amount** of shareholders' funds should be shown on the face of the balance sheet.

(ii) Shareholders' funds should be **analysed** between the amounts attributable to **equity interests and non-equity interests.**

(iii) The **total amount of non-equity interests** should be analysed between each class of non-equity shares and warrants for non-equity shares.

(iv) A **summary of the rights** attaching to each class of share should be shown, making it clear why they have been treated as equity or non-equity, but as a minimum including:

(1) Their rights to dividends

(2) The dates on which the shares are redeemable, and the amount payable on redemption

(3) Their priority and the amounts receivable on a winding up

(4) Their voting rights

33 PREPARATION QUESTION: FRS 13

Tutor's hint. FRS 13 is not an easy standard to examine as it is just about disclosure. However it is topical and the examiner may pick up on this. Make sure you plan your answer to avoid waffle and straying from the point.

(a) **Approach adopted by FRS 13**

FRS 13 requires **both narrative and numerical disclosures**. The narrative disclosures describe the role that financial instruments have in creating or changing the risks that the entity faces, including its objectives and policies in using financial instruments to manage these risks. The numerical disclosures show how these objectives and policies were implemented in the period and provide supplementary information for evaluating (potentially) significant exposures. Together these disclosures provide a broad overview of the entity's financial instruments and of the risk positions created by them, focusing on those risks and instruments that are of greatest significance.

Narrative disclosures

The FRS requires an explanation to be provided of the role that financial instruments play in creating or changing the risks that the entity faces in its activities. The entity should also explain the **directors' approach** to managing each of those risks, including a description of the objectives, policies and strategies for holding and issuing financial instruments.

The narrative disclosures are **mandatory**, although the FRS permits them to be given in a statement accompanying the financial statements (such as the operating and financial review or the directors' report) provided that they are incorporated into the financial statements by a suitable cross-reference.

Numerical disclosures

Although all entities within the scope of the FRS are required to provide the same type of narrative disclosures, the FRS requires **different** numerical disclosures for each of:

(i) Entities that are not financial institutions
(ii) Banks and similar institutions
(iii) Other types of financial institution

These different disclosures reflect differences in the significance of the main risks that arise from financial instruments.

The FRS requires specific numerical disclosures to be provided about:

(i) Interest rate risk
(ii) Currency risk
(iii) Liquidity risk
(iv) Fair values
(v) Financial instruments used for trading
(vi) Financial instruments used for hedging
(vii) Certain commodity contracts.

To avoid the numerical disclosures becoming so detailed that their message is obscured, the FRS encourages, and in some cases requires, a high degree of **aggregation**.

(b) **Need to introduce disclosures**

The **dynamic nature** of international financial markets has resulted in the widespread use by entities of both traditional primary financial instruments, such as bonds and shares, and various forms of derivative financial instruments, such as futures, options, forward contracts and swaps. This growth in the use of financial instruments has outstripped the development of **guidance for their accounting**. As a result, although many entities now use financial instruments in a way that can transform their financial position, financial performance and risk profile overnight, the accounting treatment of the instruments does not always portray effectively their impact and risks.

Standards on financial instruments have been issued by other national and international standard setters over the last few years; in particular, FASB in the USA has been developing its thoughts on financial instruments over the last 10 years.

FRS 13 is based on the premise that, in order to be able to make assessments about the **financial performance** and **financial position** of an entity, users of financial statements need information on the main aspects of the entity's risk profile and an understanding of how this risk profile is being managed. Since financial instruments contribute to this risk profile and are often used to manage it, they need to be dealt with fully in the disclosures provided. Although some disclosures are already required for financial instruments, they do not represent a coherent set of requirements that cover all the main risks involved. The main purpose of the FRS is therefore to build a set of such requirements.

(c) (i) **Types of risk arising from financial instruments**

The two most familiar risks arising from financial instruments are credit risk and liquidity risk. These risks can be defined as follows.

> '**Credit risk:** the possibility that a loss may occur from the failure of another party to perform according to the terms of a contract.
>
> **Liquidity risk** (also referred to as funding risk): the risk that an entity will encounter difficulty in realising assets or otherwise raising funds to meet commitments associated with financial instruments.'

These risks traditionally have been the main focus of what little disclosure on risk has appeared in financial statements. For example, some information about credit risk can be obtained from the nature of an entity's business and the numerical disclosures of debtors and provisions. Similarly, the disclosure of the terms and conditions of borrowings and broad indicators, such as the current ratio and quick ratio, provide some information about liquidity risk.

However, financial instruments also entail two other important types of risk - cash flow risk and market price risk. These can be defined as follows.

> '**Cash flow risk:** the risk that future cash flows generated by a monetary financial instrument will fluctuate in amount.
>
> **Market price risk:** the possibility that future changes in market prices may change the value, or the burden, of a financial instrument.'

The main components of market price risk likely to affect most entities are:

> '**Interest rate risk:** the risk that the value of a financial instrument will fluctuate because of changes in market interest rates.
>
> **Currency risk:** the risk that the value of a financial instrument will fluctuate because of changes in foreign exchange rates.
>
> **Other market price risk:** the risk that the value of a financial instrument will fluctuate as a result of changes in market prices caused by factors other than interest rates or currencies. This category includes risks stemming from commodity prices and share prices.'

(ii) **Benefits of information to users of financial statements**

Typically, information in financial statements on these risks has been **scant and lacking a focus**. For example, in the case of borrowings and interest-bearing assets, the fact that market price risk and cash flow risk are diametrically opposed is rarely mentioned, yet the relationship between the two has a significant impact on the risk profile.

A fixed rate interest-earning asset exposes an entity to a change in the market value of the asset as a consequence of a change in market rates of interest ('market price risk') but, as the entity is not exposed to a change in future cash flows arising from interest rate changes, credit risk aside it has no cash flow risk.

By contrast, a floating rate asset exposes an entity to a change in future cash flows if interest rates change ('cash flow risk' of reduced or increased cash receipts) but, aside from credit risk, has no risk of a gain or loss due to a change in the market value of that asset ('market price risk').

Depending on **management's attitudes** to these particular risks, transactions may be undertaken to reduce one of the risks at the expense of increasing the other. Consequently, the choice of which risk it seeks to reduce will have an important bearing on the entity's financial position, financial results and cash flows.

34 JEDDERS

Tutor's hint. This is one of those questions, which are likely to arise in this paper, covering various standards. In this case, you need to know about FRSs 4, 5 and 15 – all very important ones that are examined frequently.

(a) (i) FRS 15 does not allow selective revaluations of fixed assets: if one asset is revalued, all in that class must be revalued, thus avoiding 'cherry picking' of asset gains where others in the class may have fallen in value. In addition, non-recording of a fall in value of an asset cannot be justified on the basis that a recovery in market prices is expected in the near future.

(ii) PROFIT AND LOSS ACCOUNT (EXTRACT)

		£'000
Loss on revaluation (20% × £1.2m)		240
Depreciation charge		
Croydon	(£4.8m × 140%)/40 years	168
Dover	(£2.25m/30 years)	75
Exeter	(£1.2m × 80%)	48
		291

BALANCE SHEET (EXTRACTS)

	Cost/ revaluation	*Depre- ciation*	*NBV*
	£'000	£'000	£'000
Exeter	960	48	912
Croydon	6,720	168	6,552
Dover	2,250	75	2,175
	9,930	291	9,639

At 1 January 20X0 the accumulated depreciation of the Croydon property is £1.2m, which represents 10 years' depreciation, leaving 40 years remaining life. For the Dover and Exeter properties, the respective lives on these calculations are 30 and 20 years respectively. If there is no previous revaluation surplus on the Exeter property, then the loss in the current year is classed as an impairment and must be taken to the profit and loss account.

(b) A summary of how the debts should be treated:

Group A. These are normal non-factor debts and the provision should be calculated as usual.

Group B. Although these debts have been factored, the risks of late collection and bad debts remain with Jedders. Thus, the outstanding balance less the bad debt provision should still appear in Jedders' balance sheet, with a liability recorded for the amount received from Fab Factors. In addition, an interest charge would be made for the 1% charge for the monies advanced.

Group C. In a non-recourse situation such as this, Jedders has effectively sold its debtors for 95% of their value. The debtors would therefore be taken off Jedders' balance sheet, leaving cash and a residual finance charge.

Applying these treatments to the figures given:

PROFIT AND LOSS ACCOUNT (EXTRACT)

	£
Bad debt provision	
Group A (20% × (1,250 × 20%))	50,000
Group B (20% × (1,500 × 10%))	30,000
Group C	nil
	80,000
Finance charge	
Group A	nil
Group B (1% × 1,500) + (1% × 900) + (1% × 450)	28,500
Group C (5% × 2,000)	100,000
	128,500

BALANCE SHEET (EXTRACTS)

Debtors	*Less provision*	*Net balance*
Group A (1,250 × 20%)	20%	200,000
Group B (1,500 × 10%)	20%	120,000
Group C	nil	nil
		320,000

(c) (i) This is a capital instrument that must be accounted for under FRS 4 which determines how finance costs are charged. Those finance costs will include the amortisation of direct issue costs, discount on issue and premium on redemption. The total finance costs are found by comparing the proceeds with the total amounts paid by the company.

	£'000	£'000
Proceeds ((95% × £15m) – £0.3m)		13,950
Interest paid (10% × £15m × 4 years)	6,000	
Redemption cost (£15m + 10% premium)	16,500	
		22,500
Total finance costs		8,550

Amortise over a straight line = £2,137,500 pa

PROFIT AND LOSS ACCOUNT (EXTRACTS)

	£'000
Interest paid (10% × £15m)	1,500.00
Amortisation of finance costs	637.50
Total finance costs	2,137.50

BALANCE SHEET (EXTRACTS)

	£'000
Creditors due after more than one year	
Net proceeds of issue	13,950.0
Provision for amortisation of finance charges	2,137.5
	16,087.5

(ii) Fab Factors have made a suggestion that is only partially correct. FRS 4 does not allow anticipation of a conversion into equity shares, however favourable. The finance costs of the convertible loan stock is only the nominal interest (coupon) rate on the loan stock (ignoring issue costs). The cost to the company of the conversion is thus effectively ignored, so that in theory a negative finance cost may be possible where there is a low or nil interest rate and a redemption value that is less than the issue proceeds.

Further, this treatment by FRS 4 precludes convertible loan stock being treated as equity until conversion. It must be shown as a liability in the company's balance sheet and thus would affect gearing. However, the existence of the convertible loan stock will impact on diluted earnings per share, under FRS 14.

35 PREPARATION QUESTON: REVENUE RECOGNITION

> **Tutor's hint**. There is no UK standard on revenue recognition although there is an international standard. This subject can be linked to the ASB's Statement of Principles.

(a) The revenue is earned as the film is screened by Warner Cinemas in the period 1 July 20X1 to 31 December 20X1. At the year end 30 September 20X1, Telecast's accounts should reflect 15% of box office receipts, ie from 1 July to 30 September 20X1.

(b) The income is a fixed single amount. Both Telecast and Big Screen appear to have fully performed their obligations under the contract and therefore Telecast should include £10,000 in sales in the year ended 30 September 20X1.

(c) In this case Telecast should recognise the entire £4m as income in the year to 30 September 20X1 because, again, both Telecast and Global Satellite appear to have fully performed their respective obligations under the contract. (A traditional view of this contract would be that the £4m should be recognised in 10 instalments until December 20X2 and the £4m would be deferred income at 30 September 20X1.)

36 PREPARATION QUESTION: PURCHASE OF OWN SHARES

> **Tutor's hint**. If you have studied and understood this topic you will do well as it only asks for the basic rules to be followed when carrying out such a transaction. The second part of the question should present no problems, as long as you apply common sense when considering the effects of such a purchase of shares and what it may achieve.

(a) **Accounting requirement**

The accounting requirements for a public listed company when it purchases its own shares are as follows.

The basic accounting entry to effect the purchase (or redemption) is to **debit the share capital account** and **credit cash** with the **nominal value of the shares** (if they are being purchased at nominal value). Alternatively, the entry can be made to a share purchase or redemption account, which will be cleared by a cash payment when all the necessary journal entries have been made.

This transaction has caused the '**creditors' buffer**' (capital and reserves excluding debenture capital) to shrink by the nominal value of the shares purchased. This is not permitted, and to rectify the situation a transfer is made from distributable profits to a capital redemption reserve (CRR) equal to the nominal value of the shares.

The purchase must therefore be made out of **distributable profits**, or alternatively out of the **proceeds of a fresh issue** of shares. Where such shares are issued, the transfer to the CRR need only be the excess (if any) of the nominal value of the shares purchased over the proceeds of the new issue. Any premium on purchase must be charged to distributable profits, unless the shares were originally issued at a premium and there is a fresh issue of shares. In this case any premium may be charged to the share premium account.

In this last case, there is an additional restriction because it is not possible to have a debit balance on the share premium account. This means that the amount that may be charged to the share premium account is limited to the lower of:

(i) The **premium received** on the original issue of the shares now being purchased

(ii) The **proceeds of the fresh issue of shares**

(iii) The current balance on the share premium account, after accounting for any premium on the fresh issue of shares.

Other rules regarding the transaction are as follows.

(i) The **articles** of association of the company must allow the purchase.

(ii) The shares must all be **fully paid** on redemption.

(iii) The shares purchased by the company must be **cancelled**.

(iv) There must be **shares remaining** in issue after the purchase which are not redeemable.

(v) The company must make a **return to the registrar** within 28 days of the purchase stating all the details (nominal value of the shares, date of transaction, amount paid and so on).

In summary, the journal entries are as follows.

		£	£
DEBIT	Ordinary share capital	X	
CREDIT	Bank		X

Being the payment for the nominal value of the shares purchased

		£	£
DEBIT	Profit and loss account	X	
CREDIT	Capital redemption reserve		X

Being the transfer of the nominal value of the purchased shares to the CRR to maintain the creditor's buffer

DEBIT	Profit and loss account	X	
CREDIT	Bank		X

Being any premium on redemption or purchase

(b) **Advantages of purchasing own shares**

The following are advantages which a company gains when purchasing its own shares.

(i) The purchase allows the **distribution of surplus cash**, enabling the shareholders of the company to find other (perhaps better) uses for their money.

(ii) Companies with **employee share schemes** may wish to buy the employees' shares when they leave employment with the company.

(iii) It is possible to **buy out dissident shareholders**, which will allow the company to develop in the way the majority of the shareholders wish. Fewer shareholders also means that the company is less vulnerable to takeover.

(iv) By reducing the number of shares on the market, the **value of the remaining shares may rise** as part of the supply and demand mechanism, thus improving the marketability of the shares. (Note the effect on EPS and therefore the P/E ratio.)

(v) Companies which have messy and complicated capital structures may be able to simplify matters by buying whole classes of shares and issuing only one class in return.

(vi) It may be possible to reduce the level of overall dividend paid out. Retaining earnings in the business would encourage growth.

37 LED

Tutor's hint. This is quite a straightforward question. Although it covers a range of issues, the few numbers are very simple.

Prizewinner's points. You would not have needed to discuss premium on redemption to gain enough marks on part (a).

Examiner's comment. Answers to parts (a) and (b) were very narrow in character, demonstrating a lack of reading/knowledge in the area. In part (c) some candidates forgot about the CRR.

(a) **Redemption of shares – conditions and safeguards**

The conditions for the issue and redemption of redeemable shares are set out in CA 1985 ss 159 to 161. They require the following.

(i) The **articles must give authority** for the issue of redeemable shares. Articles do usually provide for this but if they do not, the articles must be altered before the shares are issued.

(ii) **Redeemable shares may only be issued if at** the time of issue the company also has **issued shares** which are **not redeemable**; a company's capital may not consist entirely of redeemable shares.

(iii) Redeemable shares may **only be redeemed if they are fully paid.**

(iv) The **terms of redemption** must provide for **payment on redemption**.

(v) **Shares which are redeemed** must be **cancelled and not reissued.**

These rules apply to all companies. Redemption may be made out of distributable profits or the proceeds of a new issue of shares.

In the case of private companies, the rules are relaxed to allow a payment out of capital to the extent of the difference between the redemption cost and the distributable profits plus the proceeds of any fresh issue made for the purpose of the purchase.

Companies will often give shareholders a **premium** when they are redeeming their shares. This premium is normally taken out of distributable profits, but in certain circumstances it may be charged to the share premium account. If the redeemable shares had originally been issued at a premium and there is a fresh issue for the purposes of redemption, then the premium on redemption can be met out of the share premium account up to the limit of the lesser of:

(i) The premium received originally on the shares now being redeemed; or

(ii) The current balance on the share premium account including any premium on the issue of the fresh issue of shares.

(b) **Reason for introduction**

The purpose of these conditions and safeguards is to prevent companies from reducing their share capital investment to such an extent that they put the **creditors of the company at risk**. If a company pays out money to its shareholders, there may be insufficient liquid funds left with in the business to pay its debts.

The Companies Act 1985 attempts to safeguard repayments to creditors of the debts owing to them by preventing 'underhand' prior payments to the shareholders.

In the case of private companies, these requirements have been relaxed to allow such companies to reduce permanent capital without having to undertake a costly and legally fraught reconstruction scheme. This relaxation was necessary to help family businesses where a family member wishes to realise his or her investment but none of the other members wishes or is able to buy their shares. A redemption is therefore allowed, but with the relevant safeguards to protect creditors' interests.

A **statutory declaration** is also required from the directors, again to reassure the creditors (and the remaining shareholders).

(c) **Balance sheet of LED Ltd after redemption of shares.**

	£	£
Ordinary shares £1 each (25,000 + 5,000)		30,000
Share premium account (W2)		8,750
Capital redemption reserve (W3)		3,750
		42,500
Sundry fixed assets		20,000
Sundry net current assets	25,000	
Bank overdraft (W4)	(2,500)	
		22,500
		42,500

Workings

1 *Permissible capital payment*

	£
Cost of redemption (12,500 × £1.10)	13,750
Less proceeds of new issue (5,000 × £1.25)	(6,250)
Profit and loss account	(5,000)
Permissible capital payment	2,500

2 *Share premium account*

	£
Balance per balance sheet	7,500
Plus premium on new issue of shares	1,250
	8,750

3 *Profit and loss account*

	£
Balance per balance sheet	5,000
Less premium on redemption	(1,250)
Transfer to CRR	(3,750)
	-

4	*Bank overdraft*	£
	Cash b/f	5,000
	Proceeds from share issue (5,000 × £1.25)	6,250
	Redemption of shares (£12,500 × 110%)	(13,750)
		(2,500)

38 GLOBELINK

Tutor's hint. Segmental reporting is not a particularly controversial issue, but segmental disclosures can provide vital information to the users of financial statements. In part (a) you would be given credit for presenting the information differently. The net assets of the associates are greater than 20% of those of the group, so they must be segmentally analysed.

Examiner's comment. This was not a popular question and was answered well by relatively few. Great analytical thought was not required; the question tested mainly computational skills.

(a) GLOBELINK PLC
SEGMENTAL ANALYSIS BY GEOGRAPHICAL AREA
FOR THE YEAR ENDED 30 NOVEMER 20X6

	United Kingdom £'000	*Asia* £'000	*Total* £'000
Turnover			
Turnover by destination			
Sales to third parties			
Continuing	150,858	70,992	221,850
Discontinued	54,853	-	54,853
	205,711	70,922	276,703
Turnover by origin			
Continuing operations			
Total sales	157,311	81,039	238,350
Inter-segment sales	(13,200)	(3,300)	(16,500)
Sales to third parties	144,111	77,739	221,850
Discontinued operations	54,853		54,853
	198,964	77,739	276,703

	United Kingdom £'000	*Asia* £'000	*Total* £'000
Profit			
Segment profit			
Continuing operations	12,920	4,080	17,000
Discontinued operations	(708)	-	(708)
	12,212	4,080	16,292
Common costs			(2,400)
Profit before tax of associated undertakings	3,575	-	3,575
Operating profit			17,467
Profit/loss on disposal			(1,998)
Interest payable and income from investments			216
Profit on ordinary activities before taxation			15,685
Net assets			
Net assets by segment			
Continuing operations (W)	48,116	25,806	73,922
Unallocated liabilities			(7,800)
			66,122
Net assets of associate	26,670		26,670
Total net assets			92,792

Working: net assets

	Apportionment	*United Kingdom* £'000	*Asia* £'000	*Total* £'000
Intangible fixed assets	75 : 25	2,010	670	2,680
Tangible fixed assets	75 : 25	32,955	10,985	43,940
Current assets	70 : 30	50,330	21,570	71,900
Creditors < 1 year (32,530 – 7,800)	70 : 30	(17,311)	(7,419)	(24,730)
Creditors > 1 year		(16,338)		(16,338)
Government grants		(3,530)		(3,530)
		48,116	25,806	73,922

(b) Any four of the following.

(i) It is often asserted that the benefits of segmental reporting are largely illusory and that the **costs are excessive**. The benefits cannot easily be measured and, since the definition of geographical and business segments is largely that of the management, it is unlikely that information will be disclosed which would present directors in a bad light. Yet one of the objectives of segmental reporting is to facilitate assessment of the efficiency of management as well as of the inherent relative merits of the business segments.

(ii) There is **no standardisation of geographical or business segments**, even between companies in the same industry, so that inter-firm comparison is not assisted by segmental reporting.

(iii) The **costs of segmental reporting are both direct and indirect**. The direct costs comprise the costs of collecting, analysing and publishing the data. Since much of the data for major international companies will be analysed by computers, the programming and processing costs can be substantial. These will be further increased should any changes in the analysis be required, since prior year comparative data will have to be derived. The costs of providing the information are borne by the preparers while the benefits are obtained by the users. Consequently, the users have no incentive to limit their demands for additional information and for changes in its composition and analysis.

(iv) The indirect costs relate to the **commercial damage** that a company may suffer if confidential information becomes public. For example, the disclosure that margins in a particular geographical or business segment are above average could prompt a company's competitors to enter the market or the host government to increase taxation.

(v) It is also argued that **management may adopt a more conservative** stance if segmental analyses are published because they do not wish to risk making losses which cannot be hidden by other segments' profits. This could inhibit innovation and encourage a short-term outlook amongst analysts and investors as well as managers.

Marking guide

		Marks	
(a)	Turnover by destination	3	
	Turnover by origin	3	
	Segment profit	3	
	Common costs	1	
	Profit-associated undertakings	1	
	Non-operating items	1	
	Interest payable and income	1	
	Net assets by segments	6	
	Unallocated liabilities	1	
	Net assets of associate	1	
	Minority interest	1	
	Unallocated liabilities	1	
	Available	23	
	Maximum		21
(b)	Classes of business	1	
	Transfer pricing	1	
	Common costs	1	
	Exceptional items	1	
	Changes in group	1	
	Definition of net assets	1	
	Available	6	
	Maximum		4
	Total maximum		25

39 DIVERSITY

Tutor's hint. For large conglomerate companies, segmental information can be vital to understanding the results of the business, which is what this question is trying to get at. You might choose to do the numbers part of the question in (c) first, to re-familiarise yourself with the mechanics, before going on to the written parts in (a) and (b), but you must not neglect these parts, that represent over 50% of the marks available.

(a) **Main disclosure requirement**

SSAP 25 requires disclosure, for each business class or geographical segment, of its turnover, results and net assets. It must also define its segments. The geographical analysis is required both in terms of the source (ie location of manufacturer/supply) and destination of sales (ie the areas to which the goods or services are supplied). The totals of the segmental information should agree with the primary statements and where they do not a reconciliation should be given. Comparatives are also required.

(b) **Need for and benefits of segmental reporting**

(i) The modern business environment has been characterised by the growth of global businesses with highly diversified operations. There are companies that operate in almost every country in the world and there are companies that carry out operations as diverse as car manufacturing and leasing, banking and insurance services.

In these cases it is not possible to gain a **full understanding** of a company's **results** from the **combined figures** shown in the **consolidated accounts**. This is of particular importance to those users of accounts that are attempting to use past performance to assess the **future potential performance** of a group; to do so based only on the consolidated accounts would produce misleading results because of the **different risk profiles** and profitability of the various components of the group.

It is important to recognise that it is **not the legal entity level** that is important in showing **segmental information,** but rather grouping together those parts of the business with particular profiles, whether as classes of businesses or geographically. Some subsidiaries may themselves operate in several geographical areas; whereas several subsidiaries may carry out the same types of business. The **choice of legal entity structure** for the group should **not affect the segmental information shown.**

It is also important that **sufficient information** be disclosed for each segment so that it is possible to see not only turnover and profits absolutely, but also to **assess profitability** by **comparing segment profit as a return on net assets.** Unfortunately this does not extend to actual cash flows, because FRS 1 (revised) *Cash flow statements* does not require similar segmental information for cash flows.

(ii) **Problems furnishing segmental information**

There are various problems relating to giving segmental information and to SSAP 25 in particular.

The **definition** of a segment is **fundamental** to this point. Although SSAP 25 gives a reasonable amount of guidance, it leaves a great deal to the **discretion of management** on how it **defines segments** and groups information together. This is understandable, because segmental information tends to flow from how management has structured and runs the business for both control and reporting. However, it does lead to a **lack of comparability** between different entities.

The standard calls for allocation of overheads between segments in a reasonable manner, but again this leaves scope for a great deal of management discretion, with scope for manipulation of segmental results. Some businesses may decide not to allocate common costs at all and hence **inter-company comparisons** might be more **difficult.**

SSAP 25, which pre-dates FRS 3, only **implicitly requires** the **segmental breakdown on exceptional items.** Some companies do offer such a breakdown but others do not, to the extent that the Review Panel has had to step in to clarify the situation.

A further definitional problem in SSAP 25 is that of **net assets** and when **interest-bearing assets and liabilities** must be **excluded** because **interest** has been **excluded** from the **segmental profits.**

One other problem is **intra-segment trading and balances.** Although the standard requires them to be disclosed, there is **no requirement to disclose transfer pricing policies** (although this is required at the legal entity level under FRS 8 *Related party disclosures*).

(c) DIVERSITY PLC

SEGMENTAL REPORT FOR YEAR ENDED 31 MARCH 20X4

Classes of business	*Engineering*	*Chemicals*	*Supermarkets*	*Total*
	£m	£m	£m	£m
Turnover				
Total sales	420	340	200	
Inter-segment	(20)	(40)	(nil)	
Third party sales	400	300	200	900
Segmental profit (W1)	45	79	25	149
Common costs				
Central admin				(37)
Interest				(12)
Profit before tax				100
Net assets				
Segmental net assets (W2)	188	162	100	450
Unallocated liabilities				(120)
				330

Workings

1 *Segmental profit*

		Engineering		*Chemicals*		*Supermarkets*
Cost of third party sales	80% of 400 =	320	60% of 300 =	180	75% of 200 =	150
Inter-segment cost of sales		20	60% of 40 =	24		nil
Distribution		24		38		25
Goodwill amortisation		6		14		nil
Interest cost (22 – 12) allocated 50:50)		5		5		nil
Total apportioned costs		375		261		175
Total sales		(420)		(340)		(200)
Segmental profit		45		79		25

2 *Segmental net assets*

		Engineering		*Chemicals*	*Supermarkets*
Goodwill	(60 × 30%)	18	(60 × 70%)	42	nil
Owned fixed assets		150		120	100
Leased assets	(150 × 60%)	90	(150 × 40%)	60	nil
Current assets		70		60	30
Current liabilities		(40)		(20)	(30)
Lease obligations	(200 × 50%)	(100)	(200 × 50%)	(100)	nil
Segmental net assets		188		162	100

Treatment of finance lease interest

While it may seem logical to allocate the finance lease interest to those segments with the finance lease obligations, this is inconsistent with the treatment of the debenture interest, which cannot be allocated in the same way. Thus it is more appropriate, as SSAP 25, to treat interest as a common cost.

Treatment of goodwill

It may be argued that it is arbitrary to apportion goodwill in this way, but the alternative would be to treat it as a common cost; however, this would overstate the profit of the engineering and chemical operations relative to the supermarkets' profit, which would be misleading.

Marking guide

			Marks
(a)		Main disclosure items	3
(b)	(i)	Problems caused by growth of diversified companies	1
		Difficulty of assessing past and future performance:	
		- profitability	1
		- growth	1
		- risk	1
		Defects of using individual companies' financial statements	1
		Success of whole is a function of success of individual segments	1
		Reference to problem of no segmental cash flows	1
		Available	7
		Maximum	5
	(ii)	Problem in defining a reportable segment	1
		Common costs	1
		Interest received/paid	1
		Exceptional/extraordinary items	1
		Definition of net assets; problem of consistency with interest	1
		Inter-segment trading – related party effect	1
		No information on transfer pricing policy	1
		Available	7
		Maximum	6
(c)		Total sales	1
		Inter-segment sales	1
		Segmental profit	3
		Common costs	1
		Segmental net assets	5
		Note on apportionment policies	2
		Available	13
		Maximum	11
		Maximum for question	25

40 PREPARATION QUESTION: CONSOLIDATED FINANCIAL STATEMENTS

> **Tutor's hint**. Answers to this type of question must be well-structured and argued logically; avoid rambling answers.

The individual accounts of a parent company are inadequate by themselves for the information needs of shareholders and other interested parties.

(a) The parent company accounts do not reveal the **true size and importance** of the economic entity in which shareholders have invested.

(b) They show investments in subsidiaries at **historical cost**, which may be a very poor indication of the resources actually controlled by the group.

(c) Parent company profit will consist only of its own operating profit, other investment income and so on and dividends received from subsidiaries. Shareholders will not know the amount of **profits retained by subsidiaries**.

(d) Creditors cannot assess, from the parent company accounts alone, the **liquidity and solvency** of the group as a whole.

The preparation of group accounts helps to overcome these difficulties and therefore provides fuller information than would be available from the parent company accounts. The statement in the question cannot be strictly justified: since individual accounts must still be prepared for each group company, the consolidated accounts are an **additional** source of information which can only be helpful to accounts users.

However, it is true that group accounts taken by themselves suffer from serious shortcomings.

(a) They **conceal the liquidity and solvency position** of individual group companies. Similarly, the losses of some group companies may be concealed by the overall profitability of the group.

(b) They aggregate assets which may be very **disparate in nature**.

(c) They do not reveal the extent of **intra-group trading and intra-group indebtedness**.

(d) They are **unsuitable for detailed ratio analysis** because they do not indicate which sectors of the group's activities are generating a high level of return and which are less satisfactory.

Some of these objections have been reduced in recent years by statutory provisions on the disclosure of segmental information, but the Companies Act 1985 does not go very far in this direction. SSAP 25 *Segmental reporting* has increased the amount of information to be disclosed in this way although the basis of inter-segmental pricing need not be disclosed.

41 PREPARATION QUESTION: CONSOLIDATED BALANCE SHEET

Tutor's hint. This is a simpler question than any you are likely to meet with in the examination. It is designed as part of a gentle introduction to the basic principles of consolidation, illustrating the calculation and accounting treatment of goodwill. Make sure that you lay out the proforma balance sheet and workings for goodwill, general reserve, unappropriated profit and minority interest.

(a) PAPPA PLC CONSOLIDATED BALANCE SHEET AS AT 31 DECEMBER 20X4

	£'000	£'000
Intangible fixed assets		
Goodwill (W2)		435
Tangible fixed assets		
Buildings	6,000	
Plant	3,939	
Vehicles	716	
	10,655	
Current assets		
Stock	3,408	
Debtors (less £23,000 inter-company)	2,746	
Cash	41	
	6,195	
Creditors: amounts falling due within one year		
Overdraft	2,016	
Trade creditors (less £23,000 inter-company)	1,941	
Tax	758	
Dividend	280	
	4,995	
Net current assets		1,200
Total assets less current liabilities		12,290
Creditors: amounts falling due after more than one year		
10% debentures	4,000	
15% debentures	500	
		4,500
		7,790
Capital and reserves		
Called up share capital		
Ordinary shares of 50p each		5,000.0
Minority interest (W3)		522.5
Reserves		
Share premium account	500.0	
General reserve (W4)	1,490.0	
Unappropriated profit (W4)	277.5	
		2,267.5
		7,790.0

(b) Pappa plc has made a profit of 15/115 × £23,000 = £3,000 on its sale of goods to Lima plc. Lima plc has not yet sold goods to an outside party and the profit is therefore unrealised as far as the group is concerned. The adjustment is necessary to reduce the balance of unappropriated profit, and the value of stocks by £3,000.

Workings

1 *Group structure*

Pappa

$\frac{1,450}{2,000} = 72.5\%$

Lima reserve £400,000
Unappropriated profit £nil

2 *Goodwill*

	£'000	£'000
Cost of investment		1,450
For:		
Shares	1,000	
General reserve	400	
Unappropriated profit	-	
	1,400	
	× 72.5%	
		(1,015)
Goodwill at acquisition/balance sheet date		435

3 *Minority interest*

	£'000
Net assets financed by	
Share capital	1,000
General reserves	800
Unappropriated profit	100
	1,900
	× 27.5%
Minority interest	522.5

4 *Reserves – unappropriated profit*

	Pappa	*Lima*
	£'000	£'000
Per question	205	100
Pre acquisition		(-)
Share of post acquisition		100
(100 × 72.5%)	72.5	
	277.5	

- general

	Pappa	*Lima*
	£'000	£'000
Per question	1,200	800
Pre question		(400)
		400
Share of post acquisition		
(400 × 72.5%)	290	
	1,490	

42 HAMPLE

Tutor's hint. This is a typical exam standard question with fair value adjustments, accounting policy adjustments and inter-group trading complications.

Examiner's comments. Problem areas were fair value adjustments and failure to include share premium in the goodwill and minority interest calculations.

HAMPLE PLC
CONSOLIDATED BALANCE SHEET AS AT 31 MARCH 20X9

	£'000	£'000
Fixed assets		
Intangible: software (W2)	1,440	
Goodwill (W3)	480	
		1,920
Tangible: land and buildings (600 + 900 – 120 + 30) (W2)	1,410	
plant and equipment (1,520 + 1,090)	2,610	
		4,020
Investments (65 + 210)		275
		6,215
Current assets		
Stocks (719 + 560 – 5) (W4)	1,274	
Debtors (524 + 328)	852	
Cash (20 + 55 cash in transit)	75	
	2,201	
Liabilities: amounts due within one year		
Trade creditors (475 + 472)	947	
Taxation (228 + 174)	402	
Overdraft	27	
Dividend payable	100	
	(1,476)	
Net current assets		725
Liabilities: amounts due after one year		
Government grants (230 + 40)		(270)
Net assets		6,670
Share capital and reserves		
Ordinary shares of £1 each		2,000
Share premium		2,000
Profit and loss account (W5)		2,320
		6,320
Minority assets (W6)		350
		6,670

Workings

1 *Group structure*

Hample
| 90% + loan note
| 1.4.X8
Sopel P/L reserve £2,200,000

2 *Fair value adjustments*

	At acquisition £'000	Movement £'000	At balance sheet date £'000
Leasehold property (4 yr life) – see note below	(120)	30	(90)
Software – see note below	(180)	(180)	(360)
	(300)	(150)	(450)

Note

Leasehold property

	CF	*DF*	*PV*		*NBV*		*FV adj*
T_0	80	1	80				
$T_{1\text{-}3}$	80	2.5	200				
			280	-	400	=	(200)

Computer software

	1.4.X8	*31.3.X9*	
	£'000	£'000	
Fair value (2,400 × 4/5)	1,920	1,440	(2,400 × 3/5)
Net book value (2,400 × 7/8)	2,100	1,800	(2,400 × 6/8)
FV adj	(180)	(360)	

3 *Goodwill*

	£'000	£'000
Cost of investment - shares		4,110
For: (net assets including loan)		
Share capital	1,500	
Share premium	500	
P/L reserve	2,200	
Fair value adj (W2)	(300)	
	3,900	
	× 90%	(3,510)
Goodwill		600
Amortised (1/5)		(120)
Unamortised		480

4 *Unrealised profit*

	£'000	%
Sales	25	125
Cost of sales	20	100
	5	25

5 *Profit and loss account*

	Hample	*Sopel*
	£'000	£'000
Per question	2,800	1,955
FV adj (W2)		(150)
Unrealised profit		(5)
Pre acquisition		(2,200)
		(400)
Share of post acquisition loss ((400) × 90%)	(360)	
Less: goodwill amortised (W3)	(120)	
	2,320	

6 *Minority interest*

	£'000
Net assets per question	3,955
Less: unrealised profit	(5)
FV adj (W2)	(450)
	3,500
	× 10%
	350

7 *Current accounts*

In Hample's books	75
Cash in transit	(15)
In Sopel's books	60
Intra group loan	
In Hample's books	200
Cash in transit	(40)
In Sopel's books	160

> **Tutor's hint.** This is an alternative format which some people find easier to understand because it integrates the various aspects of the question.
>
> It is a format which groups use in practice, as you will realise, because once the spreadsheet is set up, they can go on adding subsequent years to it.
>
> Use the method which suits your way of thinking and are likely to find most efficient in an examination environment.

8 *Goodwill and minority interests*

	Total	*At acquisition*	*Post acquisition*	*Minority interests*
	100%	90%	90%	10%
	£'000	£'000	£'000	£'000
At acquisition				
Share capital	1,500	1,350	-	150
Share premium	500	450	-	50
Profits to beginning of year	2,200	1,980	-	220
Fair value adjustment - software (480) – 300)	(180)	(162)	-	(18)
- property	(120)	(108)	-	(12)
	3,900	3,510	-	390
Cost of investment		4,110	-	
Goodwill		600		
Post acquisition movements				
Current year loss (1,955 – 2,200)	(245)	-	(220)	(25)
Additional depreciation	(180)	-	(162)	(18)
Over depreciation	30	-	27	3
Unrealised profit	(5)	-	(4)	(1)
Minority interest per P&L a/c*				(41)
Minority interest per B/S				349

Post acquisition profits of Sopel attributable to Hample	(359)
Add Profit and loss account of Hample	2,800
Goodwill amortisation (600 ÷ 5)	(120)
Consolidated profit and loss account (B/S)	2,321

* Not separately required for this particular question.

43 HARDY AND SIBLING

> **Tutor's hint**. This is a fairly straightforward consolidation. If you approached it in a systematic way then you should not have encountered any great difficulties. Part (c) tested your understanding of fair values. This was a reasonable question and should not have caused any great difficulty.
>
> **Examiner's comments.** This question was generally well answered in part (a). Part (b) was not. A number of candidates did not attempt it. Part (c) was poorly answered as well.

(a) HARDY PLC
CONSOLIDATION BALANCE SHEET AS AT 31 MARCH 20X8

	£'000	£'000
Fixed assets		
Goodwill (W3)		992
Land and buildings (22,000 + 12,000 + 3,500) (W1)		37,500
Plant and equipment (20,450 + 10,220 + 1,600) (W1)		32,270
		70,762
Current assets		
Stock (9,850 + 6,950 – 75) (W2)	16,365	
Debtors (11,420 + 3,830 – 240)	15,010	
Cash	490	
	31,865	
Creditors: amounts falling due within one year		
Creditors (5,600 + 3,810 – 240)	9,170	
Bank overdraft	570	
Taxation (2,470 + 1,980)	4,450	
Dividends: ordinary (800 + 500 – 400)	900	
preference (200 – 50)	150	
	15,240	
Net current assets		16,625
Creditors due after one year		
10% debentures 20Y1 (12,000 + 4,000)		(16,000)
Net assets		71,387
Share capital and reserves		
Ordinary shares of £1 each		10,000
Revaluation reserve (W1)		1,200
Profit and loss reserve (W3)		53,766
Minority interest (W5)		6,421
		71,387

Working

1 *Fair value adjustment table*

	At acquisition		*Movement*		*At B/S date*
	£'000		£'000		£'000
Land	2,000		–		2,000
Plant	4,000	($^3/_5 \times 4{,}000$)	(2,400)	($^2/_5 \times 4{,}000$)	1,600
	6,000		(2,400)		3,600

Note: post acquisition movement in revaluation reserve for land is £1.5m (£8.5m – £7m).

2 *Provision for unrealised profit*

£450,000 × $^{20}/_{120}$ = £75,000

3 *Goodwill*

		£'000	£'000
Paid (18,000 + 500)			18,500
For:			
Preference shares (2,000 × 25%)			(500)
Ordinary shares			
Share capital		5,000	
P/L reserve		8,400	
FV adjustment (W1)		6,000	
		19,400	
Group share		× 80%	(15,520)
			2,480
Amortised to date		2,480 × $^3/_5$	(1,488)
Unamortised			992

4 *Profit and loss reserve*

	Hardy	Sibling
	£'000	£'000
Per question	51,840	14,580
Dividends receivable		
Preference (200 × 25%)	50	
Ordinary (500 × 80%)	400	
URP on stock (W2)		(75)
FV adjustment movement (W1)		(2,400)
Pre acquisition		(8,400)
		3,705
Share of post acquisition (3,705 × 80%)	2,964	
Goodwill amortisation (W3)	(1,488)	
~~Goodwill~~ P&L reserve	53,766	

5 *Minority interest*

	£'000	£'000
Net assets at balance sheet date	21,580	
Owned by preference shareholders	(2,000)	
Revaluation reserve	1,500	
FV adjustment (W1)	3,600	
URP on stock (W2)	(75)	
	24,605 × 20% =	4,921
Net assets owned by preference shareholders	2,000 × 75% =	1,500
		6,421

(b) *Minority interest in the adjusted profits*

	£'000
Profit before taxation	5,400
Depreciation on plant for the year	(800)
Stock: PURP	(75)
Adjusted profit before taxation	4,525
Taxation	(1,600)
Adjusted profit after taxation	2,925

Minority interest of the above

75% of preference shares (200 × 75%)	150
20% of ordinary shares (2,925 – 200 @ 20%)	545
	695

(c) *Importance of fair values upon consolidation*

FRS 7 considers it important to consolidate the fair values of assets and liabilities of an acquired subsidiary upon consolidation as this treatment would best reflect the correct value of the subsidiary at the time of its acquisition. This would also be consistent with the concept of historic cost as items are shown at their value when acquired.

The alternative would be to consolidate the book values of the assets and liabilities. This treatment would lead to out of date values being used for some of the balance sheet items and therefore a different goodwill figure would arise which would in effect incorporate any fair value adjustments. Put simply this would lead to a misallocation of fair value adjustments to the intangible fixed assets caption.

Fair values allow the users of the accounts to see the value of the items acquired and the resulting goodwill figure.

44 CLAYMORE PLC

Tutor's hint. This question may look intimidating because it involves an acquisition part of the way through the year (something you should always check in the exam), some FRS 7 issues and both the consolidated profit and loss account and balance sheet. It is, however, fairly straightforward. You should not have overlooked FRS 3 aspects in the consolidated profit and loss account.

(a) CLAYMORE GROUP PLC
CONSOLIDATED BALANCE SHEET AS AT 30 NOVEMBER 20X6

	£'000	£'000
Fixed assets		
Tangible assets (700 + 140 + 60) (W2)		900
Goodwill (W4)		114
		1,014
Current assets		
Stocks	240	
Debtors	180	
Cash at bank and in hand	120	
	540	
Creditors: amounts falling due within one year	260	
Net current assets		280
Total assets less current liabilities		1,294
Creditors: amounts falling due after one year		490
		804
Capital and reserves		
Ordinary share capital		300
Share premium (W7)		130
Profit and loss account (W6)		238
		668
Minority interests (equity) (W5)		136
		804

CLAYMORE GROUP PLC
CONSOLIDATED PROFIT AND LOSS ACCOUNT
FOR THE YEAR ENDED 30 NOVEMBER 20X6

	£'000	£'000
Turnover		
Continuing operations	1,260	
Acquisitions ($^2/_{12} \times 708$)	118	
		1,378
Cost of sales (644 + ($^2/_{12} \times 426$))		(715)
Gross profit		663
Distribution costs	255	
Administrative expenses (W8)	147	
		(402)
Operating profit		
Continuing operations	235	
Acquisitions (156 ÷ 6)	26	
		261
Interest payable (28 + 2)		(30)
Profit on ordinary activities before taxation		231
Tax on profit on ordinary activities (113 + 9)		(122)
Profit after tax		109
Minority interests (equity) (W9)		(6)
		103
Dividends paid		(15)
Retained profit for the financial year attributable to the group		88

Workings

1 *Group structure*

Claymore

| 60%

College 1.10.X6

2 *Revaluation surplus*

	£'000
College Ltd: tangible fixed assets at market value	200
Carrying value	140
Revaluation surplus	60

FRS 7 *Fair values in acquisition accounting* states that **open market values** should be used to **value tangible fixed assets**, and it is this figure which is compared with the carrying value here, rather than the net realisable value. The latter is lower because the costs of realisation are deducted. However, as the group does not intend to dispose of the asset, the market value is more appropriate.

3 *Pre-acquisition dividend*

Dividend paid by College to Claymore: £18,000

Pre-acquisition element $^{10}/_{12} \times$ £18,000 = £15,000

4 *Goodwill*

	£'000	£'000
Cost of investment (£1.75 × 200)		350
Less pre-acquisition dividend (W2)		(15)
		335
Share capital	40	
Share premium	60	
Revaluation surplus (W2)	60	
Profit and loss account		
Prior year: (180 – 60)	120	
Current year: ($^{10}/_{12} \times$ 60)	50	
	330	
Group share: 60%		198
Goodwill		137
Less: amortisation (137 × 1/6)		(23)
		114

5 *Minority interest (balance sheet)*

	£'000
Net assets per question	280
Fair value adj (W2)	60
	340
Minority interest (40% × 340)	136

6 *Reserves*

	Claymore £'000	College £'000
Per question	250	180
Share issue costs	20	
Pre acquisition (180 – 60 × 2/12)		(170)
Less: pre-acquisition dividend (W3)	(15)	10
Share of post acquisition profits (60% × 60 × 2/12)	6	
Less: goodwill amortisation (W4)	(23)	
	238	

7 *Share premium account*

	£'000
Claymore plc	150
Less issue costs	(20)
	130

8 *Administrative expenses*

	£'000
Claymore plc	130
College Ltd ($^2/_{12} \times 84$)	14
Goodwill written off	23
	167
Less issue costs	(20)
	147

9 *Minority interests (p & l)*

$90{,}000 \times {}^2/_{12} \times 40\% = £6{,}000$

(b) **Estimation of fair value**

FRS 7 *Fair values in acquisition accounting* states that **quoted shares** should be valued at **market price** on the **date of acquisition.** However, the standard acknowledges that the market price may be difficult to determine if it is **unreliable** because of an **inactive market**. In particular, where the shares are **not quoted**, there may be **no suitable** market. In such cases the value must be estimated using:

(i) The value of **similar quoted securities**
(ii) The **present value of the cash flows** of the shares
(iii) Any **cash alternative** which was offered
(iv) The value of any **underlying security** into which there is an option to convert.

It may be necessary to **undertake a valuation** of the company in question should **none of the above methods prove feasible.**

Marking guide

		Marks	
(a)	Cost of control (ie goodwill calculation)	6	
	Revaluation to fair value	2	
	Group reserves	5	
	Minority interest	4	
	College Ltd reserves	3	
	Intangible assets	2	
	Tangible assets	2	
	Net current assets and creditors more than one year	2	
	Share capital	1	
	Share premium	2	
	Turnover	2	
	Cost of sales	2	
	Distribution costs	2	
	Administrative expenses	4	
	Interest payable	2	
	Taxation	2	
	Minority interests	3	
	Dividends paid	2	
	Available	48	
	÷2 =	24	
	Maximum		21
(b)	Similar shares – quoted	1	
	Present value of cash flows	1	
	Cash alternative	1	
	Value of underlying security	1	
	Valuation of company	1	
	Available	5	
	Maximum		4
	Total maximum		25

45 PREPARATION QUESTION: BASIC CONSOLIDATION

Tutor's hint. This is a very easy question giving you practice in all the basics of consolidation which are needed in all questions.

BEAVER GROUP
CONSOLIDATED PROFIT AND LOSS ACCOUNT
FOR THE YEAR ENDED 31 DECEMBER 20X8

	£'000
Sales (5,000 + 1,000 – 100)	5,900
Cost of sales (2,900 + 600 – 80)	3,420
Gross profit	2,480
Other expenses (1,700 + 320)	2,020
Net profit	460
Tax (130 + 25)	155
Profit after tax	305
Minority interest (20% × £55,000)	11
Group profit for the year	294
Dividend proposed (Beaver only)	130
Retained profit for the year	164
Retained profit brought forward (260 + 80% of 185)	408
Retained profit carried forward	572

CONSOLIDATED BALANCE SHEET AS AT 31 DECEMBER 20X8

	£'000	£'000
Fixed assets (2,000 + 200 – 80)		2,120
Current assets		
Stock (500 + 120 + 80)	700	
Trade debtors (650 – 100 + 40)	590	
Bank and cash (390 + 35)	425	
	1,715	
Current liabilities		
Trade creditors (910 + 30)	940	
Dividend payable: Beaver plc	100	
to minority in Gorilla Ltd	8	
Tax (130 + 25)	155	
	1,203	
Net current assets		512
Total assets less current liabilities		2,632
		2,632
Capital and reserves		
Share capital (Beaver only)		2,000
Profit and loss account (W5)		572
Minority interest (W4)		60
		2,632

Workings

1 *Group structure*

Beaver
| 80%
Gorilla P/L reserve £nil

2 *Goodwill*

	£'000	£'000
Cost of investment β		80
For:		
Share capital	100	
P/L reserve	-	
	× 80%	(80)
Goodwill		Nil

3 *Unrealised profit*

	£'000
Sales	100
Cost of sales	(80)
	20

4 *Minority interest*

	£'000
Net assets per question	300
Minority interest (20% × 300)	60

5 *Reserves*

	Beaver	Gorilla
	£'000	£'000
Per question	400	200
Add: dividend income (40 × 80%)	32	
Less: unrealised profit	(20)	
pre acquisition		(Nil)
Share of post acquisition		200
(200 × 80%)	160	
	572	

46 PREPARATION QUESTION: MERGER

> **Tutor's hint**. Using this simple example make sure that you understand the differences between acquisition accounting and merger accounting.

KOOL LIMITED
CONSOLIDATED BALANCE SHEET AS AT 30 SEPTEMBER 20X8

(a) *Acquisition method*

	£'000	£'000
Freehold properties		325
Goodwill (W4)		104
Other fixed assets (3,650 + 420)		4,070
Net current assets (1,160 + 51)		1,211
		5,710
Capital and reserves		
Ordinary share capital (W2)		2,500
Share premium on new issue of shares (W2)		400
Reserves (W5)		2,810
		5,710

(b) *Merger method*

	£'000	£'000
Freehold properties		210
Other fixed assets		4,070
Net current assets		1,211
		5,491
Capital and reserves		
Ordinary share capital (W1)		2,500
Reserves (W3)		2,991
		5,491

(a) *Workings*

1 *Group structure*

Kool
| 100%
Groovy

2 *Kool Ltd's share capital*

	£'000
Shares in issue before combination	2,000
Issued to shareholders in Groovy Ltd	
(5/3 × 300,000)	500
	2,500

Share premium on new issue = £400,000 (£900,000 – £500,000).

3 *Fair values – freehold properties*

	£'000
Fair value	325
Book value	210
Adj	115

4 *Goodwill*

	£'000	£'000
Cost of investment		900
For:		
Share capital	300	
Reserves (221 + 160)	318	
Fair value adj	115	
	796	
	× 100%	(796)
Goodwill		104

5 *Reserves*

	Kool £'000	Groovy £'000
Per question (2,600 + 210)	2,810	381
Pre acquisition		(381)
		Nil
	2,810	

(b) *Workings*

1 *Group structure*

As part (a)

2 *Merger adjustment*

	£'000
Nominal value of shares issued (300 × 5/3)	500
Nominal value of shares acquired (300 × 100%)	300
Merger adjustment	200

This adjustment is needed because, under the merger method, the amount at which Kool Ltd records its investment in the shares of Groovy Ltd is the nominal value of shares issued as consideration (£500,000). No share premium need be recorded because merger relief is available under s 131 CA 1985. The shares acquired, however, against which the investment of £500,000 is to be cancelled, have a nominal value of £300,000. The £200,000 imbalance is simply deducted from reserves to make the balance sheet balance.

3 *Reserves*

	Kool £'000	Groovy £'000
Per question	2,810	381
Share of all reserves (381 × 100%)	381	
Less: merger difference (W2)	(200)	
	2,991	

47 HILL AND GLEN

Tutor's hint. In this question remember that the acquisition was mid-year therefore profit and loss account figures must be time apportioned. Take care with the pre-acquisition dividend and remember to deal with the fair value adjustments.

Examiner's comment. Common mistakes in (a) included the following:

(1) Incorrect treatment of the pre-acquisition dividend
(2) Inclusion of the full year's results of the subsidiary in the consolidated accounts
(3) Use of proportional consolidation in the balance sheet
(4) Failing to include the subsidiary's proposed dividend in the group reserves

(a) HILL PLC
CONSOLIDATED PROFIT AND LOSS ACCOUNT
YEAR ENDED 30 SEPTEMBER 20X7

	£'000
Turnover 1,000 + (6/12 × 1,000)	1,500
Cost of sales (W4)	1,005
Gross profit	495
Operating expenses 120 + (6/12 × 100)	170
Operating profit before tax	325
Taxation 50 + (6/12 × 40)	70
Operating profit after tax	255
Dividends	80
Retained profit for the year	175
Retained profit b/f (410 – 120)	290
Retained profit c/f (W6)	465

CONSOLIDATED BALANCE SHEET AT 30 SEPTEMBER 20X7

	£'000	£'000
Fixed assets		
Intangible assets: goodwill (100 – 20) (W5)		80
Tangible assets (440 + 670 + 125 (revaluation))		1,235
		1,315
Current assets		
Stock (240 + 280)	520	
Debtors (170 + 210)	380	
Bank (20 + 40)	60	
	960	
Creditors: amounts falling due within one year		
Creditors (170 + 160)	330	
Taxation (50 + 40)	90	
Dividends	40	
	460	
Net current assets		500
		1,815
Creditors: amounts falling due after more than one year		
Debentures		150
		1,665
Capital and reserves		
£1 ordinary shares (200 + 150 × 4/3)		400
Share premium (150 × 4/3 × 4)		800
Profit and loss account (W6)		465
		1,665

Workings

1 *Group structure*

Hill
| 1.4.X7
Glen

2 *Reserves at acquisition*

	£'000
Reserves b/f (640 – 140)	500
Current year (140 × 6/12)	70
	570

3 *Fair value*

	At acquisition £'000	*Movement* £'000	*At balance sheet date* £'000
Land	125	-	125
Stock	25	(25)	Nil
	150	(25)	125

4 *Cost of sales*

		£'000
Per Hill plc		630
Glen Ltd (660 × 6/12)	330	
Adjustment to fair value of opening stock, increases cost of sales	25	
Goodwill amortisation (W2)	20	
		375
		1,005

5 *Goodwill*

	£'000	£'000
Cost of investment (150 × 4/3 × £5)		1,000
Less: pre acquisition dividend (60 × 6/12)		(30)
		970
For:		
Share capital	150	
Reserves (W2)	570	
FV adj (W3)	150	
	870	
	× 100%	(870)
Goodwill at acquisition		100
Amortisation (1/5 × 100)		(20)
Unamortised		80

6 *Reserves*

	Hill £'000	Glen £'000
Per question	410	640
FV adj movement (W3)		(25)
Dividend receivable (6/12 × 60 × 100%) (W5)	30	
Pre acquisition (W2)		(570)
		45
Share of post acquisition (45 × 100%)	45	
Less: goodwill amortised (W4)	(20)	
	465	

(b) **Consolidated reserves**

No fair value adjustments are needed and no distinction is drawn between pre- and post-acquisition profits.

	£'000
Hill plc reserves	410
Add dividend from Glen Ltd	60
Glen Ltd reserves	640
	1,110
Merger adjustment (W)	(50)
	1,060

Working: merger adjustment

	£'000
Nominal value of shares issued (150 × 4/3)	200
Nominal value of shares acquired	150
Merger difference to consolidated reserves	50

48 HOLDING

> **Tutor's hint.** For part (a) there are a number of adjustments to be made for pre-acquisition dividends and fair values. In part (b) the consolidated profit and loss account is fairly standard but take care with the 15 month accounting period.
>
> **Examiner's comment**. This was an anticipated and therefore well answered consolidation question. Problem areas included:
>
> - Failure to take the dividend out of pre-acquisition profits
> - Incorrect calculation of the plant's fair value
> - Incorrect apportionment of the subsidiary's profits
> - Amortising 12 months of goodwill instead of nine months
> - Not fully eliminating intergroup trade (especially unrealised profits in stock)
> - Omitting depreciation on the additional fair value amounts
> - Incorrectly including the subsidiary's dividend in the profit and loss account

(a) 18 million of the issued 24 million ordinary shares purchased.

$$\frac{18\text{ million}}{24\text{ million}} = 75\%\text{ ownership.}$$

	£m	£m
Cost of investment (18m × £10)		180
Less: pre acquisition dividend (W2)		(6)
		174
For:		
Share capital	24	
P&L reserves (W3)	80	
Fair value adjustment (W4)	44	
Revaluation reserve	20	
	168	
	× 75%	(126)
Goodwill at acquisition		48

Workings

1 *Group structure*

Holding

$$\frac{18\text{m}}{24\text{m}} = 75\%$$

1.11.X9

Subside

2 *Subside plc: dividend*

	£m
Holding plc's share £20m × 75% =	15
Of which 6 months (1 July 20X8 to 1 January 20X9) is pre acquisition: 6/15× £15m =	6

3 *Reserves at acquisition*

	£m
P/L reserve b/f	64
Current (40 × 6/15)	16
	80

4 *Fair value adjustment*

	£'000
Property	4
Plant (see note below)	40
	44

Plant	£m	£m
Fair value @ 1.1.X9		90
Net book value at 30.6.X8	60	
Depreciation to 1.1.X9 (25m × 6/15)	(10)	
		50
Fair value adjustment		40

(b) HOLDING PLC
CONSOLIDATED PROFIT AND LOSS ACCOUNT
FOR THE YEAR TO 30 SEPTEMBER 20X9

	£m
Turnover (W1)	488
Cost of sales (W2)	(286)
Gross profit	202
Operating expenses (W5)	(99)
Interest payable (10 + [5 × $\frac{9}{15}$])	(13)
Profit before tax	90
Taxation (22 + (10 × $\frac{9}{15}$))	(28)
Profit after tax	62
Minority interest (W6)	(6)
Profit after tax and minority interest	56
Dividend – final proposal	(25)
Refined profit for the year	31

Workings

1 *Turnover*

	£m
Holding plc	350
Subside plc (280 × $\frac{9}{15}$)	168
Inter-group sales	(30)
	488

2 *Cost of sales*

	£m
Holding plc	200
Subside plc (170 × $\frac{9}{15}$)	102
Intra-group sales	(30)
Provision for unrealised profit (W3)	2
Additional depreciation on plant and equipment (W4)	12
	286

3 *Stock*

	£m
Unrealised profit	
Stock held: $\frac{1}{3}$ of £30m	10
Of which $\frac{25}{125}$ is profit	2

4 *Plant and equipment*

Fair value adjustment was at 1 January 20X9.
This leaves 30 months (3 years–6 months) estimated useful life on plant and equipment.
Additional depreciation charge is £40m × 9/30 = £12m

5 *Operating expenses*

	£m
Holding plc	72
Subside plc (9/15 of 35)	21
Amortisation of goodwill [(48/6 years) × $\frac{9}{12}$]	6
	99

6 *Minority interest*

	£m
Subside's profit after tax 60 × $\frac{9}{15}$	36
Depreciation adjustment on plant	(12)
	24
Minority interest @ 25%	6

Marking guide

		Marks	
(a)	Investment at cost	1	
	Calculation of pre-acquisition dividend	1	
	Accounting treatment of pre-acquisition dividend	1	
	Share capital	1	
	Revaluation reserve	3	
	Pre-acquisition profits	2	
	Available	9	
	Maximum		8
(b)	Turnover	3	
	Cost of sales	5	
	Operating expenses	3	
	Interest	2	
	Taxation	2	
	Minority interest	3	
	Dividends	1	
	Available	19	
	Maximum		17
	Maximum for question		25

49 FRUIT AND VEGETABLES

Tutor's hint. You may find it easier to do the acquisition accounting consolidation first as this is likely to be more familiar territory. Remember to leave enough time to answer part (b).

(a) FRUIT PLC
SUMMARISED CONSOLIDATED PROFIT AND LOSS ACCOUNT
FOR THE YEAR ENDED 31 DECEMBER 20X4

	Working	*Merger accounting*	*Acquisition accounting*
		£	£
Profit before depreciation £(568,310 + 437,070)		1,005,380	1,005,380
Depreciation (91,290 + 40,035)/(91,290 + 75,000)		131,325	166,290
Amortisation of goodwill	3(b)	-	15,594
		874,055	823,496
Profit/(loss) on sale of investments			
£(138,465 – (318,750 – 140,250))		138,465	(40,035)
		1,012,520	783,461
Taxation £(119,255 + 149,940)		269,195	269,195
		743,325	514,266

FRUIT PLC
CONSOLIDATED BALANCE SHEET
AS AT 31 DECEMBER 20X4

	Working	*Merger accounting* £	*Acquisition accounting* £
Goodwill	3(b)	-	140,346
Freehold property	5	2,231,250	2,486,250
Plant and machinery	6	526,320	601,890
Net current assets £(249,390 + 874,905)		1,124,295	1,124,295
		3,881,865	4,352,781
Share capital (1,275,000 + (765,000 ÷ 2))		1,657,500	1,657,500
Share premium/merger reserve	7	-	1,530,000
Merger reserve	2(a)	382,500	-
Retained earnings	3(a) 4(b)	1,841,865	1,165,281
		3,881,865	4,352,781

Workings

1 *Group structure*

Fruit
│ 100% 1.1.X4
Vegetables Reserves £447,525

2 *Merger difference*

	£
Nominal value of investment (765,000 × $\frac{1}{2}$ × £1)	382,500
Nominal value of shares acquired (765,000 × 100%)	(765,000)
Merger difference (capital reserve)	(382,500)

3 *Retained earnings*

	Fruit £	*Vegetables* £
Per question	1,008,780	833,085
Share of reserves (833,085 × 100%)	833,085	
	1,841,865	

(b) *Workings*

1 *Group structure*

As part (a)

2 *Fair value adjustments*

	At acquisition £	*Movement* £	*At balance sheet date* £
Investments (318,750 – 140,250)	178,500	(178,500)	-
Freehold premises (828,750 – 573,750)	255,000		255,000
Plant (300,000 – 189,465)	110,535	(34,965)	75,570
	544,035	(213,465)	330,570

Note: Depreciation charged for the year on

	£
Plant and machinery	40,035
Fair value depreciation 300,000 ÷ 4 years remaining	(75,000)
Movement – additional FV depreciation	34,965

3 *Goodwill*

	£	£
Cost of investment (765,000 × £5)		1,912,500
For: Share capital	765,000	
Reserves	447,525	
Fair value adj	544,035	
	1,756,560	
	× 100%	(1,756,560)
Goodwill at acquisition		155,940
Amortisation (1/10)		(15,594)
		140,346

4 *Retained earnings*

	Fruit £	*Vegetable* £
Per question	1,008,780	833,085
Fair value adjustment (W2)		(213,465)
Pre acquisition		(447,525)
		172,095
Share of post acquisition reserves (172,095 × 100%)	172,095	
Less: goodwill amortised (W3)	(15,594)	
	1,165,281	

5 *Land and buildings*

	£	£
Fruit plc	1,657,500	1,657,500
Vegetables plc: cost/fair value	573,750	828,750
	2,231,250	2,486,250

6 *Plant and machinery*

6

	Merger Accounting £	*Acquisition Accounting* £
Fruit plc		
At cost	653,055	653,055
Depreciation	(276,165)	(276,165)
Vegetables plc		
At net book value £(316,965 – 167,535)	149,430	-
At depreciated fair value £(300,000 – 75,000)	-	225,000
	526,320	601,890

7 *Share premium account*

	£
Fair value of shares issued	1,912,500
Nominal value of shares issued	382,500
Share premium	1,530,000

(b) **Asset values**

Under merger accounting all assets are recorded in the consolidated accounts at their book values. Under the acquisition method, assets of the subsidiary are recorded in the consolidated balance sheet at an estimate of their fair values at the time of the acquisition. This treatment recognises that the consideration given for the acquired business will have related to the true value of the assets rather than their book value.

Goodwill (positive or negative) may arise under acquisition accounting but not under merger accounting because there is no fair value exercise.

Reserves

Under merger accounting, a merger reserve (credit balance) may arise when the nominal value of the shares acquired exceed the nominal value of the shares issued to acquire them. Conversely, a debit balance may arise.

Under acquisition accounting a share premium account will normally arise when the fair value of the shares issued exceeds their nominal value.

Under s 131 CA 85, however, merger relief may be granted in the holding company's accounts so that no share premium need be recorded in respect of the excess of the fair value of shares issued over assets acquired. In this case, if acquisition accounting is to be adopted, the best accounting practice is to record the investment at fair value and to credit a merger reserve with the difference between the carrying value of the investment and the nominal value of shares issued. In this case, the merger reserve would be consolidated (like any other reserve).

This business combination would appear to qualify under s 131 as:

(i) Over 90% of the nominal value of Vegetables' equity shares has been purchased by Fruit

(ii) The consideration consists of equity shares in Fruit

Under acquisition accounting pre-acquisition retained earnings are not consolidated, whereas in merger accounting the distinction is irrelevant. Consolidated reserves are also adjusted for the extra or reduced depreciation arising on assets restated at fair values, adjustments to profits or losses on disposal of such assets and the amortisation of goodwill. Tax charges also require adjustment.

50 BACUP

Tutor's hint. As in all questions of this nature, lay out the proforma balance sheet first, fill in the easy numbers and then lay out neat workings for the harder figures, cross-referencing them to the balance sheet as you slot the figures in.

Examiner's comment. In general a well-answered question, although the calculations for goodwill and the treatment of associates caused problems. In part (b), some candidates assumed, wrongly, that a holding company must always support an insolvent subsidiary.

(a) BACUP PLC
BALANCE SHEET AS AT 31 MARCH 20X7

	£'000	£'000
Fixed assets		
Intangible: goodwill (460 – 92) (W2)	368	
Tangible (3,820 + 4,425)	8,245	
Investment in associated undertaking (W3)	409	
		9,022
Current assets		
Stock (2,740 + 1,280 – 40)	3,980	
Debtors (1,960 + 980 – 250)	2,690	
Bank (1,260 + 50 cash in transit)	1,310	
	7,980	

Creditors: amounts falling due within one year		
Creditors (1,620 + 2,870 – 200)	4,290	
Bank overdraft	2,260	
Taxation (400 + 150)	550	
Proposed dividend	500	
Proposed dividend (minority interest) (W4)	40	
	7,640	
Net current assets		340
		9,362
	£'000	£'000
Capital and reserves		
25p ordinary shares fully paid		4,000
Reserves: Share premium		800
Profit and loss account (W7)		4,329
Shareholders' funds		9,129
Minority interest (W6)		233
		9,362

Workings

1 *Group structure*

Bacup —— Rishworth

40%

80%

Townley

2 *Goodwill in Townley*

		£'000
Cost of investment (1.6m shares × 75p)		1,200
Share of net assets acquired		
Ordinary shares	500	
Share premium	125	
Pre-acquisition profits (380 – 80)	300	
	925	
Group share (80%)		740
Goodwill		460
Amortisation (1/5)		92
		368

3 *Investment in associated undertaking*

		£'000	£'000
(i)	*Goodwill*		
	Cost of investment in Rishworth		400
	Net assets at date of acquisition (1.10.X6)	800	
	Less (6/12 × 150)	(75)	
		725	
	Group share (40%)		290
			110
	Amortisation to 31.3.X7 (6/12 × 1/5 × 110)		11
			99

(ii) *Share of net assets of Rishworth*

40% × (net assets – unrealised profit in stock)	
= (40% × 800 – 25) (W5)	310
Plus goodwill unamortised (110 – 11)	99
	409

Note. The investment in the associated company can also be arrived at as follows.

	£'000
Cost	400
Share of post acquisition profit (40% × 150 × 6/12)	30
Goodwill amortisation (as before)	(11)
Unrealised profit in stock (40% × 25)	(10)
	409

4 *Proposed dividend to minority*

	£'000
£200,000 × 20% =	40

5 *Unrealised profit*

	£'000	%
Bacup purchases		
Sales	200	125
Cost of sales	160	100
Profit	40	25
Rishworth purchases		
Sales	125	125
Cost of sales	100	100
Profit	25	25

6 *Minority interest*

	£'000
Net assets per question	1,405
Less: unrealised profit (W5)	(40)
accounting policy adj (development expenditure)	(200)
	1,165
Minority interest (20%)	233

7 *Reserves*

	Bacup	*Townley*	*Rishworth*
Per question	4,060	780	600
Less: unrealised profit (W5)		(40)	
(25 × 40%)	(10)		
development expenditure		(200)	
pre acquisition (380 – 80)		(300)	(525)
dividend		240	75
(200 × 80%)	160		
Share of post acquisition			
(240 × 80%)	192		
(75 × 40%)	30		
Less: goodwill amortisation (W2: 92 + 11)	(103)		
	4,329		

(b) (i) **Credit control uses**

The usefulness of the group balance sheet for assessing the creditworthiness of Townley plc is limited because the group does not possess a **separate legal identity** and therefore only the financial statements of Townley itself *as an entity* are relevant. Only the assets of Townley are available to the **creditors** of that company, *not* those of the entire group.

The group financial statements are intended to show the results of the group as a single entity **only for reporting purposes.**

It may be that the holding company has given a **guarantee** of financial support to banks or other creditors who have dealings with a subsidiary. Alternatively, the holding company may decide to support a subsidiary in financial difficulties for the purposes of good **public relations** (although there is **no legal obligation** to do so), in order to maintain the goodwill of the group.

(ii) **Further investigations recommended**

Nordern Manufacturing plc should make the following investigations.

(1) Calculate appropriate **financial ratios** using the accounts of Townley plc. (Townley appears to be in an illiquid position.)

(2) Obtaining **traders**' references and **bankers**' references.

(3) Request that the holding company does underwrite dealings with Townley.

(4) Ensure that goods are only sold **subject to payment** with order on stage payments.

(5) Consider the supply of goods subject to '**reservation of title**'.

(6) Sell the goods to Bacup who would then deal with Townley **intra group**.

51 REN

Tutor's hint. The tricky aspect here is the treatment of the pre-acquisition dividends, which is tested both as a written question and as a computational question.

Examiner's comment. Candidates generally performed quite well on part (a) of this question. However, many ignored the difficult areas, namely the treatment of the pre-acquisition dividend and the premium on the issue of the preference shares. Part (b) on the treatment of pre-acquisition dividends was well answered, even by those candidates who did not get this aspect right in part (a).

(a) REN GROUP PLC
CONSOLIDATED BALANCE SHEET AS AT 31 MAY 20X6

	£'000	£'000
Fixed assets		
Tangible assets (W10)		30,580
Investment in associate (W9)		2,700
		33,280
Current assets		
Stocks	4,622	
Debtors (W11)	2,731	
Cash at bank and in hand	997	
	8,350	
Creditors: amounts falling due within one year (W12)	3,362	
Net current assets		4,988
Total assets less current liabilities		38,268
Creditors: amounts falling due after one year		6,820
		31,448
Capital and reserves		
Share capital		20,000
Share premium		4,950
Profit and loss account (W7)		1,560
		26,510
Minority interest (W8): equity	2,110	
non-equity	2,828	
		4,938
		31,448

Workings

1 *Group structure*

```
                30%
Ren plc ——— Malic Ltd
   |        80% ordinary + 30% preference
   |
Sino plc
```

2 *Preference shares*

	£'000
Total payments	
Terminal (4,000 × 1.10)	4,400
Dividend (4,000 × 7% × 10 yrs)	2,800
	7,200
Original cash inflow	(4,000)
Total finance charge	3,200
Actual finance charge per annum	320
Posted through Sino accounts (4,000 ×7%)	280
Adj	40

3 *Dividend income*

	£'000
Ordinary (8,000 × £0.01 × 80%)	64
Preference (4,000 × 7% × 30%)	84
	148

4 *Goodwill*

Sino plc	£'000	£'000
Cost of investment		13,200
Less: pre acquisition dividend (W3)		(148)
		13,052
For:		
Preference shares (30% × 4,000)		(1,200)
Ordinary shares	8,000	
Share premium	350	
P/L reserve	3,000	
	11,350	
	× 80%	(9,080)
Goodwill at acquisition		2,772
Fully amortised		(2,772)
		Nil

Malic Ltd	£'000	£'000
Cost of investment		3,000
For: share capital	5,000	
fair value adj (9,000 – 5,000)	4,000	
	9,000	
	× 30%	(2,700)
Goodwill at acquisition		300
Fully amortised		(300)
		Nil

5 *Unrealised profit*

	£'000	%
Proceeds	2,400	120
Net book value	2,000	100
	400	20

6 *Depreciation adj*

	£'000
Ren plc has charged (2,400 × 20%)	480
Original charge (2,000 × 20%)	400
Excess depreciation	80

7 *Profit and loss account*

	Ren	*Sino*	*Malic*
	£	£	£
Per question	5,328	2,640	Nil
Pre acquisition dividend (W3)	(148)		
Excess depreciation (W6)	80		
Preference share adj (W2)		(40)	
Dividend due to Ren (40 × 30%)	12		
Unrealised profit (W5)		(400)	
Pre acquisition		(3,000)	(Nil)
		(800)	Nil
Share of post acquisition losses			
(800 × 80%)	(640)		
Goodwill amortisation - Sino (W4)	(2,772)		
- Malic (W4)	(300)		
	1,560		

8 *Minority interest*

	£'000	£'000
Equity		
Share capital	8,000	
Share premium	350	
Profit and loss account (2,640 – 40)	2,600	
	10,950	
× 20%		2,190
Less intercompany profit		80
		2,110
Non equity		
Preference shares	4,000	
Premium on redemption	40	
	4,040	
× 70%		2,828
		4,938

9 *Investment in associate*

	£'000
Cost of investment	3,000
Share of fair value of investments acquired (30% × 9,000)	2,700
Goodwill	300

As the goodwill has been amortised, the investment in associate in the consolidated balance sheet will be the share of net assets at fair value, ie £2,700,000.

10 *Tangible fixed assets*

	£'000
Ren	16,400
Less intercompany profit	(400)
Add back excess depreciation	80
	16,080
Sino	14,500
	30,580

11 *Debtors*

	£'000
Ren	2,036
Sino	1,195
Less intercompany	(500)
	2,731

12 *Creditors: amounts falling due within one year*

	£'000
Ren	2,502
Sino	1,360
Less intercompany	(500)
	3,362

(b) **Treatment of dividends received ex pre acquisition profits**

Generally, a **dividend** paid out of **pre-acquisition profits** should be applied to **reduce the cost of the investment** in the balance sheet of the holding company. It should not be treated as realised profit.

The thinking behind this is that the holding company cannot credit the dividend to profit because **no profit has been made**. The holding company was willing to pay 'over the odds' for its investment in the presumption that part of its cost would be immediately re-paid. When the dividend is paid, this presumption must be pursued to its conclusion by treating the dividend as a reduction of the cost of investment or a return of capital.

However, this accounting treatment is **no longer a legal requirement**, and it is possible to argue that, provided the investment will eventually recover the value that has been removed from it by the distribution, then it is unnecessary to write it down and the dividend to the holding company may be distributed. This implies that, provided the level of profits made by the subsidiary is to be maintained, those profits may be distributed by the holding company.

According to FRS 6 *Acquisitions and mergers,* a dividend must be applied to reduce the carrying value of the investment in a subsidiary only to the extent that this is necessary to provide for any diminution in value. Any other amount is realised profit in the hands of the parent company.

Marking guide

			Marks
(a)	Cost of control (ie goodwill calculation)	5	
	Profit/loss account - Sino plc	3	
	Minority interest	3	
	Group profit/loss account	3	
	Share premium account Sino plc	1	
	Pre-acquisition dividend	2	
	Inter company profit	2	
	Inter company debt	1	
	Associated company	2	
	Equity v non equity interests	2	
	Stock, cash, creditors more than 1 year	1	
	Share capital/share premium of group	1	
	Available	26	
	Maximum		21
(b)	Reduce cost of investment	1	
	Return of capital	1	
	Treat as realised profit	1	
	Diminution in value of investment	1	
	FRS 6 position	2	
	Available	6	
	Maximum		4
	Total maximum		25

52 JASMIN

Tutor's hint. Make sure you work out the group structure properly. If you have problems in dealing with associated companies, learn how to do it now - this is something that students often have problems with in the exam.

Examiner's comment. Part (a) was well answered. In part (b), many candidates correctly identified the status of the companies, but did not know how to treat an associated company in the consolidated accounts. Part (c) was very poorly answered.

(a) **Conditions for exclusion from consolidation**

FRS 2 *Accounting for subsidiary undertakings* states that a subsidiary must be excluded from consolidation in the following circumstances.

(i) **Severe long-term restrictions** are substantially hindering the exercise of the parent's rights over the subsidiary's assets or management.

(ii) The group's interest in the subsidiary's undertaking is held exclusively with a view to **subsequent resale** *and* the subsidiary has not been consolidated previously.

(iii) The subsidiary undertaking's **activities are so different** from those of other undertakings to be included in the consolidation that its inclusion would be incompatible with the obligation to give a true and fair view.

The FRS requires the circumstances in which subsidiary undertakings are to be excluded from consolidation to be interpreted strictly.

The Companies Act 1985 allows an additional ground for exclusion, namely that the information cannot be obtained 'without disproportionate expense or undue delay', but this is not allowed by FRS 2.

The directors of Jasmin (Holdings) plc have no grounds under FRS 2 for excluding Kasbah plc from consolidation. The activities of Kasbah plc are not materially different from those of Jasmin (Holdings) plc, in fact they are quite similar. It is apparent that the real reason the directors of Jasmin (Holdings) plc wish to exclude this subsidiary is because it is making losses: this is not sufficient reason under FRS 2.

(b) JASMIN (HOLDINGS) GROUP PLC
CONSOLIDATED BALANCE SHEET AS AT 31 MARCH 20X4

	£'000	£'000
Fixed assets		
Tangible fixed assets (W2)		379,400
Intangible fixed assets (W3)		30,640
Investment in associate (W9)		8,438
		418,478
Current assets		
Stocks (285,600 + 151,400 – 300 (W4))	436,700	
Cash (319,000 + 500)	319,500	
	756,200	
Creditors due in under one year		
(289,600 + 238,500)	528,100	
Net current assets		228,100
Total assets less current liabilities		646,578
Capital and reserves		
Share capital: £1 ordinary shares		60,000
Revaluation reserve (W8)		39,584
Profit and loss account (W7)		543,854
		643,438
Minority interests (W6)		3,140
		646,578

Workings

1 *Group structure*

(a) *Kasbah plc*

Jasmin (Holdings) plc owns 90% of the ordinary shares of Kasbah plc, so Kasbah is a subsidiary of Jasmin. Jasmin also owns 20% of the 10% preference shares of Kasbah.

(b) *Fortran plc*

	Jasmin	*Others*	*Total*
Shares			
'A' shares	80%	20%	100%
	4,800,000	1,200,000	6,000,000
'B' shares	10%	90%	100%
	400,000	3,600,000	4,000,000
Overall	52%	48%	100%
	5,200,000	4,800,000	10,000,000
Votes			
'A' shares	4,800,000	1,200,000	6,000,000
'B' shares	800,000	7,200,000	8,000,000
Overall	5,600,000	8,400,000	14,000,000
%	40%	60%	100%

Fortran plc should be classified as an associate because Jasmin (Holdings) plc does not control over 50% of the voting power in the company. However, Jasmin (Holdings) plc is entitled to 52% of the profits of Fortran plc, so the calculation of profits and losses attributable to the shares is based on this amount.

2 *Tangible fixed assets*

	£'000
Jasmin	289,400
Kasbah	91,800
Impairment (W5)	(1,800)
	379,400

3 *Goodwill*

	£'000	£'000
Kasbah		
Cost of investment		
- ordinary shares		96,000
- preference shares		1,600
For:		
Preference shares (20% × 4,000)		(800)
Ordinary shares	20,000	
Profit and loss	45,000	
	65,000	
	× 90%	(58,500)
Goodwill at acquisition		38,300
Amortisation (1/5 × 38,300)		(7,660)
Goodwill at balance sheet date		30,640

	£'000	£'000
Fortran		
Cost of investment		8,000
For:		
Share capital	10,000	
Revaluation reserve	2,000	
Profit and loss reserve	1,600	
	13,600	
	× 52%	(7,072)
Goodwill at acquisition		928
Amortisation (1/5 × 928)		(186)
Goodwill at balance sheet date		742

4 *Unrealised profit*

	£'000	%
Sales	1,200	133 $^1/_3$
Cost of sales	900	100
Profit	300	133 $^1/_3$

5 *Revaluation of Kasbah's fixed assets*

	£'000
Market value at 31.3.X4	90,000
Net book value at 31.3.X4	91,800
Impairment taken to profit and loss account	(1,800)

6 *Minority interest*

	£'000
Net assets at 31.3.X4	5,200
Less: impairment of fixed assets (W4)	(1,800)
	3,400

	£'000
Minority interest	
Preference (4,000 × 80%)	3,200
Ordinary ((3,400 – 4,000) × 10%)	(60)
	3,140

7 *Profit and loss reserve*

	Jasmin	*Kasbah*	*Fortran*
	£'000	£'000	£'000
Per question	610,000	(18,800)	3,600
Less: unrealised profit (W4)	(300)		
Impairment (W5)		(1,800)	
Pre acquisition profits		(45,000)	(1,600)
		(65,000)	2,000
Share of post acquisition profits			
((65,600) × 90%)	(59,040)		
(2,000 × 52%)	1,040		
Less goodwill amortisation (W3)			
(7,660 + 186)	(7,846)		
	543,854		

8 *Revaluation reserve*

	Jasmin	*Fortran*
	£'000	£'000
Per question	40,000	1,200
Pre acquisition		(2,000)
		(800)
Share of post acquisition ((800) × 52%)	(416)	
	39,584	

9 *Investment in associate*

	£'000
Net assets per question	14,800
Group share (52% × 14,800)	7,696
Unamortised goodwill (W3)	742
	8,438

(c) **Impact of losses**

The impact of the substantial losses at Kasbah plc may require the value of Jasmin's holding in Kasbah to be written down. This would reflect any **impairment** of the investment (according to FRS 11 *Impairment of fixed assets and goodwill:* see *Updating Notes*). This would also apply to the goodwill figure in the group accounts. The question may also arise as to whether Kasbah plc is still a **going concern**, and consequently on what basis the company's accounts should be prepared and whether group support of the company may be necessary.

53 AUGMENT PLC

Tutor's hint. The examiner is likely to examine the more recent standards. FRS 10 is a fairly straightforward standard and should not have caused you many problems. The treatment of negative goodwill may have caught you out as too may the consolidation of a joint venture. If they did then you need to revise these areas. Joint ventures are included in consolidated financial statements using the gross equity method.

Examiner's comments. The journals in part (a) were well done in most cases. A few candidates did not answer this section though. The consolidation in part (b) was also well answered. Difficulties arose in the treatment of goodwill and the consolidation of the joint venture. Candidates were aware of how goodwill may arise in part (c) but less confident describing its treatment.

(a) *Journal entries*

		£'000	£'000
DEBIT	Investment in Caldershaw Ltd	24,000	
CREDIT	8% debenture loans		14,000
CREDIT	Ordinary shares of £1		4,000
CREDIT	Share premium		6,000
DEBIT	Investments in Debut Ltd	18,750	
CREDIT	Ordinary shares of £1		7,500
CREDIT	Share premium		11,250

Workings

1 *Caldershaw Ltd*

	£'000
Consideration	
8% debenture loans	14,000
Ordinary shares (4m @ £2.50) being	
Ordinary share capital (4m × £1)	4,000
Share premium (4m × £1.50)	6,000
(12 × £2m profit)	24,000

2 *Debut Ltd*

	£'000
Consideration (7.5m × £2.50) being	
Ordinary share capital (7.5m × £1)	7,500
Share premium (7.5 × £1.50)	11,250
(£37.5m/2)	18,750

(b) AUGMENT PLC
CONSOLIDATED BALANCE SHEET AS AT 30 SEPTEMBER 20X8

	£'000	£'000
Fixed assets		
Intangible fixed assets		
Negative goodwill (W5)		(1,920)
Tangible fixed assets (34,260 + 27,000)		61,260
Investment in joint venture		
Ownership of gross assets (W4)	26,680	
Ownership of gross liabilities (14,860/2)	(7,430)	
		19,250
		78,590
Current assets		
Stocks (9,640 + 7,200 – 250) (W2)	16,590	
Trade debtors (11,200 + 5,060 – 1,250)	15,010	
Cash (3,410 + 1,250)	4,660	
	36,260	
Creditors falling due within one year		
Trade creditors (13,120 + 5,270)	18,390	
Overdraft	1,540	
Taxation (5,640 + 2,400)	8,040	
Proposed dividend	4,000	
	31,970	
Net current assets		4,290
Creditors falling due after one year		
8% debentures		(14,000)
Net assets		68,880

	£'000	£'000
Capital and reserves		
Ordinary shares of £1 each (W1)		21,500
Share premium (6,000 + 11,250) (from part (a))		17,250
Profit and loss account (W6)		30,130
		68,880

Workings

1

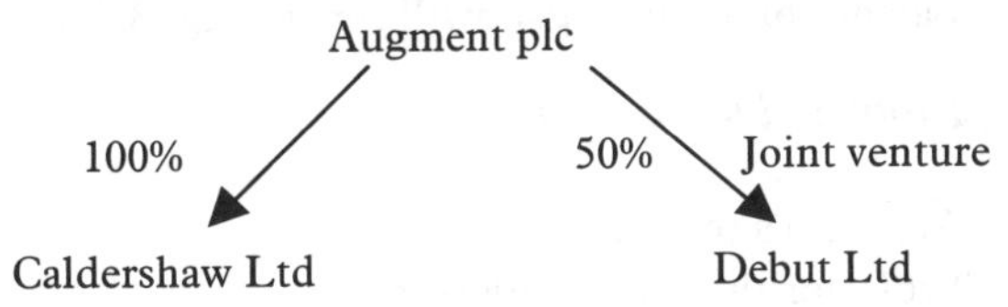

		£'000
Share issues (from (a))	Caldershaw	4,000
	Debut	7,500
	Existing	10,000
		21,500

2 *PURP*

$$£1{,}250{,}000 \times \frac{25}{125} = £250{,}000$$

3 *Investments*

	£'000	£'000
Caldershaw Ltd		
Consideration (from (a))		24,000
Assets acquired		
Share capital	20,000	
Pre acquisition profits (15,000 – 8,000)	7,000	
		(27,000)
Negative goodwill		(3,000)
Debut Ltd		
Consideration (from (a))		18,750
Assets acquired		
Share capital (25,000 × 50%)	12,500	
Pre acquisition profits (4,500 – 2,000 @ 50%)	1,250	
		13,750
Goodwill		5,000

4 *Gross assets in joint venture*

	£'000
Half share in fixed assets (21,060 × 50%)	10,530
Half share in current assets (23,300 × 50%)	11,650
Goodwill (5,000 – 500)	4,500
	26,680

5 *Treatment of negative goodwill*

	£'000	£'000
From (W4)		3,000
Non-monetary assets		
Fixed assets	24,000	
Stocks	6,000	
	30,000	

Apportionment

$\frac{3,000}{30,000} = 10\%$

All stocks sold (6,000 × 10%)	600
Depreciation on fixed assets (24,000/5 × 10%)	480
Negative goodwill recognised for the year	1,080
Balance of negative goodwill remaining (3,000 – 1,080)	1,920

6 *Profit and loss account*

	£'000
Augment's reserves	20,800
Profit for the year: Caldershaw	8,000
Debut (2,000/2)	1,000
Stock PURP	(250)
Amortisation of goodwill	(500)
Negative goodwill recognised	1,080
	30,130

7 *Profit and loss – alternative working*

	Augment	*Caldershaw*	*Debut*
	£'000	£'000	£'000
Per question	20,800	15,000	4,500
PURP on stock (W2)	(250)		
Pre question		(7,000)	(2,500)
		8,000	2,000
Share of post acquisition			
Caldershaw (8,000 × 100%)	8,000		
Debut (2,000 ×50%)	1,000		
Amortisation of goodwill	(500)		
Write back of negative goodwill	1,080		
	30,130		

(c) **Negative goodwill – scenarios and treatments**

Negative goodwill arises during the purchase of a business when the consideration paid is below the fair value of the net assets of the business.

The reason for the consideration being lower may be that the business is very specialised and so there are few potential buyers. The business may be in difficulties with poor cashflows for instance and it may require a quick sale in order to turn it around. It may well be that the acquirer has developed a strong competitive edge and therefore not to sell could see the business suffering heavy losses and so falling in value anyway, therefore it is beneficial to the owner to sell at a loss.

FRS 10 *Goodwill and intangible assets* states that the assets of the acquisition should be reviewed for impairment and the liabilities checked for overstatement. Any remaining negative goodwill should be shown in the top half of the balance sheet as a negative asset in intangible fixed assets.

This negative goodwill should be credited to the profit and loss whenever any non-monetary asset acquired in the deal is depreciated or sold.

54 PREPARATION QUESTION: CHANGING PRICES

> **Tutor's hint**. In this question the current cost adjustments are given to you but you must understand how they are calculated.

(a) CURRENT COST OPERATING PROFIT FOR 20X6

	£m	£m
Historical cost operating profit		15
Current cost adjustments:		
Depreciation adjustment	3	
Cost of sales adjustment	5	
		(8)
Current cost operating profit		7

SUMMARISED CURRENT COST BALANCE SHEET
AS AT 31 DECEMBER 20X6

	£m	£m
Fixed assets		85
Current assets		
Stocks	21	
Debtors	30	
Bank	2	
	53	
Current liabilities	30	
		23
		108
Long-term liability		(20)
		88
Capital and reserves		88

(b) (i) **Interest cover**

HC accounts: 15 ÷ 3 = 5 times
CC accounts: 7 ÷ 3 = 2.3 times

(ii) **Return on shareholders' equity**

HC accounts: 12 ÷ 62 = 19.4%
CC accounts: 4 ÷ 88 = 4.5%

(iii) **Debt/equity ratio**

HC accounts: 20 ÷ 62 = 32.3%
CC accounts: 20 ÷ 88 = 22.7%

(c) (i) **Interest cover**

Companies must maintain their capital base if they wish to stay in business. The significance of the interest cover calculation is that it indicates the extent to which profits after tax are being eaten into by payments to finance external capital. The figures calculated above indicate that only one-fifth of historical cost profit is being absorbed in this way, while four-fifths are being retained to finance future growth. On the face of it, this might seem satisfactory; however, the current cost interest cover is only 2.3 times indicating that, after allowing for the impact of rising prices, interest payments absorb nearly half of profits after tax.

(ii) **Return on shareholders' equity**

This is the ratio of profits earned for shareholders (ie profits after interest) to shareholders' equity. Once again, the position disclosed by the historical cost accounts is more favourable than appears from the current cost ratio. The historical cost profit is higher than the current cost profit because no allowance is made for the adverse impact of rising prices; and at the same time the denominator in the historical cost fraction is lower because shareholders' capital is stated at historical values rather than their higher current values.

The significance of the ratio is that it enables shareholders to assess the rate of return on their investment and to compare it with alternative investments that might be available to them.

(iii) **Debt/equity ratio**

The significance of this ratio is as a measure of the extent to which the company's net assets are financed by external borrowing and shareholders' funds respectively.

In times of rising prices it can be beneficial to finance assets from loan capital. While the assets appreciate in value over time (and the gain accrues to shareholders), the liability is fixed in monetary amount. The effect of this is that current cost accounts tend to give a more favourable picture of the debt/equity ratio than historical cost accounts. In the ratios calculated above, the amount of debt is £20m in both balance sheets. This represents nearly one-third of the historical cost value of shareholders' funds, but only one-fifth of the equity calculated on a current cost basis.

55 RECOST

> **Tutor's hint**. This question covered an area ignored by many students. Part (a) should not have presented too many problems as HCA is familiar territory. If you knew your stuff you could pass the remaining two sections. The figures in part (c) were pretty straightforward.
>
> **Examiner's comments**. This was not a popular question. Some candidates appeared to have opted for this question as they were weak on computational questions. Answers were either very good or poor. Parts (a) and (b) were badly answered. Part (c) was even worse. Answers failed to display an understanding of HCA and the two alternatives. Aspects of the alternative answers were confused and answers were far too short.

(a) Historic cost accounts (HCAs) state the value of items at the time of acquisition and as a result have a number of limitations when used to assess an entity's performance. The items affected in the primary statements are as follows.

Balance sheet

There are a number of non-monetary items in the balance sheet which will potentially be stated at a misleading value.

(i) **Fixed assets.** Many fixed assets are held in use for a number of years. The most obvious example is land and buildings which are likely to have been purchased when the entity came into being. Generally the current value of land and buildings will be higher than the historic cost.

(ii) **Current assets.** Most current assets are monetary and due to their liquid nature should not present any great limitations. Stock can be a significant exception depending on the value held and the rate of turnover. An entity may have bought great quantities of stock at a time when the market was depressed and its current value may far exceed that stated.

(iii) **Liabilities.** Again current liabilities are monetary and so present no issue. Long term liabilities may be an issue if, say, they are fixed rate and the current rate is significantly different.

Profit and loss account

The limitations of the historic cost profit and loss account stem mainly from balance sheet items.

(i) **Cost of sales**. The adjustments made due to opening and closing stock levels introduce potentially out of date items to the profit and loss account.

(ii) **Depreciation and amortisation**. These charges are made on relatively old items. Understated fixed asset costs are mingled with current costs.

General criticisms

As a result of the effect of historic cost accounting on the above items a number of criticisms can be made of HCA. In times of greater economic volatility (ie high inflation) the limitations are more pronounced.

Relevant costs

HCAs effectively mix a number of different values together. Depreciation on a forty year old building is charged to the same profit and loss account as expenditure made on heat and light in the current year. This ultimately means that profit is made up of varying values and is therefore not a consistent measure.

Comparability

Following on from the above, the variations in the costs recorded may be even more pronounced from year to year and from company to company. In theory, two very similar competitors may have very different HCAs as one of them was relocated at minimal cost in recent years. The land and buildings values, although identical at current value, would be stated at different values in the balance sheet.

Users of the accounts

Users of the accounts may be misled by HCAs.

(i) **Shareholders**. If the fixed assets are understated then so too are shareholder funds. A lower asset base will actually appear favourable as proportionately more profit is generated by each £1 invested.

(ii) **Long-term lenders**. If a long term lender were to use HCAs to assess the security for a loan the likely result would be that the current asset values would be far in excess of the balance sheet values.

(iii) **Employees**. Profits may not reflect the true costs of fixed assets or cost of sales. This would lead employees to demand higher wage increases.

Note. You may have used other user groups in your answer. As long as the user group and matching example were valid then you would get the marks.

(b) **Current purchasing power (CPP)**

The advantages of CPP are as follows.

(i) Comparability is enhanced. The asset values and results of one company can be compared with another, as can year on year results (provided comparatives are restated).

(ii) Valuation is objective as a single price index is used.

(iii) CPP provides a stable monetary unit with which to value assets and profits.

(iv) As profit is stated at a current value it is easier to forecast future results.

(v) CPP is based on historical cost so raw data can easily be obtained and verified.

The criticisms of CPP are as follows.

(i) Generalised purchasing power as measured by the retail price index is a theoretical tool. It does not exist in reality.

(ii) By using indices, approximations will be needed to measure value.

(iii) The assets in a CPP balance sheet are less relevant than those in a current value balance sheet.

Current cost accounting (CCA)

The advantages of CCA are as follows.

(i) As holding gains are excluded from profit users can readily see whether a dividend will reduce the operating capability of a business.

(ii) Management are required to value assets whilst considering future economic benefit and opportunity cost. CCA is a useful tool for management in deciding whether to retain or sell assets.

(iii) CCA can be implemented fairly easily by using historic cost as a base and making adjustments.

(iv) CCA is relevant to users of accounts as it highlights management's ability to maintain and increase the overall value of the business. Users can also assess the future prospects of business more readily.

The criticisms of CCA are as follows.

(i) The valuations made are subjective.

(ii) Assets are valued on an individual basis at economic value, net realisable value or replacement cost. This mixture of values may lead to misleading overall asset value.

(iii) The estimate of replacement cost is problematic. Depreciation based on this value does not necessarily spread the cost of the asset over its estimated life. Neither can it be a means of providing sufficient funds for replacement as technology and the business environment are too dynamic to allow for accurate valuation, so the depreciation charged is for the maintenance of the assets in place at the balance sheet date.

(iv) Deprival value is an unrealistic theoretical device as the entity is not deprived of the asset it merely estimates the effect deprival would have.

(c) (i) **Turnover**

Using the general price measure the change in turnover is as follows.

	£'000
Adjusted 20X7 turnover £18.2m @ RPI of 1.1 =	20,020
20X8 turnover	(19,965)
Decrease	55
Expressed as a percentage	0.3%

Using specific price measures the change in turnover is as follows.

	£'000
Adjusted 20X7 turnover £18.2m @ 0.95	17,290
20X8 turnover	(19,965)
Increase	2,675
Expressed as a percentage	15.47%

Note. The 20X7 turnover would be 5% less as selling price has fallen by this much in 20X8.

(ii) **Current cost earnings per share**

	£'000
Net profit (HCA)	3,200
Increase to cost of sales (14.7 – 13.1)	(1,600)
Increase to depreciation (2,000 – 1,500)	(500)
Current cost earnings	1,100
Current cost EPS (1,100/40,000)	2.75p

Note. The figures for cost of sales and depreciation are given in points (ii) and (iii) of the question.

(iii) **Current cost return on capital employed**

Adjustments are required for the return and the capital figures.

	£'000
Return	
Current cost earnings (see above)	1,100
Add back: taxation	300
interest	200
	1,600
Capital	
Fixed assets ((iii) in the question)	20,000
Current assets (10,000 + 500)	10,500
Current liabilities	(5,000)
	25,500
ROCE (1,600/25,500 × 100%)	6.3%

56 ACCOUNTING THEORIES

Tutor's hint. Students often find discussion questions most difficult - there is often a great tendency to waffle.

Prizewinners' points. Most of the marks in this question (13 out of 25) are for a discussion of two rather obscure and theoretical topics. You should not attempt a question like this unless you are confident on the subject (if you are given a choice!).

Other points. Even if you are uncertain about these topics, it would be good revision for you to read through this solution.

Examiner's comment. Candidates who had read articles in the *Students' Newsletter* performed well. In part (b), credit was given for points of relevance that were not in the model answer. In part (c), candidates could have produced reasonable answers to this question if they had simply thought of the advantages and disadvantages of any conceptual framework or document.

(a) (i) **Agency theory**

Agency theory is concerned with the **contractual relationships between members of a company**. The theory assumes that the 'team members' in a company are rational economic persons motivated solely by self-interest. But the individual's well-being depends not only on the well-being of the rest of the team, but also the team's performance in competition with other teams. Each group with an interest in the company acts in a way to maximise the position of their group.

The **company** is thus seen as a **set of contracts among the different factors of production**: each contract recognises the rights of different agents. What this theory at least partly attempts to explain is why companies sometimes take decisions which do not seem to conform to the expectations of **maximising**

shareholder wealth. For example the agents may award themselves large salary increases not commensurate with performance.

As far as choice of accounting policy is concerned, one effect of an 'agency theory' attitude is to encourage 'creative accounting'. As an interest group, the directors are in a position to control the way a company's results are presented to another interest group, for example shareholders and creditors. They will obviously wish to present those results in a flattering light. As regards development of accounting standards, for the same reason, directors may wish to encourage those standards which allow flexibility and discourage those standards which do not.

(ii) **Positive accounting theory**

Positive, or descriptive, concepts are based on an approach which is essentially concerned with **what accountants do in practice**. Observations are made and general conclusions are drawn from these observations to develop a theory. In effect, the observer will look for similarity of treatment. Once sufficient instances have occurred, assurance is gained to the extent that a theory can be developed about the practice in question.

The theory thus developed allows explanations and predictions to be made about accountants' behaviour, particularly about how specified items will be treated.

The basic concepts underlying this approach define assets, liabilities, capital, revenue, expenses, income and transactions. The descriptions are very much based on the way each of these items would arise in practice, for example, **liabilities** are the debts of the business.

The belief which underlies the positive approach is that the objective of financial statements is to **report on the stewardship aspect of the management** role, and thus a report by the directors to the shareholders on the utilisation of the assets of the business is required. The ASC used the descriptive approach in the development of many of their accounting standards.

When it comes to choice of accounting policy, **positive accounting theory** takes a '**real world**' approach, taking into account such factors as the political sensitivity of the enterprise. For example, it is important for such companies as British Gas not to be seen to be making too much profit, hence the accounting policies chosen will be ones which give a low profit figure or low profitability ratios.

As regards accounting standards, positive accounting theory would suggest a similarly realistic approach: potential accounting standards should be tested by soliciting the reactions of real companies, and reactions to accounting standards already issued should be evaluated.

(b) **Impact of accountancy research**

It has often been said that academic research on accountancy is of little use to an accountancy practitioner. When faced with a problem relating to a client's accounts, the practitioner is unlikely to look to an academic journal for guidance.

However, the fact that accountancy research has no **immediate** relevance does not necessarily mean that it is not important in the long term. Research does not aim to answer a specific practical problem but, arguably to aid our understanding so that in the long term solutions will be available for a range of problems.

The ASB, in producing such documents as the *Statement of Principles* might be seen as a 'go between', bringing together academic research and accounting practice. Without a sound academic and theoretical background, the *Statement of Principles* could not have been produced; in turn the *Statement*, by means of financial reporting standards, has a direct impact on the work done in accounting practice.

However, there does indeed seem to be a gulf between academic research and accounting practice. This may be a result of the personalities and/or educational background of the types of people who make a career in these two fields. Academics could do something to bridge the gap by endeavouring to make their research more intelligible to the professional accountant.

(c) **Merits of ASB's SOP**

The **merits of the ASB's Statement of Principles** should, ideally, be summarised in its objective, which is given in the *Foreword to Accounting Standards*:

> 'to provide a framework for the consistent and logical formulation of individual accounting standards (and to provide) a basis on which others can exercise judgement in resolving accounting issues.'

The following points may be made in favour of the *Statement of Principles.*

(i) The principles have in fact been **used in the formulation of standards**, for example its definitions of assets and liabilities have been used in FRS 5 *Reporting the substance of transactions*.

(ii) The *Statement* helps **reduce scope for individual judgement** and the potential subjectivity that this implies.

(iii) **Financial statements should be more comparable** because, although alternative treatments will still be available, there will be a consistent and coherent framework on which to base one's choice of a particular alternative.

(iv) The *Statement* puts forward a **consistent terminology** and consistent objectives, for example in the definitions and the qualitative characteristics.

It could be argued that the *Statement of Principles* is too theoretical. It is certainly general rather than particular. However, as has been seen with FRS 5, the general principles can be applied to very specific issues in accounting standards. Moreover, in areas not at present covered by accounting standards, the statement can give general guidance. Nevertheless, in the short term, the principles in the *Statement* may conflict with some accounting standards which had already been issued before it was written. However these are gradually being withdrawn and replaced by new Financial Reporting Standards.

57 PREPARATION QUESTION: ANALYTICAL REVIEW

> **Tutor's hint**. Try not to calculate too many ratios. The question gives a big hint as to those you should provide. Remember however that it is your analysis which is as important as the ratios.

(a)

		20X7	*20X6*	*20X5*	*20X4*	*20X3*
1	Net profit before tax: sales	18.3%	11.1%	14.0%	9.4%	6.9%
2	Net profit before tax: total assets less current liabilities	31.6%	20.8%	28.0%	19.5%	14.7%
3	Working capital ratio	×1.77	×1.68	×1.40	×1.77	×1.65
4	Liquidity ratio	0.60	0.50	0.54	0.68	0.70
5	Sales: fixed assets	×2.65	×3.00	×2.77	×3.54	×3.48
6	Stock turnover (cost of sales:stock ratio)	×1.78	×1.50	×2.03	×2.29	×2.53

		20X7	20X6	20X5	20X4	20X3
7	Debtors collection period (average debtors ÷ sales × 365) (Average debtors taken as average value of opening and closing debtors)	51 days	53 days	62 days	62 days	-
8	Age of stock (average stock ÷ cost of sales × 365)	199 days	198 days	162 days	143 days	-
9	Sales growth (% pa)	21%	35%	18%	16%	-
10	Cost of sales growth (% pa)	25%	16%	11%	15%	-
11	Net profit growth (% pa)	100%	7%	75%	60%	-
12	Plant/machinery growth (% pa)	60%	67%	50%	33%	-
13	Working capital per £1 sales	20p	20p	14p	20p	18p
		20X7	20X6	20X5	20X4	20X3
14	Gearing ratio (debt including overdraft:equity ratio)	90%	130%	60%	89%	126%
15	Gross profit/sales	46%	47%	39%	35%	34%
16	Creditors*/cost of sales × 365	98 days	139 days	174 days	93 days	84 days

*excluding overdraft

(b) (i) **Analysis of the financing proposals**

The company needs some long-term funds, to redeem the debenture stock in 20X9 and to finance further sales growth.

The amount of **extra long-term capital** required is uncertain; £1.5m is needed to redeem the stock. The sales growth has been fairly strong for the last four years, and if similar growth rates continue, the company will need funding for extra working capital and for new fixed assets.

It is perhaps significant that the **percentage growth** in **fixed assets** has been well **in excess of sales growth**, indicating perhaps that the company is having to purchase more expensive equipment to remain competitive. Both gross profit/sales and net profit/sales have improved over the years, indicating that in spite of the growth in fixed assets, profitability is improving (due perhaps to greater productivity).

However, **sales as a proportion of fixed assets** was relatively **low** in 20X7, suggesting perhaps that asset utilisation is below capacity and could be improved, thus reducing the requirement for fixed asset purchases.

The source of **additional long-term capital will be debt capital or equity**. The company's net profits are probably insufficient to provide finance from retained profits, and so extra finance will be needed from debt capital or a new issue of equity.

The company's **financial gearing**, although fluctuating, has been **high**. This raises doubts about whether sufficient debt capital can be raised to meet all the company's finance requirements. Presumably, the existing debentures are secured; a new issue of debentures maturing in 20X9 will also need security. The bank overdraft will probably also be secured by a charge, perhaps a floating charge on the company's stocks and debtors. Plant and machinery does not usually provide good security, and so there would be doubts about whether the company could raise sufficient extra loan capital, because of inadequate security (and excessive gearing).

(ii) **Reasonableness of figures**

The **five-year results** show a continuing growth in sales and profits, with a return and profit ratio currently higher than the industry average.

A comparison with the average statistics for the industry indicates that the **control of working capital** by AB plc is not as good as it might be. Although the company has maintained a fairly steady ratio of working capital per £1 of sales at around 20p, its current ratio and liquidity ratio are lower than the industry average.

In spite of this, **turnover of stock is slower** than the industry average, the average **debt collection period** a little **longer** and the **age of stock greater**. This suggests that the company is taking longer-than-average credit from suppliers, in spite of the improvement in 20X7. The figures therefore suggest that some attention should be given to working capital and cash flow, with a view to improving stock turnover, better credit management and improving liquidity. The stock valuation may not be accurate, which would affect the profit figure.

58 HEYWOOD BOTTLES

Tutor's hint. Remember that the answer should have been in the form of a report.

Examiner's comment. Weak answers to (a) failed to analyse movement in the figures.

REPORT

To: The directors of Heywood Bottles plc
From: Business Consultant
Date: June 20X7
Subject: *Company performance year to 31 March 20X7*

Introduction

This report was commissioned in order to assess the financial performance of Heywood Bottles plc for the year to 31 March 20X7 in the light of the strategic actions taken in April 20X6.

Specific areas addressed include profitability, liquidity and solvency. An appendix sets out the calculations of selected ratios used.

Profitability

(a) Return on capital employed has fallen from 32% (good) to 3.6% (poor).

(b) Strategic actions were intended to increase sales and utilisation of assets at the expense of reduced margins.

(c) Gross profit has declined from 25% to only 10%.

(d) Sales increased by 150%.

(e) Net asset turnover increased from 1.9 times to 5.5 times.

(f) Unfortunately the volume required to recoup lost margins has not been achieved. Overall a net loss has resulted.

(g) Note that the deferred marketing costs have reduced current year losses by £6 million. This is, however, a very questionable accounting technique.

Liquidity and working capital

(a) Current and liquid ratios have deteriorated from 1.8/1.3 to 0.9/0.8.

(b) On average in 20X6 debtors took 76 days to pay which is almost 2 weeks longer than the standard trading terms of 60 days. Increasing the allowed credit period to 90 days has led to a 114 day payment period. This has in turn led to additional financing requirements met from delayed payments to creditors and a change from a credit balance of £8 million at the bank to a £34 million bank overdraft figure.

(c) Stock turnover has improved (7.5 times to 15 times). Delayed creditor payments may mean that suppliers are cutting down on deliveries so the actual volumes of stock may be dangerously low.

Solvency

(a) A marked downturn in liquidity is discussed above.

(b) Gearing levels have deteriorated, with an impact upon interest charges. (Interest cover 10 times 20X6, nil in 20X7).

(c) Extra production has meant increased fixed asset investment, principally through finance leases.

(d) The overdraft has exceeded its limit.

(e) There is little prospect of reducing the level of overdraft.

Conclusions

(a) The company is overtrading and will fail without an immediate injection of new capital.

(b) The board actions in April 20X6 were, with hindsight, disastrous.

(c) Increased turnover and market shares are only worthwhile whilst the company is trading profitably.

(d) It will be very difficult to retain the loyalty of customers if prices are increased and relationships with suppliers and other creditors are severely strained.

APPENDIX

Selected ratios

	Calculation	*20X6*	*Calculation*	*20X7*
ROCE	20/(44 + 19) × 100	31.7%	2/(23 + 32) × 100	3.6%
Net asset turnover	120/63	1.9	300/55	5.5
Fixed asset turnover	120/43	2.8	300/63	4.8
Gross profit margin	30/120 ×100	25%	30/300 × 100	10%
Net profit margin (before interest/tax)	20/120 ×100	16.7%	2/300 × 100	0.7%
Current ratio	45/25	1.8	118/126	0.9
Acid test	33/25	1.3	100/126	0.8
Stock turnover	90/12	7.5 times	270/18	15 times
Debtor days	25/120 × 365	76	94/300 × 365	114
Gearing	19/44 × 100	43%	32/23 × 100	139%
Interest cover*	20/2	10 times	2/10	0.2 times

*(Profit before interest/tax ÷ equity + debt (finance obligations) at year end)

59 CURRENT COST ACCOUNTING AND RATIOS

Tutor's hint. Written questions in Paper 2.5 are not 'soft options'. While you would not be expected to produce as long an answer as ours, you would certainly need to demonstrate a thorough understanding of this difficult topic.

Examiner's comment. In part (a) many candidates did not take account of the fact that the current cost adjustments would affect the profit and loss account items as well as the balance sheet. In part (b) some candidates spoke generally about the limitations of ratio analysis rather than the specific ratios in the question. Part (c) was reasonably well answered.

(a) (i) **Return on capital employed**

The ratio is calculated as:

$$\frac{\text{Profit before interest and tax}}{\text{Long - term capital employed}}$$

If derived from current cost accounts, the ratio would differ from its historical cost equivalent in the following ways.

(1) The numerator would be 'current cost operating profit' and would have been affected by the cost of sales adjustment, the monetary working capital adjustment and the depreciation adjustment, but not the gearing adjustment.

(2) The denominator would reflect capital employed as represented by the current value of the assets rather than the historical cost or revalued amount. Alternatively, from the point of view of shareholders' funds, it would contain a current cost reserve.

(ii) **Stock turnover**

Stock turnover is calculated as:

$$\frac{\text{Cost of sales}}{\text{Year end stock}} \text{ or as } \frac{\text{Stock}}{\text{Cost of sales}} \times 365$$

In either case, the choice of current cost accounting rather than historical cost accounting affects both the numerator and the denominator. The cost of sales figure will include the cost of sales adjustment, and the stock will be valued at current cost.

(iii) **Debtors turnover**

This ratio can be calculated as:

$$\frac{\text{Debtors}}{\text{Credit sales}} \times 365 \text{ or as } \frac{\text{Credit sales}}{\text{Debtors}}$$

In neither case would the ratio be affected by a change from historical cost accounting to current cost accounting. Neither credit sales nor debtors are adjusted in preparing current cost accounts. There is a monetary working capital adjustment, but this affects working capital as a whole, not just debtors.

(iv) **Gearing ratio**

The gearing ratio shows the relationship between debt and equity capital and may be calculated as follows.

$$\frac{\text{Long - term debt and preference share capital}}{\text{Total capital}}$$

The numerator for this fraction would be the same under current cost accounting and historical cost accounting. However, as with ROCE, the figure for total capital will be different, and therefore the result of the ratio calculation will be different.

(b) **Limitations of specified HC ratios**

In general terms, the usefulness of ratios is limited by various factors, the most important being the fact that one is not always comparing like with like. Accounting policies may be used to manipulate a company's results, and this, in turn will affect the ratios. Furthermore, ratios are not always defined in standard form.

(i) **Return on capital employed**

This is a widely used measure of a company's profitability. It is calculated as follows.

$$\frac{\text{Profit before interest and tax}}{\text{Long - term capital employed}}$$

Both the numerator and the denominator of this fraction have problems.

Problems with the 'return' derive from the fact that there are many different ways of arriving at profit before interest and tax. The following are just a few examples.

(1) Depreciation methods used can vary.

(2) Goodwill can be amortised through the profit and loss account over different time scales.

(3) The method of stock valuation used has an effect on profit.

Problems with the 'capital employed' part of the ratio include the following.

(1) A company which revalues its assets will have a higher 'capital employed' figure and have a lower ROCE than one which does not.

(2) Capital employed may be understated by means of off balance sheet financing schemes. However, FRS 5 addresses this issue.

(ii) **Stock turnover**

This ratio is calculated as follows.

$$\frac{\text{Cost of sales}}{\text{Year end stock *}}$$

* per question

Possible problems are as follows.

(1) The year end stock figure may not be representative of the company's normal stockholding.

(2) Different firms might have different stock valuation practices, for example different ways of arriving at cost and net realisable value.

(3) Provisions for obsolete stock can be based on subjective assumptions.

(4) The stock figure may include long term contract balances, which are not always straightforward to calculate.

(5) Variations between firms may exist in the treatment of consignment stock.

(6) The value for cost of goods sold can be calculated in different ways.

(iii) **Debtors turnover**

This ratio suffers from the following limitations.

(1) The ratio is calculated as

$$\frac{\text{Debtors}}{\text{Credit sales}} \times 365$$

Very often the figure for credit sales is not available in the published accounts. Turnover is often used as an approximation for credit sales; this is usually realistic, but may not be.

(2) The debtors figure in the published accounts is net of the provisions for doubtful debts. However, the calculation of such provisions can be subjective.

(3) The debtors figure in published financial statements gives no indication of the age of particular debts, and hence the risk of non payment.

(4) Factoring of debts may distort the picture, particularly where the factor has recourse to the company for bad debts. In the past this meant that the debtors collection period looked better than it really was. However, this distortion should be remedied by FRS 5 *Reporting the substance of transactions* which states that in such circumstances the debts should be shown as an asset of the company.

(5) Year-end debtors may be unrepresentative.

(iv) **Gearing ratio**

The gearing ratio is calculated as:

$$\frac{\text{Prior charge capital (ie debentures and preference shares)}}{\text{Total capital}}$$

This ratio suffers from several limitations.

(1) An arbitrary distinction is made between interest bearing debt and interest free debt. The latter could arguably include money owed to trade creditors, but it does not.

(2) Off balance sheet finance may distort the picture.

(3) It is difficult to determine whether convertible capital instruments should be classed as debt or equity. FRS 4 *Capital instruments* has clarified the issue to some extent, but uncertainties remain.

(4) The denominator in the gearing ratio is affected by the amortisation of goodwill and the revaluation of assets.

(c) **Comments on CC ratios**

In many ways, current cost accounting ratios are a better indicator of a company's performance than ratios which derive from historical cost accounts.

(i) A **drawback of historical cost ratios** highlighted above was the fact that the **numerator and the denominator of a ratio did not match up**. For example, net profit is not expressed in terms of current prices; capital employed is also at historical cost but not necessarily the same historical cost, because assets may have been revalued. If cost of goods sold is compared with year end stock, the comparison may be distorted by the fact that older items of stock are included in cost of goods sold. Both of these problems can be avoided by the use of current cost accounting.

(ii) If current cost accounting is used, the **ROCE figure will provide a much better indication of management's efficiency** in using resources. For example, if asset values and operating costs were based on replacement costs, the ratio would provide an indication of management's ability to generate sufficient funds to replace assets as they are used.

(iii) Current cost accounting shows profit after the operating capacity of a company has been maintained, so **profitability ratios are more meaningful**.

However, some criticisms could be made of ratio analysis based on current cost accounts. These include the following.

(i) The **current cost adjustments** to the profit and loss account have been **criticised**, particularly the monetary working capital adjustment, monetary working capital being difficult to define.

(ii) Current cost accounting depends on **certain assumptions** which **may be subjective**, not least the valuation of assets.

(iii) Current cost accounting is **difficult to understand**, especially for the shareholder or potential investor who is not an accountant. Historical cost accounts and the ratios derived from them are easier to understand, perhaps because we are used to them.

It appears that, for the foreseeable future, most ratio analysis will be on a historical cost basis, but the person performing the analysis should be aware of the limitations of historical cost accounting.

60 OMEGAR

> **Tutor's hint**. You should not have ignored the requirement to calculate alternative versions of the ratios where appropriate. The calculations are fairly straightforward and you should have proceeded briskly to allow plenty of time for the narrative. However, this is a longer question than you would face in an exam.

(a) REPORT ON PERFORMANCE OF OMEGAR PLC

This report analyses the performance of Omegar plc, primarily on the basis of certain ratios, from the point of view of potential equity investors and that of holders of long-term debt. Attached is an appendix showing how the ratios are calculated.

Potential equity investors

The following ratios will be of particular interest to potential equity investors.

(i) Debt/equity
(ii) Earnings per share
(iii) Post tax return on equity
(iv) Price/earnings

(i) **Debt/equity**

The debt/equity ratio is an important indication of the **degree of risk** involved in holding equity shares in a company. Debt generally carries a fixed rate of interest, hence there is a given amount, often large, to be paid out from profits to holders of debt before arriving at a residue available for distribution to the holders of equity. The greater the proportion of debt to equity, the greater the percentage of change in profit available for ordinary shareholders for any given change in profit before interest and tax.

The calculations show that, whether or not the deferred tax provision is taken into account and whether or not intangible assets and the revaluation reserve are excluded, the debt/equity ratio gives little concern to ordinary shareholders, who would only need to worry in the case of a ratio of 50% or more. The ratio has, moreover, remained fairly constant.

The main reason why the **debt/equity ratio** is **not always** a **useful tool** for analysis is that there are **many different ways of calculating it**. Here we have shown two: inclusion or exclusion of the deferred tax provision, intangibles and the revaluation reserve. Other variables include, for example, the inclusion or exclusion of a revaluation reserve from 'shareholders' or the use of 'off balance sheet finance'. It is important that like is compared with like, whether year on year or between companies.

(ii) **Earnings per share**

Earnings per share is widely used by investors as a measure of a company's performance and is of particular importance in **comparing the results of a company over a period of time or comparing the performance of one company's equity shares against the performance of another company's equity**, and also against the returns obtainable from loan stock and other forms of investment.

The calculations show that earnings per share has improved significantly for Omegar plc, whether or not the deferred tax provision is incorporated. The reclassification of reorganisation costs as exceptional does not affect EPS, now that it is calculated on earnings after extraordinary items.

Earnings per share suffers from certain disadvantages as a performance indicator, of which the following are but a few.

(1) The **way** in which **EPS** is **calculated** can **vary**. Should the deferred tax provision be included, for example?

(2) FRS 3 *Reporting financial performance* required that **EPS** be calculated **after extraordinary items** (as now required by FRS 14). The thinking behind this was to avoid manipulation of the figure, but it could be argued that it is misleading to include in the earnings figure an item which is totally unrepresentative of the company's performance. However extraordinary items have been virtually outlawed by FRS 3 so this is no longer a major issue.

(3) The **number of shares issued** by a company **varies widely**; the variation in earnings per share may therefore have little to do with the financial health of the companies concerned.

(iii) **Post tax return on equity**

This ratio relates profits to the amount of funds (capital) that were employed in making the profits. It is an indication of the **efficiency** or otherwise with which the company has **managed its resources**.

The figures show a comfortable post tax return on equity, and an increase on previous years.

The ratio suffers as a performance indicator from the fact that there are **different opinions** as to **what constitutes equity**.

(iv) **Price/earnings**

The price/earnings ratio is the ratio of a company's current share price to the earnings per share. A high P/E ratio indicates strong shareholder confidence in the company and a lower P/E ratio indicates lower confidence.

The **limitations** of this ratio derive largely from those **associated** with **earnings per share**. In addition, share price is not an absolute indicator of company performance but can reflect, for example, the **general state** of the **market**.

In the case of Omegar plc, the P/E ratio has fallen slightly. If full provision is made for deferred taxation, the ratio also falls.

Potential holders of long-term debt

The following ratios are of interest to potential debt holders.

(i) The debt/equity ratio
(ii) The interest cover
(iii) The current ratio

(i) **The debt/equity ratio**

The purpose and limitations of the debt/equity ratio have been discussed above.

The fall in the ratio should be seen in a favourable light by potential long term loan creditors, as a low ratio indicates to them that their debt will not be at risk.

(ii) **Interest cover**

The interest cover ratio shows whether a company is earning enough profits before interest and tax to pay its interest costs comfortably, or whether its interest costs are high in relation to the size of its profits. The calculations show a very favourable interest cover both this year and in the previous year giving no apparent cause for concern.

The ratio has a number of drawbacks as a performance indicator, not least the fact that **interest** is **paid out of cash rather than book profits**, and the interest cover ratio gives **no information** about **cash resources**. Furthermore there are different opinions as to what should be included in both the 'profit' and 'interest' components of the ratio.

(iii) **Current ratio**

The current ratio is the standard test of a company's liquidity. The idea behind this is that a company should have enough current assets that give a promise of '**cash to come**' to meet its future commitments to pay off its current liabilities. Ideally the ratio should be comfortably in excess of 1 although **what is 'comfortable' varies between different types of businesses.**

Omegar plc's current ratio has remained steady. However, it is difficult to say without some idea of the nature of the product manufactured and sold, whether the company is likely to have a problem with **unsaleable stock**.

APPENDIX: RATIO CALCULATIONS BEFORE ADDITIONAL FINANCE

(i) **Current ratio**

$$\frac{\text{Current assets}}{\text{Current liabilities}}$$

1st version

	20X1	*20X0*
$\frac{679 + 511 + 117}{308 + 190 + 80}$	2.3:1	
$\frac{684 + 471 + 80}{336 + 140 + 80}$		2.2:1

2nd version

The ratio can be re-calculated after adjustments have been made to write off the obsolescent stock, stock subject to reservation of title and bad debts and to include contingent liabilities.

	20X1	20X0
$\frac{679-(40+28)+(511-40)+117}{308+190+80+85}$	1.8:1	
$\frac{684-(40+28)+(471-40)+80}{336+140+80+80}$		1.8:1

(ii) **Interest cover**

$\frac{\text{Operating profit}}{\text{Interest payable}}$

1st version

	20X1	20X0
$\frac{698}{55}$	13 times	
$\frac{636}{45}$		14 times

2nd version

Interest can be calculated on the basis of profit before tax, interest and depreciation as follows.

	20X1	20X0
$\frac{698+150}{55}$	15.4 times	
$\frac{636+110}{45}$		16.6 times

(iii) **Debt/equity ratio**

$\frac{\text{Long term debt}}{\text{Capital and reserves}}$

1st version

	20X1	20X0
$\frac{450+100}{1{,}981}$	28%	
$\frac{450}{1{,}608}$		28%

2nd version

This version is after providing for deferred tax and it excludes intangibles and the revaluation reserve.

	20X1	20X0
$\frac{450+100+7}{1{,}981-298-144}$	36%	
$\frac{450+8}{1{,}608-247-144}$		38%

(iv) **Earnings per share**

$\frac{\text{Profit after tax and extraordinary item}}{\text{Ordinary shares}}$

	20X1	*20X0*
1st version		
$\frac{453}{800}$	57p	
$\frac{451-90}{800}$		45p

2nd version

This is after providing for deferred taxation and re-classifying the reorganisation costs as exceptional in accordance with FRS 3.

$\frac{453-7}{800}$	56p	
$\frac{451-90-8}{800}$		44p

(v) **After tax return on equity**

$\frac{\text{Profit after tax}}{\text{Capital and reserves}}$

	20X1	*20X0*
1st version		
$\frac{453}{1,981}$	23%	
$\frac{451-90}{1,608}$		22%

Note. The re-organisation costs have been re-classified as exceptional in accordance with FRS 3.

2nd version

This is after adjusting for write off of obsolescent stock, stock subject to reservation of title and bad debts.

$\frac{453-(40+28+40)}{1,981}$	17.4%	
$\frac{451-(40+28+40)-90}{1,608}$		16%

Note. The re-organisation costs have been re-classified as exceptional.

(vi) **Price/earnings**

$\frac{\text{Market price of share}}{\text{Earnings per share}}$

	20X1	*20X0*
1st version		
$\frac{2.50}{0.57}$	4.4	
$\frac{2.20}{0.45}$		4.9

2nd version

This is based on full provision for deferred taxation and reclassification of the extraordinary item as exceptional (see (iv)).

	20X1	20X0
$\frac{2.50}{0.56}$	4.5	
$\frac{2.20}{0.44}$		5

(b) (i) **Rights issue**

(1) **Debt/equity ratio**

$$\frac{\text{Long term creditors}}{\text{Capital and reserves (W2)}} = \frac{450 + 100}{3{,}038} = 18.1\%$$

(2) **Interest cover**

$$\frac{\text{Operating profit (W1)}}{\text{Interest payable (W1)}} = \frac{903}{55} = 16 \text{ times}$$

(3) **Post tax return on equity**

$$\frac{\text{Profit after tax (W1)}}{\text{Capital and reserves (W2)}} = \frac{551}{3{,}038} = 18.1\%$$

(ii) **Loan**

(1) **Debt/equity ratio**

$$\frac{450 + 100 + 800}{2{,}230} = 60.5\%$$

(2) **Interest cover**

$$\frac{903}{175} = 5 \textit{ times}$$

(3) **Post tax return on equity**

$$\frac{473}{2{,}230} = 21.2\%$$

On the face of it, the directors should opt for the loan since returns are higher. Furthermore, the associated increase in risk is not significant; interest cover is still high and the debt/equity ratio is still acceptable.

Other aspects which the directors need to consider are whether the additional funds will generate enough *cash*, as opposed to profits, to meet the loan repayments and the interest payments and whether there are any restrictions on borrowing powers in the company's articles of association.

Workings

1 *Forecast profit and loss account*

	Rights issue	*Loan*
	£'000	£'000
20X1 operating profit	698	698
Gain on disposal	(95)	(95)
Increase in profit due to additional funds	300	300
	903	903
Interest payable: 55/(55 + (800 × 15%))	55	175
Profit before tax	848	728
Taxation @ 35%	(297)	(255)
Profit after tax	551	473
Dividends	(150)	(80)
Retained profit	401	393

2 *Forecast balance sheet: share capital and reserves*

	Rights issue	*Loan*
	£'000	£'000
Share capital 20X1	800	800
Rights issue 800/2	400	-
	1,200	800
Share premium	400	-
Profit and loss account 20X1	1,037	1,037
Retained profit	401	393
	3,038	2,230

Financial Reporting
BPP Mock Exam 1:
December 2001

Question Paper:	
Time allowed	**3 hours**
This paper is divided into two sections	
Section A	**This question is compulsory and MUST be attempted**
Section B	**THREE questions ONLY to be answered**

paper 2.5

DO NOT OPEN THIS PAPER UNTIL YOU ARE READY TO START
UNDER EXAMINATION CONDITIONS

Section A - This question is compulsory and MUST be attempted

1 Hanford plc acquired six million of Stopple plc's ordinary shares on 1 April 20X1 for an agreed consideration of £25 million. The consideration was settled by a share exchange of five new shares in Hanford plc for every three shares acquired in Stopple plc, and a cash payment of £5 million. The cash transaction has been recorded, but the share exchange has not.

The draft balance sheets of the two companies at 30 September 20X1 are:

	Hanford plc		*Stopple plc*	
	£'000	£'000	£'000	£'000
Fixed assets				
Land and buildings		32,060		9,400
Plant and equipment		46,480		17,780
Investment in Stopple plc		5,000		nil
		83,540		27,180
Current assets				
Stock	7,450		4,310	
Debtors	12,960		4,330	
Cash and bank	nil		520	
	20,410		9,160	
Creditors: amounts falling due within one year				
Creditors and accruals	5,920		4,160	
Bank overdraft	1,700		nil	
Provision for taxation	1,870		1,380	
Proposed final dividend	1,200		800	
	(10,690)		(6,340)	
Net current assets		9,720		2,820
Creditors: amounts falling due after more than one year				
8% Debentures 20X4		nil		(6,000)
Net assets		93,260		24,000
Share capital and reserves				
Ordinary shares of £1 each		20,000		8,000
Reserves				
Share premium	10,000		2,000	
b/f 1 October 20X0	51,260		6,000	
For the year to 30 September 20X1	12,000	73,260	8,000	16,000
		93,260		24,000

The following information is relevant:

(i) The fair value of Stopple plc's land at the date of acquisition was £4 million in excess of its carrying value. Stopple plc's financial statements contain a note of a contingent asset for an insurance claim of £800,000 relating to some stock that was damaged by a flood on 5 March 20X1. The insurance company is disputing the claim. Hanford plc has taken legal advice on the claim and believes that it is highly likely that the insurance company will settle it in full in the near future.

The fair values of Stopple plc's other net assets approximated to their carrying value.

(ii) At the date of acquisition Hanford plc sold an item of plant to Stopple plc for £2.4 million. This plant had cost Hanford plc £2 million. Stopple plc has charged depreciation of £240,000 on this plant since it was acquired.

(iii) Hanford plc's current account debit balance of £820,000 with Stopple plc does not agree with the corresponding balance in Stopple plc's books. Investigations revealed that on 26 September 20X1 Hanford plc billed Stopple plc £200,000 for its share of central administration costs. Stopple plc has not yet recorded this invoice. Inter company current accounts are included in debtors or creditors as appropriate.

(iv) Stopple plc paid an interim dividend of £400,000 on 31 March 20X1. The profit and total dividends (interim plus final) of Stopple plc are deemed to accrue evenly throughout the year. Stopple's retained profit of £8 million for the year to 30 September 20X1 as shown in its balance sheet is after the deduction of both its interim and final dividends. Hanford plc's policy is to credit to income only those dividends received or receivable from post acquisition profits. Hanford plc has not yet received or accounted for any dividends from Stopple plc.

(v) Consolidated goodwill is written off on a straight-line basis over a five year life, with time apportionment in the year of acquisition.

Required:

(a) Prepare the consolidated balance sheet of Hanford plc at 30 September 20X1 (20 marks)

(b) Suggest reasons why a parent company may not wish to consolidate a subsidiary company, and describe the circumstances in which non-consolidation of subsidiaries is permitted. (5 marks)

(25 marks)

Section B – THREE questions ONLY to be attempted

2 The following trial balance relates to Telenorth plc at 30 September 20X1:

			£'000	£'000
Turnover				283,460
Stock 1 October 20X0			12,400	
Purchases			147,200	
Distribution expenses			22,300	
Administration expenses			34,440	
Debenture interest paid			300	
Interim dividends	- ordinary		2,000	
	- preference		480	
Investment income	- UK dividends received (note (ii))			1,080
	- interest received (net) (note (ii))			420
25 year leasehold building – cost			56,250	
Plant and equipment – cost			55,000	
Computer system – cost			35,000	
Investments – at valuation			34,500	
Depreciation 1 October 20X0 (note (iii))		- leasehold		18,000
		- plant and equipment		12,800
		- computer system		9,600
Trade debtors (note (iv))			35,700	
Bank overdraft				1,680
Trade creditors				17,770
Deferred tax (note (v))				5,200
Ordinary shares of £1 each				20,000
Suspense account (note (vi))				26,000
6% Debentures (issued 1 October 20X0)				10,000
8% Preference shares				12,000
Revaluation reserve (note (v))				3,400
Profit and loss reserve 1 October 20X0				14,160
			435,570	435,570

The following notes are relevant.

(i) Stocktaking could not be conducted by Telenorth plc until 4 October 20X1 due to operational reasons. The value of the stock on the premises at this date was £16 million at cost. Between the year end and the stock take the following transactions have been identified:

Normal sales at a mark up on cost of 40%	£1,400,000
Sales on a sale or return basis at a mark up on cost of 30%	£650,000
Goods received at cost	£820,000

All sales and purchases had been correctly recorded in the period in which they occurred.

(ii) Dividends received had related tax credits of £120,000; and the interest received was net of a withholding tax of 25%.

(iii) Telenorth plc has the following depreciation policy:

- leasehold – straight-line;
- plant and equipment – five years straight line with residual values estimated at £5,000,000'
- computer system – 40% per annum reducing balance.

Depreciation of the leasehold and plant is treated as cost of sales; depreciation of the computer system is an administration expense.

(iv) The outstanding balance (debtor) of a major customer amounting to £12 million was factored to Kwickfinance on 1 September 20X1. The terms of the factoring were:

- Kwickfinance will pay 80% of the gross debtor outstanding account to Telenorth plc immediately;
- the balance will be paid (less the charges below) when the debtor is collected in full. Any amount of the debt outstanding after four months will be transferred back to Telenorth plc at its full book value.
- Kwickfinance will charge 1.0% per month to the net amount owing from Telenorth plc at the beginning of each month. Kwickfinance had not collected any of the factored debtor by the year end.

Telenorth plc debited the cash from Kwickfinance to its bank account and removed the debtor from its sales ledger. It has prudently charged the difference as an administration costs.

(v) A provision for corporation tax, excluding the amount of any withholding taxes, of £23.4 million for the year to 30 September 20X1 is required. The deferred tax liability is to be increased by £2.2 million, of which £1 million is to be charged direct to the revaluation reserve.

(vi) The suspense account contains the proceeds of two share issues:

- the exercise of all the outstanding directors' share options of four million shares on 1 October 20X0 at £2 each;
- a fully subscribed rights issue 1 July 20X1 of 1 for 4 held at a price of £3 each. The stock market price of Telenorth plc's shares immediately before the rights issue was £4.

(vii) The company has proposed an ordinary dividend of 15p per share.

Required:

Prepare:

(a) (i) The profit and loss account of Telenorth plc for the year to 30 September 20X1; and (9 marks)

(ii) A balance sheet as at 30 September 20X1 in accordance with the Companies Acts and current Accounting Standards as far as the information permits. (11 marks)

Notes to the financial statements are not required.

(b) Calculate the Earnings per Share in accordance with FRS 14 for the year to 30 September 20X1 (ignore comparatives) (5 marks)

(25 marks)

3 The broad principles of accounting for tangible fixed assets involve distinguishing between capital and revenue expenditure, measuring the cost of assets, determining how they should be depreciated and dealing with the problems of subsequent measurement and subsequent expenditure. FRS 15 'Tangible Fixed Assets' was issued in February 1999 with the intention of improving consistency in these areas.

Required:

(a) Explain:

(i) how the initial cost of tangible fixed assets should be measured; and (4 marks)

(ii) **the circumstances in which subsequent expenditure on those assets should be capitalised.** (3 marks)

(b) **Explain FRS 15's requirements regarding the revaluation of fixed assets and the accounting treatment of gains and losses on both the revaluation and the disposal of fixed assets.** (8 marks)

(c) (i) Broadoak plc has recently purchased an item of plant from Plantco plc, the details of this are:

	£	£
Basic list price of plant		240,000
trade discount applicable to Broadoak plc		12.5% on list price
Ancillary costs:		
shipping and handling costs		2,750
estimated pre-production testing		12,500
maintenance contract for three years		24,000
site preparation costs		
electrical cable installation	14,000	
concrete reinforcement	4,500	
own labour costs	7,500	26,000

Broadoak plc paid for the plant (excluding the ancillary costs) within four weeks of order, thereby obtaining an early settlement discount of 3%.

Broadoak plc had incorrectly specified the power loading of the original electrical cable to be installed by the contractor. The cost of correcting this error of £6,000 is included in the above figure of £14,000.

The plant is expected to last for 10 years. At the end of this period there will be compulsory costs of £15,000 to dismantle the plant and £3,000 to restore the site to its original use condition.

Required

Calculate the amount at which the initial cost of the plant should be measured. (Ignore discounting). (5 marks)

(ii) Broadoak acquired a 12 year lease on a property on 1 October 20X0 at a cost of £240,000. The company policy is to revalue its properties on an existing use value (EUV) at the end of each year, and calculate annual amortisation on the carrying value at the beginning of the year. The valuations (EUV) of the property on 30 September 20X1 and 20X2 were £231,000 and £175,000 respectively.

Required

Prepare extracts of the profit and loss account, the Statement of Total Recognised Gains and Losses and the balance sheet of Broadoak plc for the years to 30 September 20X1 and 20X2 in respect of the leasehold properties. (5 marks)

(25 marks)

4 The summarised financial statements of Charmer plc for the year to 30 September 20X1, together with a comparative balance sheet are:

Profit and loss account	*£'000*
Turnover	7,482
Cost of sales	(4,284)
Gross profit	3,198
Operating expenses	(1,479)
Interest payable	(260)
Investment income	120
Profit before tax	1,579
Taxation	(520)
	1,059
Dividends	(500)
Retained profit for period	559

	30 September 20X1:			*30 September 20X0:*		
	£'000	*£'000*	*£'00*	*£'000*	*£'000*	*£'000*
Fixed Assets:	*Cost/valuation*	*Depreciation*	*NBV*	*Cost/valuation*	*Depreciation*	*NBV*
Tangible:						
Land and Buildings	2,000	760	1,240	1,800	680	1,120
Plant	1,568	464	1,104	1,220	432	788
	3,568	1,224	2,344	3,020	1,112	1,908
Investment			690			nil
			3,034			1,908
Current Assets						
Stock		1,046			785	
Trade debtors		935			824	
Short term treasury bills		120			50	
Bank		nil			122	
		2,101			1,781	
Creditors: amounts falling due within one year:						
Trade creditors		644			760	
Accrued interest		40			25	
Provision for negligence claim		nil			120	
Proposed dividends		350			30	
Taxation		480			367	
Government grants		100			125	
Overdraft		136			nil	
		(1,750)			(1,427)	
Net current assets			351			354
Creditors: amounts falling due after more than one year:						
Deferred tax		439			400	
Government grants		275			200	
10% Convertible Loan Stock		nil	(714)		400	(1,000)
			2,671			1,262
Share Capital and Reserves						
Ordinary shares £1 each			1,400			1,000
Reserves:						
Share premium		460			60	
Revaluation		90			40	
Profit and loss account		721	1,271		162	262
			2,671			1,262

The following information is relevant:

(i) Fixed assets

On 1 October 20X0 Charmer plc recorded an increase in the value of its land of £150,000.

During the year an item of plant that had cost £500,000 and had accumulated depreciation of £244,000 was sold at a loss (included in cost of sales) of £86,000 on its carrying value.

(ii) Government grant

A credit of £125,000 for the current year's amortisation of government grants has been included in cost of sales.

(iii) Share capital and loan stocks

The increase in the share capital during the year was due to the following events:

(i) On 1 January 20X1 there was a bonus issue (out of the revaluation reserve) of one bonus share for every 10 shares held;

(ii) On 1 April 20X1 the 10% convertible loan stock holders exercised their right to convert to ordinary shares. The terms of conversion were 25 ordinary shares of £1 each for each £100 of 10% convertible loan stock; and

(iii) The remaining increase in the ordinary shares was due to a stock market placement of shares for cash on 12 August 20X1.

(iv) Provision for negligence claim:

In June 20X1 Charmer plc made an out of court settlement of a negligence claim brought about by a former employee. The dispute had been in progress for two years and Charmer plc had made provisions for the potential liability in each of the two previous years. The unprovided amount of the claim at the time of settlement was £30,000 and this was charged to operating expenses.

Required:

Prepare a Cash Flow Statement for Charmer plc for the year to 30 September 20X1 in accordance with FRS 1 'Cash Flow Statements'.

Note: you are NOT required to prepare an analysis of, or reconciliation of the movement in, net debt.

(25 marks)

5 You have been asked to assist the financial accountant of Myriad plc in preparing the company's financial statements for the year to 30 September 20X1. The financial accountant has asked for your advice in the following matters:

(a) A review of the company policy on the treatment of deferred development expenditure has come to the conclusion that it would be preferable for the company to change its current accounting policy of immediate write off of all development costs. The new policy, to be first applied for the financial statements to 30 September 20X1, is to recognise development costs as an intangible asset where they meet the recognition criteria in SSAP 13 'Accounting for Research and Development'. Amortisation of all 'qualifying' development expenditure is on a straight-line basis over a four-year period (assuming a nil residual value). Recognised development expenditure 'qualifies' for amortisation when the project starts commercial production of the related product. The amount of recognised development expenditure, and the amount qualifying for amortisation each year is as follows:

	£'000 amount recognised as an asset	£'000 amount qualifying for amortisation
In the year to 30 September 20W9	420	300
In the year to 30 September 20X0	250	360
In the year to 30 September 20X1	560	400
	1,230	1,060

No development costs were included by Myriad plc prior to 20W9.

Required:

(i) **Explain the circumstances when a company should change its accounting policies; and** (4 marks)

(ii) **Prepare extracts of Myriad plc's financial statements for the year to 30 September 20X1 including the comparative figures to reflect the change in accounting policy.** (6 marks)

Note: Ignore taxation.

(b) Myriad plc owns several properties which are revalued each year. Three of its properties are rented out under annually renewable operating leases. Details of these properties and their valuations are:

Property	*Type*	*Cost*	*Value 30 September 2000*	*Value 30 September 2001*
		£'000	*£'000*	*£'000*
A	50 year lease	150	240	200
B	50 year lease	120	180	145
C	15 year lease	120	140	150

All three properties were acquired on 1 October 20W9. The valuations of the properties are based on their age at the date of the valuation. Myriad plc's policy is to carry all non-investment properties at cost. Annual amortisation, where appropriate, is based on the carrying value of assets at the beginning of the relevant period.

Property A is let to a subsidiary of Myriad plc on normal commercial terms. The other properties are let on normal commercial terms to companies not related to Myriad plc.

Required

(i) **Explain why investment properties require a different accounting treatment to owner-occupied properties; and** (3 marks)

(ii) **Prepare extracts of the financial statements of Myriad plc for the year to 30 September 20X1 reflecting the appropriate treatment of the above properties.** (6 marks)

(c) Myriad plc manufactures and sells high quality printing paper. The auditor has drawn the company's attention to the sale of some packs of paper on 20 October 20X1 at a price of £45 each. These items were included in closing stock on 30 September 20X1 at their manufactured cost of £48 each. Further investigations revealed that during stocktaking on 30 September 20X1 a quantity of packs of A3 size paper had been damaged by a water leak. The following week the company removed the damage by cutting the paper down to A4 size (A4 size is smaller than A3). The paper was then repackaged and put back into stock. The cost of cutting and repackaging was £4 per pack. The normal selling price of the paper is £75 per pack for the A3 and £50 per pack for the A4, however on 12 October 20X1 the company reduced the selling price of all its paper by 10% in response to similar price cuts by its competitors.

Securiprint plc, one of the customers that bought some of the 'damaged' paper had used it to print some share certificates for a customer. Securiprint plc informed Myriad plc that these share certificates had been returned by the customer because they contained marks that were not part of the design. Securiprint plc believes the marks were part of a manufacturing flaw on the part of Myriad plc and is seeking appropriate compensation.

Required

Discuss the impact the above information may have on the draft financial statements of Myriad plc for the year to 30 September 20X1. (6 marks)

(25 marks)

ANSWERS

DO NOT TURN THIS PAGE UNTIL YOU HAVE COMPLETED THE MOCK EXAM

WARNING! APPLYING THE BPP MARKING SCHEME

If you decide to mark your paper using the BPP marking scheme, you should bear in mind the following points.

1 The BPP solutions are not definitive: you will see that we have applied the marking scheme to our solutions to show how good answers should gain marks, but there may be more than one way to answer the question. You must try to judge fairly whether different points made in your answers are correct and relevant and therefore worth marks according to our marking scheme.

2 If you have a friend or colleague who is studying or has studied this paper, you might ask him or her to mark your paper for you, thus gaining a more objective assessment. Remember you and your friend are not trained or objective markers, so try to avoid complacency or pessimism if you appear to have done very well or very badly.

3 You should be aware that BPP's answers are longer than you would be expected to write. Sometimes, therefore, you would gain the same number of marks for making the basic point as we have shown as being available for a slightly more detailed or extensive solution.

It is most important that you analyse your solutions in detail and that you attempt to be as objective as possible.

Professional Examination - Paper 2.5 **Marking Scheme**

Financial Reporting

This marking scheme is given as a guide to markers in the context of the suggested answer. Scope is given to markers to award marks for alternative approaches to a question, including relevant comment, and where well-reasoned conclusions are provided. This is particularly so in the case scenario questions where there may be more than one definitive solution.

A PLAN OF ATTACK

Managing your nerves

As you turn the pages to start this mock exam a number of thoughts are likely to cross your mind. At best, examinations cause anxiety so it is important to stay focused on your task for the next three hours! Developing an awareness of what is going on emotionally within you may help you manage your nerves. Remember, you are unlikely to banish the flow of adrenaline, but the key is to harness it to help you work steadily and quickly through your answers.

Working through this mock exam will help you develop the exam stamina you will need to keep going for three hours.

Managing your time

Planning and time management are two of the key skills which compliment the technical knowledge you need to succeed. To keep yourself on time, do not be afraid to jot down your target completion times for each question, perhaps next to the title of the question on the paper.

Focusing on scoring marks

When completing written answers, remember to communicate the critical points, which represent marks, and avoid padding and waffle. Sometimes it is possible to analyse a long sentence into more than one point. Always try to maximise the mark potential of what you write.

As you read through the questions, jot down on the question paper, any points you think you might forget. There is nothing more upsetting than coming out of an exam having forgotten to write a point you knew!

Structure and signpost your answers

To help you answer the examiner's requirements, highlight as you read through the paper the key words and phrases in the examiner's requirements.

Also, where possible try to use headings and subheadings, to give a logical and easy-to-follow structure to your response. A well structured and sign-posted answer is more likely to convince the examiner that you know your subject.

Your approach

This paper has two sections. The first section contains one question which is compulsory. The second has four questions and you must answer three of them.

You have a choice.

- Read through and answer Section A question before moving on to Section B
- Go through Section B and select the three questions you will attempt. Then go back and answer the questions in Section A first
- Select the three questions in Section B, answer them and then go back to Section A

You must give yourself a couple of minutes at the start of the exam to go through the questions you are going to do.

Time spent at the start of each question confirming the requirements and producing a plan for the answers is time well spent.

Question selection

When selecting the three questions from Section B make sure that you read through all of the requirements. It is painful to answer part (a) of a question and then realise that parts (b) and (c) are beyond you, by then it is too late to change your mind and do another question.

When reviewing the requirements look at how many marks have been allocated to each part. This will give you an idea of how detailed your answer must be.

Generally, you need to be aware of your strengths and weaknesses and select accordingly.

Doing the exam

Actually doing the exam is a personal experience. There is not a single *right way*. As long as you submit complete answers to question 1 and any three from questions 2 to 5 after the three hours are up, then your approach obviously works.

Looking through the paper

Question 1 is on **group accounts**.

This time it is a consolidated balance sheet, but next time it could be a profit and loss account. Note that there are a further 5 marks available for discussing non-consolidation. In this first question there is invariably a secondary requirement testing a wider issue in the group section of the syllabus.

In section B you have four questions on a variety of topics, and you must choose three.

- Question 2 requires you to produce a **profit and loss account** and **balance sheet** after coping with various problems including a **suspense account**.
- Question 3 covers **FRS 15** in some detail and contains a substantial written element.
- Question 4 requires the preparation of a **cash flow statement**: an excellent source of marks for the well-prepared.
- Question 5 covers various issues, principally **FRS 18, SSAP 17, SSAP 9** and **FRS 12**.

Allocating your time

Always begin by allocating your time **according to the marks for the question.** However, you must always **use common sense.** If you've done as much as you can on a question, you are probably better off re-allocating your time and getting more marks on another question, where you can add something you didn't have time to do earlier on.

Learn from this Mock

This mock is difficult. No one said it was going to be easy. **Do not brood** on your lack of knowledge in certain areas. Make a note of holes in your knowledge and do your best to plug them. This may mean redoing the bits where you are weak.

Remember technique is important.

- Know **what you are going to do** when you open the exam on the day.
- Know that you will select questions **after a thorough review.**
- Know that you can throw down **pro formas** when you attempt the accounts preparation questions.

- Know that **written answers** are so much better when each point is presented in a **separate paragraph** (lots of white space makes the marker's job easier and you can always go back, if you have time, and add a point you have just remembered without the page looking like an ink covered spider has been break dancing all over it).
- Know that you are the **only one** who knows the best way to approach the exam

Most important of all, focus on the **positive** things you have done in attempting this exam. You may have spent the allocated time on each question. You may have realised that you only answer three questions in Section B. You may know enough to pass every question in this Mock. Only change to improve. **Good luck.**

1

> **Tutor's hint**. This consolidated balance sheet has a number of complications. Watch out for the **pre-acquisition dividend**, the recognition of the contingent asset and adjustments for unrealised profits and inter-group transactions.
>
> **Examiner's comments**. This was generally the best answered question on the paper. Most candidates had a good knowledge of the basic consolidation principles, but there were some problems with the adjusting items, notably:
>
> - incorrect treatment of the pre-acquisition dividend
> - incorrect fair value adjustment for the plant
> - failure to adjust the share capital or calculate the premium for the share exchange
> - treating invoiced administration costs as cash in transit
>
> Some candidates were confused between profit and loss account and balance sheet issues, arising from the fact that the acquisition was half way through the year.
>
> In part (b) some candidates did not consider other possible reasons why a parent company might not want to consolidate a subsidiary, even if permitted to do so.

(a) HANFORD PLC
CONSOLIDATED BALANCE SHEET AS AT 30 SEPTEMBER 20X1

	£'000	£'000
Intangible fixed assets:		
Goodwill (W1)		5,625
Tangible fixed assets:		
Land and buildings		
(32,060 + 9,400 + 4,000)		45,460
Plant and equipment (W3)		63,900
		114,985
Current assets:		
Stock (7,450 + 4,310)	11,760	
Debtors (12,960 + 4,330 - 820)	16,470	
Insurance claim	800	
Cash and bank	520	
	29,550	
Creditors: amounts falling due within one year		
Creditors and accruals		
(5,920 + 4,160 - 620)	9,460	
Bank overdraft	1,700	
Taxation (1,870 + 1,380)	3,250	
Proposed dividend - parent	1,200	
- minority (800 × 25%)	200	
	15,810	
Net current assets		13,740
		128,725
Creditors: amounts falling due after more than one year		
8% Debentures		6,000
		122,725
Share capital and reserves:		
Ordinary share capital (20,000 + 10,000)(W4)		30,000
Share premium (10,000 + 10,000) (W4)		20,000
Profit and loss account (W5)		65,565
		115,565
Minority interest (W6)		7,160
		122,725

Workings

1 *Goodwill*

	£'000	£'000
Consideration		25,000
Less: pre-acquisition dividend (W2)		(150)
		24,850
Share of net asset acquired		
Balance sheet value (24,000 – 4,000)	20,000	
Revaluation of land	4,000	
Contingent asset	800	
	24,800	
Group share 75%		18,600
Goodwill		6,250
Amortisation (6,250/5 × 6/12)		(625)
Balance sheet balance		5,625

2 *Pre-acquisition dividend*

	£'000
Interim dividend	400
Final dividend	800
Total dividend for the year	1,200
Group share (1,200 × 75%)	900
Post acquisition (900 × 6/12)	450
Dividend received (800 × 75%)	600
Pre-acquisition dividend	150

3 *Plant and equipment*

	£'000
Hanford	46,480
Stopple	17,780
Unrealised profit on sale	(400)
Additional depreciation charged	40
	63,900

4 *Ordinary share capital*

Number of shares acquired in Stopple (8,000 × 75%)	6,000
Number of shares in Hanford issued (6,000 × 5/3)	10,000
Value of shares	
	£'000
Nominal value (10,000 × £1)	10,000
Share premium (bal fig)	10,000
Total value of shares issued (25,000 - 5,000)	20,000

5 *Consolidated profit and loss reserve*

	£000	£000
Hanford		63,260
Less: unrealised profit on sale of land		(400)
Post acquisition dividend (W2)		450
		63,310
Stopple - Post acquisition (8,000 × 6/12)	4,000	
Add: depreciation adjustment	40	
Less: administration charge	(200)	
Group share 75%	3,840	2,880
		66,190
Less: goodwill amortised		625
		65,565

6 *Minority interest*

Minority interest		£000
Net assets per balance sheet		24,000
Fair value adjustment	- land	4,000
	- insurance	800
Depreciation adjustment		40
Management charge		(200)
		28,640
Minority interest (28,640 × 25%)		7,160

(b) A parent company may wish not to consolidate a subsidiary because the **Companies Act** or **FRS 2, Accounting for subsidiary undertakings**, either allow or require the subsidiary not to be consolidated. In other instances a parent company may wish not to consolidate a subsidiary due to the **poor performance** of the subsidiary which they do not wish to include in the consolidated financial statements as the parent would like the consolidated financial statements to show the position of the group in the best possible light.

If the results of a poorly performing subsidiary are consolidated then this will impact on the consolidated balance sheet and profit and loss account. Consolidation of the subsidiary may **lower the consolidated return on capital employed, worsen the perceived consolidated liquidity position or increase the consolidated gearing level**. If a subsidiary therefore has operating losses, poor liquidity or high gearing levels then the parent company may wish not to consolidate that subsidiary.

In order to ensure that consolidated financial statements are **not manipulated** to improve perceived performance by non-consolidation of subsidiaries **both the Companies Act and FRS 2 have criteria regarding the non-consolidation of subsidiary companies**.

FRS 2 requires a subsidiary to be excluded from the consolidation when the subsidiary operates under **severe long-term restrictions** as in such cases the parent no longer has control of the subsidiary. The Companies Act permits exclusion on this basis.

FRS 2 also requires a subsidiary to be excluded from consolidation where the interest in the subsidiary is **held exclusively with a view to subsequent resale** and the subsidiary has not previously been consolidated in the group accounts of the parent. The Companies Act permits exclusion for this reason.

The Companies Act allows a subsidiary to be excluded if it has significantly **different operations from those of the rest of the group**. However FRS 2 makes it clear that exclusion on this basis should never occur.

Marking guide

				Marks	
1	(a)	Balance sheet:			
		Goodwill	- calculation	3	
			- depreciation	1	
		Land and buildings		2	
		Plant and machinery		2	
		Stock		1	
		Debtors		2	
		Insurance claim		1	
		Bank/overdraft		1	
		Creditors		2	
		Dividend to minority		1	
		Tax and dividend		1	
		8% debentures		1	
		Minority interest		2	
		Share capital		1	
		Share premium		1	
		P&L reserve	- treatment of admin charge	1	
			- post acq profit	1	
			- post acq dividend	1	
			Available	25	
			Maximum		20
	(b)	For reasons of	- poor profitability	1	
			- poor liquidity/gearing	1	
			- long-term restrictions	1	
			- subsequent resale	1	
			- differing activities	1	
		First two prohibited, last three permitted		1	
			Available	6	
			Maximum		5
			Total maximum		25

2 (a) (i)

Tutor's hint. A typical **published accounts** question with a number of different adjustments covering a variety of SSAPs and FRSs. In particular knowledge of **FRS 5** is needed in the treatment of the factored debt and of **FRS 16** when dealing with withholding taxes and tax credits. Time is a problem in this question so you need to work methodically. Part b) is a fairly straightforward calculation of earnings per share.

Examiner's comments. Some candidates ran out of time on this question, and several areas of the syllabus were covered. The main areas of error were:

- failure to deal correctly with a factored debtor
- adjusting a stock figure for movements since the date of the stock count, and adjusting sales
- the treatment of the deferred tax
- failure to clear the balance on the suspense account

More serious errors were made by some candidates, notably

- not providing for the second half of the debenture interest and preference dividend, and incorrectly calculating the final ordinary dividend
- incorrect calculation of basic depreciation charges

Part (b) was generally disappointingly answered, and some candidates did not attempt it at all.

Telenorth plc - Profit and loss account for the year ending 30 September 20X1

		£000	£'000
Turnover			283,460
Cost of sales (W2)			(155,170)
Gross profit			128,290
Distribution expenses		(22,300)	
Administrative expenses (W4)		(42,200)	
			(64,500)
Operating profit			63,790
Interest payable and similar charges (W5)		(696)	
Investment income (W6)		1,640	
			944
Profit on ordinary activities before tax			64,734
Tax on profit on ordinary activities (W7)			(24,740)
Profit on ordinary activities after tax			39,994
Dividends	- preference (12,000 × 8%)	960	
	ordinary (2,000 + 4,500) (W8)	6,500	
			7,460
Retained profit for the year			32,534
Retained profit b/f			14,160
			46,694

(ii) **Telenorth plc - Balance sheet as at 30 September 20X1**

	£000	£000
Tangible fixed assets (W9)		83,440
Investments		34,500
		117,940
Current assets:		
Stock (W1)	16,680	
Trade debtors		
(35,700 + 12,000) (W3)	47,700	
	64,380	
Creditors: amounts falling due within one year (W10)	57,826	
Net current assets		6,554
		124,494
Creditors: amounts falling due after more than one year		
6% Debentures		(10,000)
Provision for liabilities and charges		
Deferred tax (5,200 + 2,200)		(7,400)
		107,094
Share capital and reserves:		
Ordinary shares of £1 each (W8)		30,000
8% Preference shares		12,000
		42,000
Share premium (W11)	16,000	
Revaluation reserve (3,400 - 1,000)	2,400	
Profit and loss account	46,694	65,094
		107,094

Workings

1 *Closing stock*

Closing stock

	£000
Value at 4 October	16,000
Add: sales (1,400 × 100/140)	1,000
sale or return (650 × 100/130)	500
Less: purchases	(820)
	16,680

2 *Cost of sales*

	£000
Opening stock	12,400
Purchases	147,200
Less: closing stock (W1)	(16,680)
	142,920
Leasehold depreciation (56,250/25)	2,250
Plant depreciation (55,000 - 5,000/5)	10,000
	155,170

3 *Debt factoring*

The risks and rewards of the debt that has been factored remains with Telenorth plc therefore the debt should not have been taken off the balance sheet. Instead the substance of the transaction is that Kwikfinance has provided a loan to Telenorth at an interest rate of 1% per month. This must be reflected in the balance sheet with subsequent adjustments in the profit and loss account.

The journal entry to reinstate the debtor and correctly record the transaction is:

		£000	£000
Debit	Debtors	12,000	
Credit	Loan		9,600
Credit	Administrative expenses		2,400
Debit	Interest payable (9,600 × 1%)	96	
Credit	Accruals		96

4 *Administrative expenses*

	£000
Per trial balance	34,440
Less: incorrect treatment of debt factoring (W3)	(2,400)
Add: computer depreciation ((35,000 - 9,600) x 40%)	10,160
	42,200

5 *Interest payable and similar charges*

	£000
Debenture interest (10,000 × 6%)	600
Debt factor finance charge (W3)	96
	696

6 *Investment income*

FRS 16, Current tax, states that dividends, interest etc, receivable or payable should include withholding taxes but exclude other taxes, such as tax credits, not payable wholly on behalf of the recipient.

	£000
UK dividends	1,080
Interest received (420 + 140)	560
	1,640

The withholding tax will then also form part of the charge for taxation (W7).

7 *Tax charge*

	£000
Provision required	23,400
Withholding tax	140
Deferred tax	1,200
	24,740

8 *Final dividend*

	Number of shares
Per trial balance	20,000
Directors share options	4,000
Rights issue (24,000/4)	6,000
	30,000

	£000
Final dividend (30,000 × 0.15)	4,500

9 *Tangible fixed assets*

	£000	£000
Leasehold		
Cost	56,250	
Depreciation (18,000 + 2,250)	20,250	
NBV		36,000
Plant and equipment		
Cost	55,000	
Depreciation (12,800 + 10,000)	22,800	
NBV		32,200
Computer system		
Cost	35,000	
Depreciation (9,600 + 10,160)	19,760	
		15,240
		83,440

10 *Creditors: amounts falling due within one year*

		£000
Bank overdraft		1,680
Trade creditors		17,770
Taxation		23,400
Proposed preference dividend		480
Proposed ordinary dividend (W8)		4,500
Loan from factor		9,600
Accruals	- debenture interest	300
	debt factor finance charge (W3)	96
		57,826

11 *Share premium account*

	£000
Issue of options (4,000 ×£1)	4,000
Rights issue (6,000 ×£2)	12,000
	16,000

(b)

	£000
Earnings available for ordinary shareholders:	
Profit after tax	39,994
Preference dividends	(960)
	39,034

Rights issue - theoretical ex-rights price

	£
4 shares @ £4	16
1 share @ £3	3
5 shares @ £3.80 (bal fig)	19

Weighted average number of shares in issue:

	000s
24,000 × 9/12 × 4/3.80	18,947
30,000 × 3/12	7,500
	26,447

$$\text{Earnings per share} = \frac{£39,034}{26,447}$$

$$= 148 \text{ pence}$$

Marking guide

				Marks	
(a)	(i)	Profit and loss account			
		Cost of sales		3	
		Turnover and distribution		1	
		Administration		2	
		Finance costs		2	
		Investment income		1	
		Taxation		2	
		Dividends		1	
			Available	12	
			Maximum		9
	(ii)	Balance sheet			
		Fixed assets		3	
		Stock		1	
		Debtors/creditor from question		1	
		Treatment of factored debtors		2	
		Tax provision		1	
		Debenture		1	
		Deferred tax		1	
		Proposed dividends		1	
		Ordinary shares		1	
		Revaluation reserve		1	
		Share premium		1	
		Profit and loss account reserve		1	
			Available	15	
			Maximum		11
(b)		Earnings attributable to ordinary shares		1	
		Calculation of theoretical ex-rights price		1	
		Weighting exercise		2	
		Calculation of earnings per share (in pence)		1	
			Maximum		5
			Total maximum		25

3

Tutor's hint. This question required fairly comprehensive knowledge of a relatively new standard, **FRS 15, Tangible fixed assets**. Remember that revaluation is not compulsory but if one asset is revalued so must all other assets in that class.

Examiner's comments. Answers to this question were rather polarised: either very good or rather poor; however in general the answers were above average. The main areas of criticism were:

- for the cost of fixed assets, many students gave the roles relating to determining whether an asset was impaired and other incorrect answer discussed the fair value of assets. Candidates should ensure that they read the question carefully so that they know what it is asking.
- many candidates thought that revaluation was compulsory (it is not) and the treatment of gains and losses was not properly understood.

In part (c) the most common errors were:

- incorrect capitalisation of maintenance costs (in some cases all three years) and the installation error
- failure to capitalise the compulsory dismantling and restoration costs
- failure to depreciate the property in part (ii) or depreciating it over the wrong period
- debiting the whole revaluation loss to the revaluation reserve rather than also partly to the profit and loss account.

(a) (i) When a tangible fixed asset is first capitalised it should be measured at its **cost.** Cost according to FRS 15 is the costs that are **directly attributable to bringing the asset into working condition for its intended use**. These directly attributable costs might include:

- Purchase price (after deducting any trade discount but not settlement discount)
- Other acquisition costs such as stamp duty, import duties and non-refundable purchase taxes
- Delivery costs
- Installation costs
- Site preparation and clearance costs
- Professional fees
- The labour costs of any of the company's own employees directly involved in the construction or acquisition of the specific tangible fixed asset
- Any costs of dismantling and removing the asset and restoring the site that would be recognised as a provision under FRS 12, Provisions, Contingent Liabilities and Contingent Assets.

Finance costs that are directly attributable to the construction of tangible fixed assets **may be capitalised** as part of this cost according to FRS 15. Companies are **not required to capitalise finance costs** but if they do adopt this policy then it **must be applied consistently.**

(ii) The key to determining whether any **subsequent expenditure** is to be capitalised is the standard of **performance** of the asset which was initially assessed to determine the asset's useful economic life and residual value. Subsequent expenditure that ensures that the asset maintains its **previously assessed standard of performance** should be recognised in the **profit and loss account** as revenue expenditure. However FRS 15 allows subsequent expenditure to be capitalised in three circumstances:

- Where the subsequent expenditure provides **an enhancement of the economic benefits** of the fixed asset in excess of the previously assessed standard of performance, (for example expenditure which lengthens the economic life of the asset or increases its production capacity).
- Where a component of the fixed asset which has been **treated separately for depreciation purposes is replaced or restored**. This relates to major elements of a fixed asset that are treated separately from the main asset such as the replacement of an engine on an aeroplane - the plane's body may be expected to last for 40 years but the engines must be replaced (say) every 8 years.
- Where the subsequent expenditure **relates to a major inspection or overhaul** of a fixed asset that restores the economic benefits of the asset that have been consumed by the entity and have already been reflected in depreciation.

(b) Companies are **not required to revalue** their fixed assets according to FRS 15 but it does allow them to revalue if the directors wish to. However if a company chooses a policy of revaluation of fixed assets then **if one asset in a class of fixed assets is revalued** then **all fixed assets in that class must be revalued**. This is to ensure that assets are not selectively revalued if the valuation is favourable but left at book value if the valuation is adverse.

The carrying value of revalued fixed assets should be their **current values at the balance sheet date**. This might imply a full valuation each year but FRS 15 allows that where properties are revalued a full valuation should take place at least every 5 years with an interim valuation in year 3 and at any other time when it is likely that there has been a material change in value.

Revaluation gains and losses are differences between the carrying value or net book value of the asset and the revalued amount. **Revaluation gains are normally recognised in the Statement of Total Recognised Gains and Losses (STRGL) and taken to a revaluation reserve.**

The treatment of revaluation losses however can be more complex and will depend upon their cause and the amount of the loss. If a revaluation loss is **clearly caused by a consumption of economic benefits,** such as damage to the asset, this loss should be **taken to the profit and loss account**. Other revaluation losses **should be taken to the revaluation reserve until the carrying amount is equivalent to depreciated historical cost** and then any further losses to the profit and loss account. However if the recoverable amount of the asset is greater than its revalued amount this amount of the loss can be taken to the revaluation reserve rather than the profit and loss account.

Any profit or loss on the disposal of a fixed asset is the **difference between the net disposal proceeds and the net book value or carrying value** of the asset at the date of disposal. This will be the case whether the asset is carried at cost or revaluation. This profit or loss should be **recognised in the profit and loss account** for the period in which the disposal takes place. There is then a reserve transfer of any remaining credit on the revaluation reserve relating to the asset disposed of to the profit and loss account reserve.

(c) Initial cost of plant

	£
Purchase price (£240,000 × 87.5%)	210,000
Shipping and handling costs	2,750
Estimated pre-production testing	12,500
Electrical cable cost (14,000 - 6,000)	8,000
Concrete reinforcement	4,500
Own labour cost	7,500
Dismantling and restoration costs (15,000 + 3,000)	18,000
	263,250

Note:

The items that are excluded from initial cost are:

- Maintenance contract as this is revenue expenditure
- Settlement discount (only trade discounts are deducted)
- The cost of the specification error - only normal costs should be capitalised.

(d) **Broadoak plc - Profit and loss account extract**

		30 September 20X1	*30 September 20X2*
		£	£
Amortisation	(£240,000/12)	(20,000)	
	(£231,000/11)		(21,000)
Impairment (W)			(25,000)

Broadoak plc - Statement of total recognised gains and losses extract

Surplus/ (deficit) on revaluation (W)	11,000	(10,000)

Broadoak plc – Balance sheet extract

Leasehold	231,000	175,000

Working

Revaluation and impairment

	£
Cost at 1 October 20X0	240,000
Amortisation to 30 September 20X1	(20,000)
Carrying value at 30 September 20X1	220,000
Revaluation gain	11,000
Valuation at 30 September 20X1	231,000
Amortisation to 30 September 20X2	(21,000)
Carrying value at 30 September 20X2	210,000
Revaluation loss to STRGL	
- down to depreciated historical cost	
(210,000 - (240,000 × 10/12))	(10,000)
Impairment loss to profit and loss account	(25,000)
Valuation at 30 September 20X2	175,000

Marking guide

					Marks
(a)	(i)	Definition of tangible fixed assets		1	
		Cost	– purchase price net of trade discount	1	
			- incidentals, transport etc	1	
			- installation	1	
			- borrowing costs	1	
			- site restoration etc	1	
			Available	6	
			Maximum		4
	(ii)	Subsequent expenditure – 1 mark per circumstance			
			Maximum		3
(b)		Must revalue whole class of assets		1	
		Must keep values up-to-date		1	
		Treatment of revaluation	- gains	2	
			- losses	3	
		Gain/loss on disposal	- basis of calculation	1	
			- treatment of previous surplus	1	
			Available	9	
			Maximum		8
(c)	(i)	Deduction of trade discount		1	
		Inclusion of	- shipping and preparation costs	1	
			- testing and installation	2	
			- dismantling	1	
		Exclusion of error, maintenance and early settlement discount		1	
			Available	6	
			Maximum		5
	(ii)	Amortisation		2	
		Impairment charge		1	
		STRGL surplus/deficit		2	
		Carrying value of leasehold at year ends		2	
			Available	7	
			Maximum		5
			Total maximum		25

4

> **Tutor's hint**. A standard cash flow statement question. There are a lot of workings for this question and take care when dealing with the cash flows arising from the various share issues in the year.
>
> **Examiner's comments**. A surprising number of candidates chose not to do this question. Cash flow statements are usually a popular choice.
>
> Significant problems were:
>
> - Confusion as to which items were non-cash operating profit reconciling items and which were actual cash flows.
> - Working capital adjustments and the loss on the sale of plant being shown as cash flows
> - Incorrect signing of cash flows (ie outflows being treated as inflows and vice versa)
> - The inclusion of items under inappropriate headings, eg the purchase of plant included as a financing item
>
> Very few candidates correctly calculated the cash flow from the issue of shares, and many thought that the conversion of loan stock to equity shares was a cash flow.

Charmer plc - Cash flow statement for the year ending 30 September 20X1

	£000	£000
Reconciliation of operating profit to net cash flow from operating activities		
Operating profit (3,198 - 1,479)		1,719
Depreciation - buildings (760 - 680)		80
plant (W1)		276
Loss on sale of plant		86
Amortisation of government grants		(125)
Negligence claim previously provided for		(120)
Increase in stocks (1,046 - 785)		(261)
Increase in debtors (935 - 824)		(111)
Decrease in creditors (760 - 644)		(116)
Net cash inflow from operating activities		1,428
Cash flow statement		
Net cash inflow from operating activities		1,428
Returns on investment and servicing of finance:		
Interest paid (260 - 40 + 25)	(245)	
Investment income	120	
		(125)
Taxation (W2)		(368)
Capital expenditure:		
Purchase of land and buildings (W3)	(50)	
Purchase of plant (W4)	(848)	
Sale of plant (500 - 244 - 86)	170	
Purchase of investments	(690)	
Receipt of government grant (W5)	175	
		(1,243)
		(308)
Equity dividends (W6)		(180)
		(488)
Management of liquid resources (120 - 50)		(70)
Financing:		
Issue of ordinary shares (W7)		300
Decrease in cash (122 + 136)		(258)

Workings

1 *Plant depreciation charge*

Plant – accumulated depreciation

	£		£
Disposal	244	Opening balance	432
Closing balance	464	P&L charge (bal fig)	276
	708		708

2 *Tax paid*

Taxation

	£		£
Cash paid (bal fig)	368	Opening balance – current	367
Closing balance – current	480	- deferred	400
- deferred	439	P&L charge	520
	1,287		1,287

3 *Purchase of land and buildings*

Land and buildings at cost

	£		£
Opening balance	1,800		
Revaluation	150		
Purchases (bal fig)	50	Closing balance	2,000
	2,000		2,000

4 *Purchase of plant*

Plant at cost

	£		£
Opening balance	1,220	Disposal	500
Purchases (bal fig)	848	Closing balance	1,568
	2,068		2,068

5 *Receipt of government grant*

Government grants

	£		£
P&L credit	125	Opening balance – current	125
Closing balance – current	100	- non-current	200
- non-current	275	Cash received (bal fig)	175
	500		500

6 *Equity dividends paid*

Equity dividends

	£		£
Cash paid (bal fig)	180	Opening balance	30
Closing balance	350	P&L charge	500
	530		530

7 *Cash from share issue*

	Number of shares 000's
30 September 20X0 - number of shares	1,000
Bonus issue	100
Convertibles (400/ 100 × 25)	100
	1,200
Market issue	200
	1,400

The convertible loan stock has a value of £400,000 and is converted into 100,000 ordinary shares of £1 each. So £300,000 is added to the share premium account for this issue.

	£'000
Share capital	200
Share premium (460 – 300 – 60)	100
	300

Marking guide

		Marks
Net profit before interest and tax		1
Depreciation adjustments		2
Loss on sale of plant		1
Amortisation of government grants		1
Negligence adjustment		1
Working capital 1 per item		3
Interest paid		2
Investment income		1
Tax		2
Equity dividends		2
Management of liquid resources		1
Purchase of	– land and buildings	2
	- plant	2
	- investments	1
Sale of plant		1
Receipt of government grant		1
Share issue		3
Decrease in cash		1
	Available	28
	Total maximum	25

5

Tutor's hint. For this question you need a reasonable knowledge of **FRS 18**, **SSAP 17, SSAP 9 and FRS 12**. You also need to be able apply the rules from these standards to the specific situations given.

Examiner's comments. This was a selection of 'mini questions'. Many candidates seemed to have chosen it because they had gambled on other topics, that did not come up. 'Question spotting' is a dangerous strategy.

In general, candidates had difficulty putting their knowledge about the areas tested into practice. A lot of candidates did not attempt the numerical sections on this question, so the overall marks were well below average.

(a) (i) According to **FRS 18, Accounting Policies,** companies should choose the **most appropriate accounting policies** for their enterprise. These accounting policies should be **reviewed regularly** to ensure that they are the most appropriate for the particular circumstances and **changed if they are no longer the most appropriate** for the enterprise. Any changes in **recognition, presentation or measurement basis** of an item in the financial statements is a **change in accounting policy**. A change in accounting policy should only occur **where the new policy is more appropriate** than the old policy or there has been a **change in accounting standards or requirements of the law**.

(ii)

		30 September 20X1	30 September 20X0 (restated)
Myriad plc - Profit and loss account extract		£'000	£'000
Amortisation (1,060 × 25%)		265	
((1,060 - 400) × 25%)			165
Myriad plc - Balance sheet extract			
Development expenditure	- cost	1,230	
	cost (1,230 – 560)		670
	amortisation (W1)	505	240
Net book value		725	430

Myriad plc - Statement of total recognised gains and losses extract

At the foot of the current years STRGL there would be a prior period adjustment of £430,000 (W2)

Workings

1 *Amortisation of development expenditure*

		£'000
Amortisation at 30 September 20X0 -		
for 1999	300 × 25% × 2 years	150
For 2000	360 × 25%	90
		240
Amortisation at 30 September 20X1		
for 1999	300 × 25% × 3 years	225
for 2000	360 × 25% × 2 years	180
for 2001	400 × 25%	100
		505

2 *Prior period adjustment*

	£'000
Development costs at 30 September 20W9	420
Amortisation at 30 September 20W9 (300 × 25%)	75
Prior period adjustment at 30 September 20W9	345
Development costs for year ended 30 September 20X0	250
Amortisation for year ended 30 September 20X0	165
Prior period adjustment at 30 September 20X0	430

(b) (i) Investment properties are properties owned by a company which are **not used within its own operations** (or the operations of any other member of its group) but instead are held for two main purposes:

- To **gain rental income** from letting
- To **gain on the capital appreciation** of the properties.

In contrast owner-occupied properties are normal operational fixed assets of a company in that they are used within the operations of the company and their economic value is therefore consumed in the process of earning revenue.

The difference in nature of these two types of property are recognised in **SSAP 19, Accounting for investment properties,** by distinguishing investment properties from other property fixed assets. The different accounting treatment for investment properties is based upon the fact that investment properties are held to earn rental income and to gain in value.

The importance of the current value of the properties is recognised by their valuation in the balance sheet at current value or **open market value**. Any changes in this market value are **taken to the Statement of Total Recognised Gains and Losses** each year and **shown in an investment revaluation reserve**. The second important difference in accounting treatment is that as the investment properties are not being consumed within the business there is **no annual depreciation charge**. Depreciation recognises the economic consumption of assets but this is not appropriate for investment properties and therefore it should not be charged. There is an exception recognised in SSAP 19 in that **leasehold properties with less than 20 years remaining on their leases should be depreciated** each year although also shown at their open market value.

(ii) **Myriad plc - Balance sheet extract**

		Cost/ valuation	*Accumulated depreciation*	*Carrying value*
		£'000	£'000	£'000
Land and buildings	– A (150/50 × 2)	150	6	144
Investment properties	– B	145	-	145
	– C	150	-	150

	£000
Investment property revaluation reserve (W1)	73

Myriad plc – Profit and loss account extract

	£'000
Depreciation (3 + 10) (W2)	13

Myriad plc – Statement of total recognised gains and losses - extract

	£'000
Unrealised loss on revaluation of investment properties (35 – 20) (W1)	(15)

Workings

1 *Investment property revaluation reserve*

		£000
1 October 2000	- B (180 - 120)	60
	- C (140 - 112)(W2)	28
		88
Year ended 30 September 2001 – STRGL		
	- B (180 - 145)	(35)
	- C (150 - 130)(W2)	20
Balance at 30 September 20X1		73

2 As investment C has less than 20 years of its lease remaining it must be depreciated according to SSAP 19.

	£000
Cost at 1 October 20W9	120
Depreciation to 30 September 20X0 (120/15)	(8)
Carrying value	112
Revaluation STRGL	28
Valuation	140
Depreciation to 30 September 20X1 (140/14)	(10)
Carrying value	130
Revaluation STRGL	20
Valuation at 30 September	150

(c) The scenario given introduces a number of issues relating to post balance sheet events, provisions and contingent liabilities.

The stock of paper had originally cost £48 per pack. It was eventually sold on 20 October at £45, being the normal price of £50 less the 10% price reduction that was introduced on 12 October due to competitive pressures. The paper was cut and repackaged due to the water damage at a cost of £4 per pack. The figures for cost and net realisable value therefore are as follows:

	Per pack
	£
Cost	48
Net realisable value (45 - 4)	41
Loss per pack	7

It therefore has to be decided whether the closing stock valuation at 30 September should be reduced to reflect this loss. The problem however is that the loss has two separate causes.

Part of the reason for the net realisable value of the paper being £7 per pack lower than its cost was that the paper had been damaged by water before the year end. This is an **adjusting post balance sheet event** and should lead to a **write down of the value of the closing stock**. However £5 of the loss per pack is due to the reduction of prices after the balance sheet date which is a **non-adjusting post balance sheet event**.

Therefore it would seem sensible that the closing stock should be written down by £2 (the adjusting post balance sheet event element) per pack at the balance sheet date with the loss being recognised in the year ending 30 September 20X1. The remaining £5 per pack loss however relates to the following year, 30 September 20X2, and should be recognised in that period. If the £5 per pack reduction in price is material then it should be **disclosed** in the 20X1 financial statements as a non-adjusting post balance sheet event.

There is then a further problem to consider, the complaint from Securiprint plc. If the marks on the paper are due to either the manufacturing process or the damage that occurred to the paper then Myriad plc will probably be liable to Securiprint for compensation. If the liability is probable then a **provision should be made in the 20X1 financial statements** for the amount likely to be payable to Securiprint. If the marks on the paper were not caused by Myriad plc then no provision would be required but at this stage it is probably difficult to determine this categorically. It is therefore likely that a **contingent liability** for compensation should be disclosed in the 20X1 financial statements to reflect the possibility of liability. It must also be considered that if the marks on the paper are due to Myriad then it is possible that the entire stock of this paper is affected. If stocks have been sold to other customers then the possibility of a provision for compensation to them should also be considered. If however the paper has not yet been sold then the year end stock value **may need to be further reduced** to reflect the reduction in value of this damaged stock.

Marking guide

				Marks	
(a) (i)	Principle of consistency/comparability			1	
	To give a fairer presentation or more useful information			1	
	Usually because of new FRS/Companies Act change			1	
	Initial implementation for new circumstances not a change			1	
			Maximum		4
(ii)	Profit and loss: amortisation			2	
	R&D in balance sheet	- cost		2	
		- amortisation		2	
	Prior period adjustment			1	
			Available	7	
			Maximum		6
(b) (i)	Reasons for different accounting treatment		Maximum		3
(ii)	Fixed asset figure	- 1 mark for each property		3	
	Revaluation reserve			2	
	Depreciation charges			2	
	STRGL			1	
			Available	8	
			Maximum		6
(c)	Total loss per pack is £7			1	
	£2 is an adjusting event			1	
	£5 is non-adjusting, perhaps requiring disclosure			1	
	If 'marks' due to water damage, provision required			1	
	If not enough information, treat as a contingency			1	
	Possibility of similar claims from other customers			1	
	May be that remaining stock should be written down			1	
			Available	7	
			Maximum		6
			Total maximum		25

Financial Reporting

BPP Mock Exam 2: June 2003

Question Paper:	
Time allowed	**3 hours**
This paper is divided into two sections	
Section A	**This question is compulsory and MUST be attempted**
Section B	**THREE questions ONLY to be answered**

Disclaimer of liability

Please note that we have based our predictions of the content of the June 2003 exam on our long experience of the ACCA exams. We do not claim to have any endorsement of the predictions from either the examiner or the ACCA and we do not guarantee that either the specific questions, or the general areas, that are forecast will necessarily be included in the exams, in part or in whole.

We do not accept any liability or responsibility to any person who takes, or does not take, any action based (either in whole or in part and either directly or indirectly) upon any statement or omission made in this book. We encourage students to study all topics in the ACCA syllabus and the mock exam in this book is intended as an aid to revision only.

paper 2.5

DO NOT OPEN THIS PAPER UNTIL YOU ARE READY TO START

UNDER EXAMINATION CONDITIONS

Section A - This question is compulsory and MUST be attempted

1 (a) On 1 October 20X0 Hepburn plc acquired 80% of the ordinary share capital of Salter Ltd by way of a share exchange. Hepburn plc issued five of its own shares for every two shares it acquired in Salter Ltd. The market value of Hepburn plc's shares on 1 October 20X0 was £3 each. The share issue has not yet been recorded in Hepburn plc's books. The summarised financial statements of both companies are:

PROFIT AND LOSS ACCOUNTS FOR THE YEAR TO 31 MARCH 20X1

	Hepburn plc		*Salter Ltd*	
	£'000	£'000	£'000	£'000
Turnover		1,200		1,000
Cost of sales		(650)		(660)
Gross profit		550		340
Operating expenses		(120)		(88)
Debenture interest		nil		(12)
Operating profit		430		240
Taxation		(100)		(40)
Profit after tax		330		200
Dividends: interim	(40)			
final	(40)			
		(80)		nil
Retained profit for the year		250		200

BALANCE SHEETS AS AT 31 MARCH 20X1

	Hepburn plc		*Salter Ltd*	
	£'000	£'000	£'000	£'000
Fixed assets				150
Land and Buildings		400		510
Plant and Machinery		220		10
Investments		20		670
		640		
Current Assets				
Stock	240		280	
Debtors	170		210	
Bank	20		40	
	430		530	
Creditors: amounts falling due within one year				
Trade creditors	170		155	
Taxation	50		45	
Dividends	40		nil	
	(260)		(200)	
Net current assets		170		330
Creditors: amounts falling after more than one year				
8% Debentures		nil		(150)
Net assets		810		1,000
		810		850
Capital and reserves				
Ordinary shares of £1 each		400		150
Profit and loss account		410		700
		810		850

The following information is relevant.

(i) The fair value of Salter Ltd's assets were equal to their book values with the exception of its land, which had fair value of £125,000 in excess of its book value at the date of acquisition.

(ii) In the post acquisition period Hepburn plc sold goods to Salter Ltd at a price of £100,000, this was calculated to give a mark-up on cost of 25% to Hepburn plc. Salter Ltd had half of these goods in stock at the year end.

(iii) Consolidated goodwill is to be written off as an operating expense over a five-year life. Time apportionment should be used in the year of acquisition.

(iv) The current accounts of the two companies disagreed due to a cash remittance of £20,000 to Hepburn plc on 26 March 20X1 not being received until after the year end. Before adjusting for this, Salter Ltd's debtor balance in Hepburn plc's books was £56,000.

Required:

Prepare a consolidated profit and loss account and balance sheet for Hepburn plc for the year to 31 March 20X1. (20 marks)

(b) At the same date as Hepburn plc made the share exchange for Salter Ltd's shares, it also acquired 6,000 'A' shares in Woodbridge Ltd for a cash payment of £20,000. The share capital of Woodbridge Ltd is made up of:

Ordinary voting A shares	10,000
Ordinary non-voting B shares	14,000

All of Woodbridge Ltd's equity shares are entitled to the same dividend rights; however during the year to 31 March 20X1 Woodbridge Ltd made substantial losses and did not pay any dividends.

Hepburn plc has treated its investment in Woodbridge Ltd as an ordinary fixed asset investment on the basis that:

(i) It is only entitled to 25% of any dividends that Woodbridge Ltd may pay

(ii) It does not have any directors on the Board of Woodbridge Ltd

(iii) It does not exert any influence over the operating policies or management of Woodbridge Ltd.

Required:

Comment on the accounting treatment of Woodbridge Ltd by Hepburn plc's directors and state how you believe the investment should be accounted for. (5 marks)

Note. You are not required to amend your answer to part (a) in respect of the information in part (b). **(25 marks)**

Section B – THREE questions ONLY to be attempted

2

Extracts from the balance sheet of Radan plc as at 1 April 20X6 are as follows.

	£'000	£'000
Ordinary shares of 25p each		4,000
8% preference shares		1,000
Reserves		
Share premium	700	
Capital redemption reserve	1,300	
Revaluation reserve	90	
Profit and loss account	750	
		2,840
		7,840
10% convertible debentures		2,000

Note. The above are extracts from the *opening* balance sheet for the current reporting year.

The following draft profit and loss account has been prepared for the year to 31 March 20X7, prior to the declaration of the proposed final ordinary dividend for the year.

	£'000	£'000
Profit before interest and tax		1,800
Debenture interest		(200)
Profit before tax		1,600
Taxation: provision for 20X7	300	
deferred tax	390	
		(690)
		910
Dividends paid:	320	
Preference	80	
		(400)
		510

The following information is relevant.

(a) A bonus issue of 1 for 8 ordinary shares was made on 7 September 20X6.

(b) A fully subscribed rights issue of 1 for 5 ordinary shares at a price of 50p each was made on 1 January 20X7. Immediately prior to the issue the market price of Radan plc's ordinary shares was £1.40 each.

(c) The terms of conversion of the 10% debentures are:

Year	*Debentures*	*Ordinary shares*
20X9 to 20Y3	£100	100
20Y4	£100	120

Corporation tax is to be taken as 33%.

(d) The profit before interest and taxation includes the following items.

(i) Stage profits of £150,000 relating to long-term contracts that have been calculated in accordance with SSAP 9 Stocks and long-term contracts

(ii) An exchange gain of £25,000 on a long-term US dollar loan

(e) The balance sheet includes an asset of deferred development expenditure of £114,000. The directors do not propose to include any note to the accounts in respect of whether or not this is a realised loss.

(f) Plant and equipment was revalued on 1 April 20X4 giving a surplus of £150,000. At that time it had a remaining life of five years. It is being depreciated, based on its revalued amount, on a straight-line basis. The excess depreciation for the years to 31 March 20X5 and 20X6 have been transferred from the revaluation reserve to the profit and loss account reserve.

(g) The earnings per share (EPS) was correctly reported in last year's accounts at 8p.

Required

(a) In relation to earnings per share, FRS 14 requires that, if the number of ordinary shares changes without a corresponding change in resources, the EPS calculations for all periods presented should be adjusted retrospectively.

(i) Give examples of circumstances in which such a change might take place that would affect the EPS calculation. (3 marks)

(ii) Calculate the basic EPS for Radan plc for the year ended 31 March 20X7, including the comparative figure. (4 marks)

(b) FRS 14 requires all listed companies to calculate and present diluted EPS.

(i) State how diluted EPS should be calculated according to FRS 14. (3 marks)

(ii) Calculate the diluted EPS figure for Radan plc for the year ended 31 March 20X7 (ignoring the comparative). (5 marks)

(iii) Explain why it is useful to disclose diluted EPS as well as basic EPS. (2 marks)

(c) Calculate the distributable profit of Radan plc at 31 March 20X7 prior to the deduction of any dividends relating to the current year, and explain how you have treated the items in notes (d), (e) and (f) above. (8 marks)

(25 marks)

3 The timing of revenue (income) recognition has long been an area of debate and inconsistency in accounting. Industry practice in relation to revenue recognition varies widely, the following are examples of different points in the operating cycle of businesses that revenue and profit can be recognised.

(i) On the acquisition of goods
(ii) During the manufacture or production of goods
(iii) On delivery/acceptance of goods
(iv) When certain conditions have been satisfied after the goods have been delivered
(v) Receipt of payment for credit sales
(vi) On the expiry of a guarantee or warranty

In the past the 'critical event' approach has been used to determine the timing of revenue recognition. The Accounting Standards Board (ASB) in its '*Statement of Principles for Financial Reporting*' has defined the 'elements' of financial statements, and it uses these to determine when a gain or loss occurs.

Required:

(a) Explain what is meant by the critical event in relation to revenue recognition and discuss the criteria used in the Statement of Principles for determining when a gain or loss arises. (5 marks)

(b) **For each of the stages of the operating cycle identified above, explain why it may be an appropriate point to recognise revenue and, where possible, give a practical example of an industry where it occurs.** (12 marks)

(c) Jenson plc has entered into the following transactions/agreements in the year to 31 March 20X1:

(i) Goods, which had cost £20,000 were sold to Wholesaler plc for £35,000 on 1 June 20X0. Jenson plc has an option to repurchase the goods from Wholesaler plc at any time within the next two years. The repurchase price will be £35,000 plus interest charged at 12% per annum from the date of sale to the date of repurchase. It is expected that Jenson plc will repurchase the goods.

(ii) Jenson plc owns the rights to a fast food franchise. On 1 April 20X0 it sold the right to open a new outlet to Mr Cody. The franchise is for five years. Jenson plc received an initial fee of £50,000 for the first year and will receive £5,000 per annum thereafter. Jenson plc has continuing service obligations on its franchise for advertising and product development that amount to approximately £8,000 per annum per franchised outlet. A reasonable profit margin on the provision of the continuing services is deemed to be 20% of revenues received.

(iii) On 1 September 20X0 Jenson plc received total subscriptions in advance of £240,000. The subscriptions are for 24 monthly publications of a magazine produced by Jenson plc. At the year end Jenson plc had produced and despatched six of the 24 publications. The total cost of producing the magazine is estimated at £192,000 with each publication costing a broadly similar amount.

Required:

Describe how Jenson plc should treat each of the above examples in its financial statements in the year to 31 March 20X1. (8 marks)

(25 marks)

4 Webster plc is a diversified holding company that is looking to acquire a suitable engineering company. Two private limited engineering companies, Cole Ltd and Darwin Ltd, are available for sale. The summarised financial statements for the year to 31 March 20X1 of both companies are as follows:

PROFIT AND LOSS ACCOUNTS

	Cole Limited		*Darwin Limited*	
	£'000	£'000	£'000	£'000
Sales (note (i))		3,000		4,400
Opening stock	450		720	
Purchases (note (ii))	2,030		3,080	
	2,480		3,800	
Closing stock	(540)		(850)	
		(1,940)		(2,950)
Gross profit		1,060		1,450
Operating expenses	480		964	
Debenture interest	80		nil	
Overdraft interest (note (v))	nil		10	
		(560)		(974)
Net profit		500		476

BALANCE SHEETS

	Cole Limited		Darwin Limited	
Fixed assets	£'000	£'000	£'000	£'000
Premises (note iii)		1,140		1,900
Plant (note iv)		1,200		1,200
		2,340		3,100
Current assets				
Stock	540		850	
Debtors	522		750	
Bank	20		nil	
	1,082		1,600	
Current liabilities				
Creditors	438		562	
Overdraft	nil		550	
	(438)		(1,112)	
		644		488
Total assets less current liabilities		2,984		3,588
10% Debenture		(800)		nil
Net assets		2,184		3,588
Share capital and reserves				
Ordinary share of 1 each		1,000		500
Reserves				
Revaluation reserve		nil		700
Profit and loss - 1 April 20X0	684		1,912	
Profit for year to 31 March 20X1	500		476	
		1,184		2,388
		2,184		3,588

Webster plc bases its preliminary assessment of target companies on certain key ratios. These are listed below together with the relevant figures for Cole Ltd and Darwin Ltd calculated from the above financial statements:

	Cole Limited		*Darwin Limited*
Return on capital employed (500 + 80)/(2,184 + 800) × 100	19.4%	(476/3,588) × 100	13.3%
Asset turnover (3,000/2,984)	1.01 times	(4,400/3,588)	1.23 times
Gross profit margin	35.3%		33.0%
Net profit margin	16.7%		10.8%
Debtors collection period	64 days		62 days
Creditors payment period	79 days		67 days

Note. Capital employed is defined as shareholders' funds plus long-term, debt at the year end; asset turnover is sales revenues divided by gross assets less current liabilities.

The following additional information has been obtained.

(i) Cole Ltd is part of the Velox Group. On 1 March 20X1 it was permitted by its holding company to sell goods at a price of £500,000 to Brander Ltd, a fellow subsidiary. Cole Ltd's normal selling price for these goods would have been £375,000. In addition Brander Ltd was instructed to pay for the goods immediately. Cole Ltd normally allows three months credit.

(ii) On 1 January 20X1 Cole Ltd purchased £275,000 (cost price to Cole Ltd) of its materials from Advent Ltd, another member of the Velox Group. Advent Ltd was also instructed to depart from its normal trading terms that would have resulted in a charge of £300,000 to Cole Ltd for these goods. The Group's finance director also authorised a four-month credit period on this sale. Normal credit terms for this industry are two months credit from suppliers. Cole Ltd had sold all of these goods at the year-end.

(iii) Fixed assets:

Details relating to the two companies' fixed assets at 31 March 20X1 are:

		Cost/revaluation	*Depreciation*	*Book value*
		£'000	£'000	£'000
Cole Ltd	- property	3,000	1,860	1,140
	- plant	6,000	4,800	1,200
				2,340
Darwin Ltd	- property	2,000	100	1,900
	- plant	3,000	1,800	1,200
				3,100

Both companies own very similar properties. Darwin Ltd's property was revalued to £2,000,000 at the beginning of the current year (ie 1 April 20X0). On this date Cole Ltd's property, which is carried at cost less depreciation, had a book value of £1,200,000. Its current value (on the same basis as Darwin Ltd's property) was also £2,000,000. On this date (1 April 20X0) both properties had the same remaining life of 20 years.

(iv) Darwin Ltd purchased new plant costing £600,000 in February 20X1. In line with company policy a full year's depreciation at 20% per annum has been charged on all plant owned at the year-end. The plant is still being tested and will not come on-stream until next year. The purchase of the plant was largely financed by an overdraft facility that resulted in the interest cost shown in the profit and loss account. Both companies depreciate plant over a five-year life.

(v) The bank overdraft that would have been required but for the favourable treatment towards Cole Ltd in respect of the items in (i) and (ii) above, would have attracted interest of £15,000 in the year to 31 March 20X1.

Required:

(a) Restate the financial statements of Cole Ltd and Darwin Ltd for the year to 31 March 20X1 in order that they may be considered comparable for decision making purposes. State any assumptions you make. (10 marks)

(b) Recalculate the key ratios used by Webster plc and, together with any other relevant points, comment on how the revised ratios may affect the relative assessment of the two companies. (10 marks)

(c) Discuss whether the information in notes (i) to (v) above would be publicly available, and if so, describe its source(s). (5 marks)

(25 marks)

5 The overriding requirement of a company's financial statements is that they should present a true and fair view and represent faithfully the underlying transactions and other events that have occurred. to achieve this, transactions have to be accounted for in terms of their 'substance' or economic reality rather than their legal form. this principle is included in the Accounting Standards Board (ASB) 'statement of principles for financial reporting', and it is also used in many standards, in particular FRS 5 *Reporting the substance of transactions* and SSAP 21 *Accounting for leases and hire purchase contracts.*

Required

(a) Describe why it is important that substance rather than legal form is used to account for transactions, and describe how financial statements can be adversely affected if the substance of transactions is not recorded. (5 marks)

(b) Describe, using an example, how the following features may indicate that the substance of a transaction is different from its legal form:

(i) Separation of ownership from the beneficial use of an asset

(ii) Linking of transactions including the use of option clauses

(iii) When an asset is sold at a price that differs to its fair value (9 marks)

(c) On 1 April 20X0 Forest plc had an inventory of cut seasoning timber which had cost £12 million two years ago. Due to shortages of this quality of timber its value at 1 April 20X0 had risen to £20 million. It will be a further three years before this timber is sold to a manufacturer of high-class furniture. On 1 April 20X0 Forest plc entered into an arrangement to sell Barret Bank the timber for £15 million. Forest plc has an option to buy back the timber at any time within the next three years at a cost of £15 million plus accumulated interest at 2% per annum above the base rate. This will be charged from the date of the original sale. The base rate for the period of the transaction is expected to be 8%. Forest plc intends to buy back the timber on 31 March 20X3 and sell it the same day for an expected price of £25 million.

Note. The above does not constitute a long-term contract under SSAP 9, and you are to ignore any costs and capitalisation of interest that may relate to stocks.

Required

Assuming the above transactions take place as expected, prepare extracts to reflect the transactions in the profit and loss accounts for the years to 31 March 20X1, 20X2 and 20X3 and the balance sheets (ignore cash) at those year ends:

(i) If Forest plc treats the transactions in their legal form

(ii) If the substance of the transactions is recorded

Comment briefly on your answer to (c) above. (11 marks)

(25 marks)

ANSWERS

DO NOT TURN THIS PAGE UNTIL YOU HAVE COMPLETED THE MOCK EXAM

WARNING! APPLYING THE BPP MARKING SCHEME

If you decide to mark your paper using the BPP marking scheme, you should bear in mind the following points.

1 The BPP solutions are not definitive: you will see that we have applied the marking scheme to our solutions to show how good answers should gain marks, but there may be more than one way to answer the question. You must try to judge fairly whether different points made in your answers are correct and relevant and therefore worth marks according to our marking scheme.

2 If you have a friend or colleague who is studying or has studied this paper, you might ask him or her to mark your paper for you, thus gaining a more objective assessment. Remember you and your friend are not trained or objective markers, so try to avoid complacency or pessimism if you appear to have done very well or very badly.

3 You should be aware that BPP's answers are longer than you would be expected to write. Sometimes, therefore, you would gain the same number of marks for making the basic point as we have shown as being available for a slightly more detailed or extensive solution.

It is most important that you analyse your solutions in detail and that you attempt to be as objective as possible.

Professional Examination - Paper 2.5 **Marking Scheme**

Financial Reporting

This marking scheme is given as a guide to markers in the context of the suggested answer. Scope is given to markers to award marks for alternative approaches to a question, including relevant comment, and where well-reasoned conclusions are provided. This is particularly so in the case scenario questions where there may be more than one definitive solution.

A PLAN OF ATTACK

Managing your nerves

As you turn the pages to start this mock exam a number of thoughts are likely to cross your mind. At best, examinations cause anxiety so it is important to stay focused on your task for the next three hours! Developing an awareness of what is going on emotionally within you may help you manage your nerves. Remember, you are unlikely to banish the flow of adrenaline, but the key is to harness it to help you work steadily and quickly through your answers.

Working through this mock exam will help you develop the exam stamina you will need to keep going for three hours.

Managing your time

Planning and time management are two of the key skills which complement the technical knowledge you need to succeed. To keep yourself on time, do not be afraid to jot down your target completion times for each question, perhaps next to the title of the question on the paper.

Focusing on scoring marks

When completing written answers, remember to communicate the critical points, which represent marks, and avoid padding and waffle. Sometimes it is possible to analyse a long sentence into more than one point. Always try to maximise the mark potential of what you write.

As you read through the questions, jot down on the question paper, any points you think you might forget. There is nothing more upsetting than coming out of an exam having forgotten to write a point you knew!

Structure and signpost your answers

As you read through the paper, highlight the key words and phrases in the examiner's requirements. This will help you focus precisely on what the examiner wants.

Also, where possible try to use headings and subheadings, to give a logical and easy-to-follow structure to your response. A well structured and sign-posted answer is more likely to convince the examiner that you know your subject.

Your approach

This paper has two sections. The first section contains one questions which is compulsory. The second has four questions and you must answer three of them.

You have a choice.

- Read through and answer the Section A question before moving on to Section B
- Go through Section B and select the three questions you will attempt. Then go back and answer the question in Section A first
- Select the three questions in Section B, answer them and then go back to Section A

You must give yourself a couple of minutes at the start of the exam to go through the questions you are going to do.

Time spent at the start of each question confirming the requirements and producing a plan for the answers is time well spent.

Question selection

When selecting the three questions from Section B make sure that you read through all of the requirements. It is painful to answer part (a) of a question and then realise that parts (b) and (c) are beyond you, by then it is too late to change your mind and do another question.

When reviewing the requirements look at how many marks have been allocated to each part. This will give you an idea of how detailed your answer must be.

Generally, you need to be aware of your strengths and weaknesses and select accordingly.

Doing the exam

Actually doing the exam is a personal experience. There is not a single *right way.* As long as you submit complete answers to question 1 and any three from questions 2 to 5 after the three hours are up, then your approach obviously works.

Looking through the paper

Question 1, as always, is on **group accounts**. This time it requires both a profit and loss account, and a balance sheet, but next time it could require just one of those financial statements. Notice also the 5 marks available in part (b) on the accounting treatment of an investment.

In Section B there are four question on a variety of topics. You must choose three.

- Question 2 is on **earnings per share**, FRS 14 and **distributable profits.**
- Question 3 is on **revenue recognition**, an important element within the syllabus.
- Question 4 involves **ratio analysis**, but with the added complication of restating the accounts before you can use them to derive meaningful information.
- Question 5 is on **substance over form**, involving both a discussion section and a numerical section.

Compulsory question

You should be very familiar with consolidated financial statements by now, so the first 20 marks are there for the taking. Part (b) is a fairly straightforward test of knowledge, straight from your textbook.

Optional questions

Ratio analysis is an area that comes up quite often as it tests your ability to think about the information presented. You will have used ratios before and so **question 4** should not be a surprise for you.

Earnings per share and distributable profits in **question 2** are quite nice self-contained topics, and if you have revised them in enough detail you should be happy with this question. The basic EPS calculation should present no problems, but there are some trickier twists as well.

If you are happy with your written skills then **question 3** would have attracted you. Some candidates avoid written questions because they cannot see whether they are picking up marks (whereas a balanced balance sheet *feels* right).

Question 5 requires an appreciation of the principle of substance over form. It may appeal to you in that it includes both a discursive element and a numerical element, so that you should be able to pick up marks on both sections. Don't fall into the trap of launching into the first part without considering whether you can also have a reasonable attempt at the second.

Allocating your time

BPP's advice is to always allocate your time **according to the marks for the question.** However, **use common sense.** If you're doing a question but haven't a clue how to do part (c), you might be better off re-allocating your time and getting more marks on another question, where you can add something you didn't have time for earlier on.

Forget about it!

Don't worry if you found the paper difficult. It is most likely that the other candidates did too. **Do not talk about the exam**. It is history and you cannot change a thing. It is probably better to go and do something you enjoy eg see a movie, have a nice meal, maybe even go on holiday!

1

> **Tutor's hint**. Technique is everything in these questions. You must *always* check for the date of acquisition in a consolidation question, to check whether it is mid-year, as in this case – you would lose a lot of marks for missing that. Don't neglect part (b): remember that it is **voting rights** which determine the level of control of an investment, not rights to dividends.

(a) HEPBURN PLC
CONSOLIDATED PROFIT AND LOSS ACCOUNT
FOR THE YEAR ENDED 31 MARCH 20X1

	£'000
Turnover (W2)	1,600
Cost of sales (W3)	(890)
Gross profit	710
Operating expenses (W4)	(184)
Debenture interest (12 × 6/12)	(6)
Operating profit	520
Taxation (100 + (40 × 6/12)	(120)
Profit after tax	400
Minority interest (20% ×200 × 6/12)	(20)
Profit after tax and minority interest	380
Dividends: interim	(40)
final	(40)
Retained profit for the year	300

HEPBURN PLC
CONSOLIDATED BALANCE SHEET
AS AT 31 MARCH 20X1

	£'000	£'000
Fixed assets		
Intangible: goodwill (W7)		180
Tangible fixed assets		
Land and buildings (400 + 150 + 125)		675
Plant and machinery (220 + 510)		730
Investments (20 + 10)		30
		1,615
Current assets		
Stock (240 + 280 – 10 (W8))	510	
Debtors (170 + 210 – 56)	324	
Bank (20 + 40 + 20)	80	
	914	
Creditors: amounts due < 1 year		
Trade creditors (170 + 155 - 36)	289	
Taxation (50 + 45)	95	
Dividends	40	
	424	
Net current assets		490
		2,105
Creditors: amounts due > 1 year		
8% Debentures		150
Net Assets		1,955
Capital and reserves		
Ordinary shares £1 each (400 + 300 (W5))		700
Share premium account (900 – 300 (W5))		600
Profit and loss account (W10)		460
		1,760
Minority interests (W9)		195
Shareholders' funds		1,955

Workings

1 *Group structure*

Hepburn

80%

Salter 1.10.X0

2 *Turnover*

	£'000
Hepburn	1,200
Salter (1,000 × 6/12)	500
Less: intercompany sale	(100)
	1,600

3 *Cost of sales*

	£'000
Hepburn	650
Salter (660 × 6/12)	330
Less: intercompany sales	(100)
Unrealised profit in stock (100 × 50% × 25/125)	10
	890

4 *Operating expenses*

	£'000
Hepburn	120
Salter (88 × 6/12)	44
Goodwill amortisation (W4)	20
	184

5 *Cost of investment in Salter Ltd*

Salter shares in issue	150
80% acquired	120
Hepburn shares issued (5 for 2)	300
	£'000
Cost at £3 a share	900

6 *Fair value adjustment*

	At acquisition £'000	*Movement* £'000	*At balance sheet date* *£'000*
Land	125	Nil	125

7 *Goodwill*

	£'000	£'000
Cost of investment (W5)		900
For:		
Share capital	150	
Reserves (700 – 200)	500	
Current year (200 × 6/12)	100	
Fair value adjustment (W6)	125	
	875	
	× 80%	(700)
Goodwill at acquisition		200
Amortisation (200 × 1/5 × 6/12)		(20)
Goodwill at balance sheet date		180

8 *Unrealised profit*

	£'000	%
Sales	100	125
Cost of sales	80	100
Profit	20	25
Proportion in stock ($\frac{1}{2}$)	10	

9 *Minority interest (BS)*

	£'000
Net assets per question	850
Fair value adjustment (W6)	125
	975
Minority interest (20%)	195

10 *Profit and loss account*

	Hepburn £'000	*Salter* £'000
Per question	410	700
Unrealised profit (W8)	(10)	
Pre acquisition profit		(600)
		100
Share of post acquisition profit (100 × 80%)	80	
Goodwill amortised (W7)	(20)	
	460	

11 *Goodwill and minority interest*

Salter Ltd

	Total (100%) £'000	*At acquisition (80%)* £'000	*Post acquisition (80%)* £'000	*Minority interest (20%)* £'000
At acquisition				
Share capital	150	120	-	30
P&L a/c at 1.4.X0	500	400	-	100
Profit 6 months to 1.10.X0	100	80	-	20
Fair value adjustment	125	100	-	25
		700		
Cost of investment		900		
Goodwill		200		
Post acquisition				
Profit 6 months to 31.3.X1	100		80	20
	1,075			195

> **Tutor's hint.** This is an alternative format which some people find easier to understand because it integrates various aspects of the key consolidation workings.
>
> It is a format which is used in practice by groups and accounting firms as you will realise, because once a spreadsheet is set up, they can go on adding subsequent years to it.
>
> Use the method which best suits your way of thinking and that you are likely to find most efficient and effective in an examination.

(b) **Status of investment in Woodbridge Ltd**

In **voting rights**, Hepburn's interest in Woodbridge Ltd is **60%**; however it is correct that it is only entitled to 6,000/24,000 = 25% of any dividends paid.

The approach taken by Hepburn to its investment in Woodbridge seems to be based on the view that, with a **25% equity holding**, the investment would normally be treated as an **associate** and **equity accounting** applied. However, Hepburn does **not exert** any **significant influence** over Woodbridge and hence under FRS 9 *Associates and joint ventures* it can **rebut** the **presumption** of **associate status.**

This overlooks the fact that FRS 2 *Accounting for subsidiary undertakings* bases the treatment of an investment in another entity on the notion of **control rather than ownership**. Hepburn can control Woodbridge by virtue of its holding the **majority of the voting rights** in the company.

Woodbridge is thus a **subsidiary** and should be **consolidated in full** in Hepburn's group accounts, **from the date of acquisition.**

Hepburn's directors may wish to avoid consolidation because of Woodbridge's **losses.** But these **losses** may indicate that the **value of the investment** in Woodbridge in Hepburn's own individual accounts may be **overstated.**

A test for **impairment**, as required by FRS 11 *Impairment of fixed assets and goodwill* may reveal that the **recoverable amount** of the investment has fallen below £20,000, thus requiring a write down in Hepburn's own accounts and a write down of Woodbridge's assets in the consolidated accounts.

	Marking guide		**Marks**
(a)	Profit and loss account:		
	Turnover		2
	Cost of sales		2
	Operating expenses including goodwill		2
	Tax		1
	Minority interest		1
	Dividends		1
	Balance sheet:		
	Goodwill		1
	Land and buildings		2
	Plant and investments		1
	Stock		1
	Debtors		1
	Bank		1
	Creditors		1
	Tax		1
	Dividend		1
	Minority interest		2
	Share capital		1
	Share premium		1
	P&L reserve		2
		Available	25
		Maximum	20
(b)	Directors seem to think it may be an associate		1
	Reasons for it not being an associate		1
	Recognising it as a subsidiary		1
	Treatment should be to consolidate Woodbridge Ltd		1
	Losses may be motivating management		1
	FRS 11 impairment		1
		Available	6
		Maximum	5
		Maximum for question	**25**

2

> **Tutor's hint**. The basic EPS calculation should have presented few problems. In (b)(ii) you must have noted in your answer that the potential ordinary shares were anti-dilutive to gain the bulk of the marks.
>
> To gain the most difficult marks you should have mentioned some of the more detailed points in FRS 14, eg mentioning share consolidations in (a)(i) or that dilution relates to net profit from *continuing operations* in (b)(i).

(a) (i) **Transaction requiring retrospective adjustment**

Examples of events or transactions requiring retrospective adjustment are convertible debt, share options and shares contingently issuable on an acquisition. A **bonus issue** is one of the most common examples of this, another being a **rights issue** at less than market value (both of which are given in the question).

It should also be noted that the adjustment must also be made when the increase or decrease in ordinary shares takes place **after the year end** but before the date of approval of the accounts.

FRS 14 also makes particular reference to **special dividends** and **share consolidations**. Basic EPS for earlier years will generally be adjusted for a share consolidation, since there will have been a change in the number of shares outstanding without a commensurate change in resources. However, when such a consolidation is coupled with a special dividend, such that the **overall commercial effect** is the same as if the company had made a share repurchase at fair value. FRS 14 states that the usual retrospective adjustment should not be made.

(ii) **Basic EPS**

Number of shares

	'000
Ordinary shares at 1.4.X6 £4,000/£0.25	16,000
1 for 8 bonus issue	2,000
	18,000
1 for 5 rights issue	3,600
Ordinary shares at 31.3.X7	21,600

Theoretical ex-rights price (initial holding of, say, 100 shares)

	£
100 shares at £1.40	140
1 for 5 rights issue at 50p (20 new shares)	10
	150
Therefore ex-rights price = £150/120 =	£1.25

Weighted average number of shares

	'000
Before rights issue (18,000 × 9/12 × 1.40/1.25)	15,120
After rights issue (21,600 × 3/12)	5,400
	20,520

Earnings	£'000
Profit after tax	910
Preference dividend	(80)
	830

$$\text{EPS} = \frac{£830{,}000}{20{,}520{,}000} = \underline{\underline{4.0 \text{ pence}}}$$

Prior year comparative: 20X6

$8p \times 8/9 \text{ (bonus)} \times \frac{1.25}{1.40} \text{ (rights)} = \underline{\underline{6.3 \text{ pence}}}$

(b) (i) **Calculating diluted EPS**

Diluted EPS is calculated by adjusting the figures used for the basic EPS calculation. The **earnings figure** is adjusted for the post-tax effect of any dividends or interest recognised in the period in relation to dilutive potential ordinary shares, and any other changes in income or expense that would arise from their conversion.

The **number of shares** used to compute diluted EPS is the number for basic EPS adjusted for the dilutive potential ordinary shares.

In both these cases (ie for both earnings and weighted average number of shares), adjustment should be made **only** for the effects of **dilutive** potential ordinary shares, ie where their conversion would decrease net profit per share from **continuing operations**.

(ii) **Diluted EPS**

From (a)(ii) above, basic EPS = $\frac{£830,000}{20,520,000} = \underline{\underline{4.0 \text{ pence}}}$

The 10% debentures will convert to:

$£2,000,000 \times \frac{120}{160} = 2,400,000 \text{ shares}$

Earnings will increase by:

$2,000,000 \times 10\% \times (100 - 33)\% = £134,000 \text{ (post-tax)}$

Diluted EPS = $\frac{£(830,000 + 134,000)}{20,520,000 + 2,400,000} = \underline{\underline{4.2 \text{ pence}}}$

This is higher than basic EPS, ie the potential ordinary shares arising on the debentures are **anti-dilutive** and so are ignored. There are no other potential ordinary shares and so no diluted EPS figure need be shown.

(iii) **Usefulness of diluted EPS disclosure**

Diluted EPS is useful to assess the impact of **future changes in capital** structure upon earnings (such as the convertible debentures of Radan plc). Share options and convertible preference shares would also affect the diluted EPS calculation.

Diluted EPS is **not a predicted EPS figure**, merely current EPS **adjusted** to reflect **potential changes** in **capital structure**, eg where there are convertible bonds in issue (which will be converted into shares at a future date).

(c) **Calculation of distributable profits**

	£'000
Profit and loss reserve 1.4.X6	750
Draft accounts profit y/e 31.3.X7	910
Adjustments	
Long-term contract profit (note 1)	no change
Exchange gain on dollar loan treated as unrealised (note 2)	(25)
Development expenditure is treated as a realised loss for distributable profits (note 3)	(114)
Adjustment to depreciation (excess depreciation) is *not* treated as a realised loss (150/5) (note 4)	30
Distributable profit	1,551

Notes

Distributable profits are computed having regard to Companies Act rules and also 'Generally Accepted Accounting Principles', hence the adjustments shown above.

1 SSAP 9 accepts stage profits as being realised when the **outcome** of a contract can be assessed with **reasonable certainty.**

2 Exchange gains are included in reported profit, to reflect the fact that **exchange movements** can be **favourable** as well as **unfavourable,** but they are not realised.

3 Development expenditure is a realised loss (Companies Act requirement) unless the directors justify the contrary. Deferment in the balance sheet it is not sufficient justification and the notes to the accounts must explain why it is not treated as realised loss. This is not the case with Radan plc.

4 The **Companies Act** specifically states that **'excess' depreciation** is **not treated as a realised loss for the purposes of determining distributable profit.**

Marking guide

					Marks
(a)	(i)	1 mark per example	Maximum		3
	(ii)	Basic for 20X7		3	
		20X6 restated		2	
			Available	5	
			Maximum		4
(b)	(i)	Earnings figure		1	
		Number of shares		1	
		Dilutive only		1	
			Maximum		3
	(ii)	Conversion of debentures		1	
		Earnings adjustment		2	
		Calculation		1	
		Anti-dilutive, no effect		2	
			Available	6	
			Maximum		5
	(iii)	1 mark per relevant point	Maximum		2
(c)		Profit b/f		1	
		SSAP 9 no effect		1	
		Exchange gain		1	
		Development expenditure		1	
		Excess depreciation		1	
		One mark for explanation of each above		4	
			Available	9	
			Maximum		8
			Total maximum		25

3

Tutor's hint. This is an important conceptual subject and it is closely linked with the ASB's *Statement of Principles,* which you should have discussed, given the UK has no accounting standard on revenue recognition. You need to use your imagination to come up with examples in (b).

(a) **Revenue recognition criteria and the critical event approach**

(i) **Description of critical event**

In revenue recognition, the '**critical event**' is the point in the earnings process or operating cycle at which the transaction is deemed to have been **sufficiently**

completed to allow the **profit** arising from the transaction, or a distinct component part of it, to be **recognised** in income in a particular period.

The revenue recognition issue needs to be addressed in order to allocate transactions and their impacts to different accounting periods. This a direct result of the **episodic nature** of financial reporting.

For most companies the **normal earnings cycle** is the purchase of raw materials which are transformed through a manufacturing process into saleable goods, for which orders are subsequently received, delivery is made and then payment received.

(ii) **Matching and prudence driven approach**

In the past, the approach has been to **match costs with revenues** and record both once the critical event has passed. In most systems this critical event has been full or near **full performance of the transaction**, so that **no material uncertainties** surround either the transaction being **completed** or the **amounts arising** from the transaction.

The above is encompassed in the notion of **prudence**, so that revenue is **recognised** only in **cash** or **near cash** form. However, any point in the cycle could be deemed to be the critical event. This approach leaves the balance sheet as a statement of uncompleted transaction balances, comprising unexpired costs and undischarged liabilities.

(iii) **Statement of principles – balance sheet driven approach**

In contrast, the *Statement of Principles* defines **gains and losses** (or income and expenses) in terms of **changes** in **assets** and **liabilities** other than those arising from transactions with owners as owners, **not** in **terms** of an **earnings** or **matching process**.

The balance sheet thus **assumes primary importance** in the **recognition** of **earnings** and **profits**. A gain **can only be recognised** if there is an **increase** in the **ownership interest** (ie net assets) of an entity not resulting from contributions from owners. Similarly, a loss is recognised if there is a **decrease** in the **ownership interest** of an entity not resulting from distributions to owners. Thus **gains arise** from **recognition** of **assets** and derecognition of liabilities, and losses arise from derecognition of assets and **recognition** of **liabilities.**

The Statement of principles explains that it is not possible to reverse this definitional process, ie by defining assets and liabilities in terms of gains and losses, because it has not been possible to formulate sufficient robust base definitions of gains and losses (partly because the choice of critical event can be subjective).

Nevertheless the **two approaches** are **linked** by the **Statement of Principles**, which says that '**sufficient evidence**' for **recognition** or **derecognition** will be met at the **critical event** in the **operating cycle.**

(b) **Recognition and stages of operating cycle**

(i) **On the acquisition of goods**

Generally, this would be **unlikely** to be a critical event for most businesses.

However, there may be specific scenarios where the acquisition of the raw materials is the most important part of the process, eg extraction of gold from a mine, or the harvesting of coffee beans. Only where the goods in question could be **sold immediately in a liquid market** would it be appropriate to recognise revenue, ie they would have to have a **commodity value**.

(ii) **During the manufacture or production of goods**

This is also **unlikely** to be the critical event for most businesses because **too many uncertainties** remain, eg of damaged goods or overproduction leading to obsolete stock.

An **exception** would be **long-term contracts** for the construction of specific assets . Here the constructing company tends to earn revenues over the length of the contract, usually in stages, ie there is a **series of critical events** in the operating cycle (according to the *Statement of Principles*). It would **not** be appropriate to recognise all the revenue at the end of the contract, because this would reflect profit earned in past periods as well as the present period. Profit is therefore recognised during manufacture or production, usually through certification of a qualified valuer. Some would argue that this is not really a critical event approach, but rather an 'accretion approach'.

(iii) **On delivery/acceptance of goods**

Goods are frequently sold on **credit**, whereby the vendor hands over the inventory asset and receives in its place a **financial asset of a debt** due for the price of the goods. At that point legal title passes and **full performance** has taken place. In general, the bulk of the risks of the transaction have gone and the only ones remaining relate to the creditworthiness of the purchaser and any outstanding warranty over the goods.

Many trade sales take place in this way, with periods of credit allowed for goods delivered, eg 30 days. This therefore tends to be the critical event for many types of business operating cycles.

(iv) **Where certain conditions have been satisfied after the goods have been delivered**

In these situations the customer had a right of return of the goods without reason or penalty, but usually within a time and non-use condition. A good example is clothes retailers who allow **non-faulty goods to be returned**. Another example is that the goods need only be paid for once they are sold on to a third party.

Traditionally, recognition of revenue is delayed until, eg the **deadline to allowed return passes**. However, in circumstances where goods are never returned, it might be argued that the substance of the transaction is a sale on delivery.

(v) **Receipt or payment for credit sales**

Once payment is received, only warranty risk remains. A company may wait until this point to recognise income if receipt is considered uncertain, eg when goods have been sold to a company resident in a country that has **exchange controls**. It would otherwise be **rare** to delay recognition until payment.

(vi) **On the expiry of a guarantee or warranty**

Many businesses may feel unable to recognise revenue in full because of **outstanding warranties**, eg a construction company which is subject to fee retention until some time after completion of the contract. Other businesses, such as car manufacturers, may make a **general provision** for goods returned under warranty as it will not be possible to judge likely warranty costs under individual contracts.

(c) **Treatment in financial statements**

(i) **Option to repurchase goods**

This agreement is worded as a **sale**, but it is fairly obvious from the terms and assessed substance that it is in fact a **secured loan**.

Jensen should therefore continue to recognise the stock in the balance sheet and should treat the receipt from Wholesaler as a loan, not revenue. Finance costs will be charged to the profit and loss account, of £35,000 × 12% × 9/12 = £3,150.

(ii) **Fast food franchise**

Years 2 to 5 of the franchise contract would be **loss making** for Jensen and hence part of the initial fee of £50,000 should be **deferred over the life of the contract**.

Since Jensen should be making a profit margin of 20% on this type of arrangement, revenues of £10,000 will be required to match against the costs of £8,000. The company will receive £5,000 pa and so a further £5,000 × 4 = £20,000 of the initial fee should be deferred, leaving £50,000 – £20,000 = £30,000 to be recognised in the first year.

However, this may not represent a liability under FRS 12 *Provisions, contingent liabilities and contingent assets*, where a liability is defined as an obligation to transfer economic benefits as a result of past transactions or events. It will be necessary to consider the terms of the initial fee and whether it is returnable.

(iii) **Magazine subscriptions**

The cost of the first 6 months' publications is £192,000 ÷ 24 × 6 = £48,000. On an accruals basis, income of £240,000 ÷ 24 × 6 = £60,000 should be recognised. This would leave deferred income of £240,000 – £60,000 = £180,000 in Jensen's balance sheet (ie as a liability).

As in (ii), however, this may not represent a liability. In fact, the liability of the company may only extend to the cost of the future publications, ie £192,000 – £48,000 = £144,000. This would allow Jensen to **recognise all the profit** on the publications **immediately**. In the absence of an accounting standard on revenue recognition, it will be necessary to consider the extent of Jensen's commitments under this arrangement.

			Marks
(a)	Discussion of critical event		2
	ASB uses balance sheet approach for gains and losses		1
	Gains based on increases in asset etc		1
	Criteria for recognition		2
		Available	6
		Maximum	5
(b)	Discussion of each stage of cycle, 2 marks each		12
		Maximum	12
(c)	Discussion of transaction/agreement - (i)		4
	- (ii)		4
	- (iii)		3
		Available	11
		Maximum	8
		Maximum for question	**25**

BPP Professional Education

4

Tutor's hint. This is a different slant on a ratio analysis question, but it highlights important issues relating to related party transactions and accounting policies and the differences these can create between company results.

(a) PROFIT AND LOSS ACCOUNTS (Restated)

	Cole Ltd		*Darwin Ltd*	
	£'000	£'000	£'000	£'000
Sales (W1)		2,875		4,400
Opening stock	450		720	
Purchases (W2)	2,055		3,080	
	2,505		3,800	
Closing stock	(540)		(850)	
		(1,965)		(2,950)
Gross profit		910		1,450
Operating expenses (W3)	520		844	
Debenture interest	80		-	
Overdraft interest	15		-	
		(615)		(844)
Net profit		295		606

BALANCE SHEETS (restated)

	Cole Ltd		*Darwin Ltd*	
	£'000	£'000	£'000	£'000
Fixed assets (W4)				
Premises		1,900		1,900
Plant		1,200		720
		3,100		2,620
Current assets				
Sales	540		850	
Debtors (522 + 375)	897		750	
Bank (W5)	-		60	
	1,437		1,660	
Current liabilities				
Creditors (438 – 275)	163		562	
Overdraft (W5)	795		-	
	958		562	
Net current assets		479		1,098
		3,579		3,718
10% debenture		(800)		-
Net assets		2,779		3,718
Share capital and reserves				
Ordinary shares £1 each		1,000		500
Revaluation reserve (800 – 40)		760		700
Profit and loss account		1,019		2,518
(684 + 295 + 40)/(1,912 + 606)		2,779		3,718

Workings

1 *Cole's sales*

	£'000
Per P&L account	3,000
Over-priced intra group sales (500 – 375)	(125)
	2,875

2 *Cole's purchases*

	£'000
Per P&L account	2,030
Under-priced intra group sales (300 – 275)	25
	2,055

3 *Operating expenses*

	£'000
Cole: as if property is revalued	
Per P&L account	480
Additional depreciation (2,000 – 1,200) ÷ 20	40
	520

Darwin's as if plant not yet acquired	£'000
Per P&L account	964
Less depreciation on plant (600 × 20%)	(120)
	844

4 *Fixed asset balance*

	Cole	Darwin
	£'000	£'000
Property	2,000	2,000
Depreciation	(100)	(100)
	1,900	1,900
Plant	1,200	1,200
Less plant not on stream (600 – (600 × 20%))	-	(480)
	1,200	720

5 *Bank balances*

	£'000
Cole	
Per balance sheet	20
Intra group sale	(500)
Intra group purchase	(300)
Overdraft interest	(15)
	(795)
Darwin	
Per balance sheet	(550)
Plant purchase reversed	600
Overdraft interest reversed	10
	60

6 *Ratios*

	Cole Limited		*Darwin Limited*	
	Original	*Restated*	*Original*	*Restated*
ROCE (W1)	19.4%	10.5%	13.3%	16.3%
Asset turnover (W2)	1.01 times	0.80 times	1.23 times	1.18 times
Gross profit margin (W30	35.3%	31.7%	33.0%	33.0%
Net profit margin (W4)	16.7%	10.3%	10.8%	13.8%
Debtors collection period (W5)	64 days	114 days	62 days	62 days
Creditors payment period (W6)	79 days	29 days	67 days	67 days

Workings

1 *ROCE*

Cole = $\frac{295 + 80}{2,779 + 800}$ = 10.5%

Darwin = $\frac{606}{3,718}$ = 16.3%

2 *Asset turnover*

Cole = $\frac{2,875}{3,579}$ = 0.80 times

Darwin = $\frac{4,400}{3,718}$ = 1.18 times

3 *Gross profit margin*

Cole = $\frac{910}{2,875}$ = 31.7%

4 *Net profit margin*

Cole = $\frac{295}{2,875}$ = 10.3%

Darwin = $\frac{606}{4,400}$ = 13.8%

5 *Debtors collection period*

Cole = $\frac{897}{2,875} \times 365$ = 114 days

6 *Creditors payments period*

Cole = $\frac{163}{2,055} \times 365$ = 29 days

(b) **Impact of revised ratios on assessments of the companies**

The general effect of the restatement is to **improve Darwin's results** in comparison to Cole's. Once the impact of the **beneficial intra-group purchases** and sales are removed, Cole is shown to have a **poorer gross profit margin** than Darwin. This has fed through to the net margin, which is also affected in Cole's case by the impact of a **higher depreciation charge**. The **cash flow** situation for Cole is significantly **worse,** thus increasing interest payable which also impacts on net profit margin.

Darwin's **return on capital** has been **improved** by removing the asset that had yet to make a contribution to the company's profitability. It is significant that the revaluation of Cole's property along the same lines as Darwin has **failed to compensate** for the increase in depreciation and the decrease in gross margin caused by the adjustments to the intra-group transactions.

These adjustments have also had a marked effect on **Cole's collection periods**; whereas these are evenly matched between debtors and creditors by Darwin; Cole's figures indicate an **imbalance,** with far longer taken to pay by debtors than Cole can take to pay its own debts to creditors.

In summary, **Darwin** looks much the **better investment opportunity**. However, Webster will also have to consider:

(i) The relative **asking prices** of the companies.

(ii) The likelihood that the **historical results** are a **true reflection** of future profitability (eg what is the likely effect of Darwin's new machinery coming on stream?).

(c) **Availability of information**

Some but **not all** of the **information** is likely to be available, although each company may **disclose voluntarily** beyond that required by legislation or standards.

Items (i) and (ii)

FRS 8 *Related party transactions* requires the disclosure of transactions and balances, between **related parties**. These would be included, but may be aggregated with other similar transactions, as permitted by the standard. Further, if Cole is 90% + owned by Velox, then an exemption from disclosure is permitted.

Item (iii)

Companies that do not follow a policy of revaluation are **not required** to state **market values,** other than in the Directors' Report, where considered significant. However, those that **do revalue** are required to give **historical cost information**; in any case, the additional depreciation would appear in the note of historical cost profits and losses.

Item (iv)

The company's **depreciation policy** would be disclosed, but not necessarily that a certain asset is yet to come on-line, nor how the purchase had been financed.

Item (v)

Without the information in (i) and (ii), it would **not** be possible to work out how much overdraft interest Cole would have to pay.

				Marks
(a)	Sales adjustment			1
	Purchase adjustment			1
	Depreciation adjustment	- Cole Ltd		2
		- Darwin Ltd		2
	Overdraft interest			1
	Fixed assets	- Cole Ltd's property		1
		- Darwin Ltd's plant		1
	Debtors	- Cole Ltd		1
	Bank	- Cole Ltd		2
		- Darwin Ltd		1
	Creditors	- Cole Ltd		1
			Available	14
			Maximum	10
(b)	1 mark per recalculated ratio maximum of			5
	1 mark per comment to a maximum of			5
			Maximum	10
(c)	Generally comments – 1 mark per point up to			3
	Comments on related parties			3
			Available	6
			Maximum	5
			Maximum for question	**25**

5

> **Tutor's hint**. Many students find written answers difficult. They are never an easy option as you invariably need to understand a concept or method and apply it accordingly. This was even harder as you needed to show an understanding then provide and explain examples and then work through the example provided.

(a) **Substance over legal form**

It is important that the substance of a transaction is reflected in the financial statements in order that a **true and fair view** of the entity's financial affairs is given. The legal form of a transaction may be very different to the underlying financial effects. FRS 5 was introduced to ensure it is the substance which is disclosed. Prior to FRS 5 the full financial affairs of an entity may not have been reflected in the accounts. There were many cases of **off balance sheet finance** for instance. By recording transactions in their legal form the **commercial reality** would be hidden. This could lead to a **more predictable level of profit** being reported every year, and more favourable ratios such as a better gearing ratio (as finance was not accounted for in the balance sheet).

(b) (i) **Separation of ownership from beneficial use**

A prime example of separation of ownership from the beneficial use of an asset would be leases. The **legal form** of a **lease** is usually such that **ownership** of an asset **remains with** the **lessor until the lease expires**. The **substance** may well be that the **lessee** has all the **rewards** and **risks of ownership** (a finance lease under SSAP 21) and so the asset should still be recorded on the balance sheet of the lessee with a corresponding finance lease liability in creditors.

(ii) **Linking of transactions**

In the case of linking of transactions which include the use of **option clauses**, a firm may **factor its debtors** to an **external agency**. The firm may at any time receive 80% of the value of the debtors. The commercial reality may be that the 80% advance is a loan which is dependent on the full debtors balance being collected. To disclose on the basis of legal form, debtors could be shown at as little as 20% of their true value which would be misleading as they have yet to pay. The disclosure taking account of the substance, would be a **linked presentation** such that the cash advance is related to the debtor balance and a **note gives the nature of the agreement**.

The debt factor may hold an option over other assets of the company allowing it to recover the cash advanced. The reality is that this option would be unlikely to be exercised as the cash advance will be recovered by the receipts from debtors. Options in this case are either very likely to be exercised (ie the option to buy back an asset sold under fair value) or very unlikely to be exercised (a financier's right to sell an asset owned but essentially held as security).

(iii) **Asset sold at price different from fair value**

An asset sold at a price that differs from its fair value is an occurrence in a number of industries. In the whisky industry a cask of single malt may require a couple of decades to mature. To finance this the distillery sells the cask to a bank with an **agreement to buy back** the cask when it has reached maturity. The legal form of the transaction would lead to a **sale being recorded in year 1**, then a **purchase and subsequent sale in year 20**.

The **substance** is that the cask was always the property of the distillery and was only **security** against a **bank loan**. It was, in effect, **sold** at a **low value** so that the **buy back** at a **higher value** will **incorporate** the **interest** and the **value** of the whisky will be **good security** for the **bank's loan**.

(c) (i) **Legal form of the transaction**

Profit and loss account for the years to 31 March

	20X1	*20X2*	*20X3*
	£'000	£'000	£'000
Sales	15,000	-	25,000
Cost of sales	(12,000)	-	(19,965)
Gross profit	3,000	-	5,035

The cost of sales in 20X3 is £15m plus three years of cumulative interest at 10%.

The balance sheets for the three years will have no disclosure after the initial reduction of stocks by £12m from the sale in 20X1.

(ii) **The substance of the transaction**

Profit and loss account for the years to 31 March

	20X1	*20X2*	*20X3*
	£'000	£'000	£'000
Sales	-	-	25,000
Cost of sales	-	-	(12,000)
Gross profit	-	-	13,000
Interest paid	(1,500)	(1,650)	(1,815)
Net profit/(loss)	(1,500)	(1,650)	11,185

Balance sheet extracts as at 31 March

	20X1	*20X2*	*20X3*
	£'000	£'000	£'000
Stocks	12,000	12,000	-
Loan	(16,500)	(18,150)	-

Note. The loan is repaid in the final year (£19,965,000).

From the above it can be seen that the overall profit made over the three years amounts to the same (£8,035,000). By taking the legal form the profit would be spread between 20X1 and 20X3. This also means that the gross margin would be around 20% in both years whereas if the substance of the transaction is reflected then the sale hits the 20X3 profit and loss and the margin is 52%. Margin is improved not only because the whole sale hits one year but also because the loan interest is an expense.

The **legal form** shows a sale to the bank which, from a **commercial viewpoint,** never took place. The bank had secured the loan on the timber and did not intend using or selling it on. The legal form disclosure also fails to disclose the stock figure and the corresponding loan liability. This in itself would improve the **financial ratios** including the stock days and gearing.

Marking guide

				Marks	
(a)	General discussion of importance of substance			2	
	Typical examples of manipulation of financial statements			3	
			Available	5	
			Maximum		5
(b)	Up to 4 marks for each example,		Available	12	
			Maximum		9
(c)	(i) Profit and loss account				
	Profit of £3,000 in 20X1			1	
	Sales of £20,000 in 20X3			1	
	Cost of sales/profit in 20X3			1	
	Nothing in balance sheet			1	
	(ii) Profit and loss account	- sales		11	
		- cost of sales		1	
		- accrued interest 1 for each year		3	
	Balance sheet	- stock		1	
		- loan		1	
		- interest		1	
	Comments on above 1 per point maximum			4	
			Available	16	
			Maximum		11
			Total maximum		25

See overleaf for information on other
BPP products and how to order

ACCA Order

To BPP Professional Education, Aldine Place, London W12 8AW
Tel: 020 8740 2211 Fax: 020 8740 1184
email: publishing@bpp.com online: www.bpp.com

Mr/Mrs/Ms (Full name)

Daytime delivery address

Postcode

Daytime Tel

Date of exam (month/year)

	6/02 Texts	1/03 Kits	1/03 Passcards	MCQ Cards	Tapes	Videos	7/02 i-Learn	7/02 i-Pass	Virtual Campus
PART 1									
1.1 Preparing Financial Statements	£20.95	£10.95	£6.95	£5.95	£12.95	£25.00	£34.95	£24.95	£90.00
1.2 Financial Information for Management	£20.95	£10.95	£6.95	£5.95	£12.95	£25.00	£34.95	£24.95	£90.00
1.3 Managing People	£20.95	£10.95	£6.95		£12.95	£25.00	£34.95	£24.95	£90.00
PART 2									
2.1 Information Systems	£20.95	£10.95	£6.95		£12.95	£25.00	£34.95	£24.95	£90.00
2.2 Corporate and Business Law	£20.95	£10.95	£6.95		£12.95	£25.00	£34.95	£24.95	£90.00
2.3 Business Taxation FA 2002 (for 2003 exams)†	£20.95	£10.95	£6.95		£12.95	£25.00	£34.95	£24.95	£90.00
2.4 Financial Management and Control	£20.95	£10.95	£6.95		£12.95	£25.00	£34.95	£24.95	£90.00
2.5 Financial Reporting	£20.95	£10.95	£6.95		£12.95	£25.00	£34.95	£24.95	£90.00
2.6 Audit and Internal Review	£20.95	£10.95	£6.95		£12.95	£25.00	£34.95	£24.95	£90.00
PART 3									
3.1 Audit and Assurance Services	£20.95	£10.95	£6.95		£12.95	£25.00			
3.2 Advanced Taxation FA 2002 (for 2003 exams)†	£20.95	£10.95	£6.95		£12.95	£25.00			
3.3 Performance Management	£20.95	£10.95	£6.95		£12.95	£25.00			
3.4 Business Information Management	£20.95	£10.95	£6.95		£12.95	£25.00			
3.5 Strategic Business Planning and Development	£20.95	£10.95	£6.95		£12.95	£25.00			
3.6 Advanced Corporate Reporting (7/02)	£20.95	£10.95	£6.95		£12.95	£25.00			
3.7 Strategic Financial Management	£20.95	£10.95	£6.95		£12.95	£25.00			
INTERNATIONAL STREAM									
1.1 Preparing Financial Statements	£20.95	£10.95	£6.95	£5.95					
2.5 Financial Reporting	£20.95	£10.95	£6.95						
2.6 Audit and Internal Review	£20.95	£10.95	£6.95						
3.1 Audit and Assurance Services	£20.95	£10.95	£6.95						
3.6 Advanced Corporate Reporting	£20.95	£10.95	£6.95						
Success in your Research and Analysis Project – Tutorial Text (8/02)	£19.95								
Learning to Learn (7/02)	£9.95								

Subtotal £

POSTAGE & PACKING

Texts/Kits

	Mail Order First	Mail Order Each extra	On-line per item	
UK	£5.00	£2.00	£2.00	£
Europe*	£6.00	£4.00	£4.00	£
Rest of world	£20.00	£10.00	£10.00	

Passcards/MCQ Cards/Success Tapes/CDs

	Mail Order First	Mail Order Each extra	On-line per-item	
UK	£2.00	£1.00	£1.00	£
Europe*	£3.00	£2.00	£2.00	£
Rest of world	£8.00	£8.00	£8.00	£

Breakthrough Videos

	Mail Order First	Mail Order Each extra	On-line per-item	
UK	£2.00	£1.00	£1.00	£
Europe*	£3.00	£2.00	£2.00	£
Rest of world	£8.00	£8.00	£8.00	

Grand Total (incl. Postage)

I enclose a cheque for £
(Cheques to *BPP Professional Education*)

Or charge to Visa/Mastercard/Switch

Card Number

Expiry date Start Date

Issue Number (Switch Only)

Signature

We aim to deliver to all UK addressess inside 5 working days; a signature will be required. Orders to all EU addresses should be delivered within 6 working days. All other orders to overseas addresses should be delivered within 8 working days.
* Europe includes the Republic of Ireland and the Channel Islands. † Available on the following dates: Texts 9/02, Kits 1/03, Passcards 1/03.

REVIEW FORM & FREE PRIZE DRAW

All original review forms from the entire BPP range, completed with genuine comments, will be entered into one of two draws 31 July 2003 and 31 January 2004. The names on the first four forms picked out on each occasion will be sent a cheque for £50.

Name: ______________________ **Address:** ______________________

How have you used this Kit?
(Tick one box only)

☐ Self study (book only)
☐ On a course: college (please state)__________
☐ With 'correspondence' package
☐ Other __________

Why did you decide to purchase this Kit? *(Tick one box only)*

☐ Have used the complementary Study Text
☐ Have used other BPP products in the past
☐ Recommendation by friend/colleague
☐ Recommendation by a lecturer at college
☐ Saw advertising in journals
☐ Saw website
☐ Other __________

During the past six months do you recall seeing/receiving any of the following?
(Tick as many boxes as are relevant)

☐ Our advertisement in *Student Accountant*
☐ Our advertisement in *Pass*
☐ Our brochure with a letter through the post
☐ Our website

Which (if any) aspects of our advertising do you find useful?
(Tick as many boxes as are relevant)

☐ Prices and publication dates of new editions
☐ Information on product content
☐ Facility to order books off-the-page
☐ None of the above

When did you sit the exam? __________

Which BPP products have you used?

Text	☐	**MCQ cards**	☐	**i-Learn**	☐
Kit	☑	**Tape**	☐	**i-Pass**	☐
Passcard	☐	**Video**	☐	**Virtual Campus**	☐

Your ratings, comments and suggestions would be appreciated on the following areas of this Kit.

	Very useful	*Useful*	*Not useful*
Effective revision and revision plan	☐	☐	☐
Exam guidance			
Websites and mindmaps			
Preparation questions	☐	☐	☐
Exam standard questions	☐	☐	☐
'Tutor's hints' section in answers	☐	☐	☐
Content and structure of answers	☐	☐	☐
Marking schemes	☐	☐	☐
'Plan of attack'	☐	☐	☐
Mock exam answers	☐	☐	☐

	Excellent	*Good*	*Adequate*	*Poor*
Overall opinion of this Kit	☐	☐	☐	☐

Do you intend to continue using BPP products? ☐ Yes ☐ No

Please note any further comments and suggestions/errors on the reverse of this page. The BPP author of this edition can be e-mailed at: philfontbin@bpp.com

Please return this form to: Katy Hibbert, ACCA range manager, BPP Professional Education, FREEPOST, London, W12 8BR

REVIEW FORM & FREE PRIZE DRAW (continued)

Please note any further comments and suggestions/errors below.

FREE PRIZE DRAW RULES

1 Closing date for 31 July 2003 draw is 30 June 2003. Closing date for 31 January 2004 draw is 31 December 2003.

2 Restricted to entries with UK and Eire addresses only. BPP employees, their families and business associates are excluded.

3 No purchase necessary. Entry forms are available upon request from BPP Professional Education. No more than one entry per title, per person. Draw restricted to persons aged 16 and over.

4 Winners will be notified by post and receive their cheques not later than 6 weeks after the relevant draw date.

5 The decision of the promoter in all matters is final and binding. No correspondence will be entered into.